THE BYFLEET MURDER & MUTILATION

A TRAIL OF BLOOD

Vol. 1 (Jan. 12, 1888)

by Mark Starr

Paperback Edition:
ISBN-13: 979-8-218-32564-0

Published by Noteworthy Editions
Los Altos, California 94022
noteworthyeditions@gmail.com

A Paperback Book,
printed in the United States of America.

This paperback book, with images printed in Standard Colors on white paper, is available for purchase on amazon.com (and on Amazon sites in various countries.)

A hardcover edition of this book, with images printed in Premium Colors on white paper, is also available for purchase on amazon.com (and on Amazon sites in various countries.)

"For nothing is secret,
that shall not be made manifest;
neither any thing hid,
that shall not be known..."

Luke 8:17, King James Version

Table of Contents

Chapter 1. Welcome to Byfleet, Surrey, U.K.

In 2022-24, when this book was researched and written, a diverse population of about 8,000 people living in approximately 3,200 households resided in the picturesque village of Byfleet. Located in the Borough of Woking in the County of Surrey, the village is now physically divided by the M25 motorway and the Wey River navigation canal into two small villages: Byfleet and West Byfleet (about 1.5 miles to the West.) This tranquil community rarely calls attention to itself. In most respects, Byfleet is indistinguishable from many other surrounding small villages in the Borough of Woking—such as Brookwood, Pyrford, and the ward of Old Woking; and from Chertsey and Addlestone in the nearby Borough of Runnymeade. Byfleet and West Byfleet are dwarfed by the nearby town of Woking (population today about 63,000 persons, or 2/3 of the Borough of Woking;) or by the town of Guildford (population about 80,000, or 3/5 of the Borough of Guildford.)

Even those who hail from elsewhere in the County of Surrey may be unfamiliar with the village's name of Byfleet—other than as a name of a train station on the Southwestern Main Line. The Southwestern is predominantly a passenger rail line, 143 miles long, that shuttles commuters between Weymouth and Waterloo

Station in central London—with numerous stops at points in between. Byfleet sits about 24 miles South-West of the center of London (see **Figure 1-1**, below.) In large part, it has evolved into a lovely residential community of well-to-do and well-educated commuters who take a train, or drive less than an hour, to work weekdays in the big city.

Figure 1-1. Map of County Surrey, showing the proximity of Byfleet (circled in red) to Greater London (area in green in North-East corner of map.)

Historic Byfleet

Beneath this modern *façade*, there remain hidden within the village's boundaries some notable relics of past ages. The combined towns of Byfleet and West

Byfleet have a long history, stretching back to Medieval times. Some features of that long history have been preserved and are still visible to the dogged and adventurous tourist. For example, St. Mary's Church, located in the center of town, dates back at least to the 14th Century, and perhaps much earlier. Several timber-framed houses on High Road were built in the 16th and 17th Centuries, and currently they have listed status.

In 1911, the population of Byfleet was a mere 2,960—and before that, it was even considerably lower. Not until 1907, with the opening of the Brooklands Motor Circuit, did the area begin to develop substantially. That construction dramatically increased Byfleet's tiny Medieval footprint. In 1911, the arrival of the Vickers factory spurred population growth, and the topographical expansion surged still further. Byfleet's rural character became more industrial during WWI when aircraft factories opened nearby. Later, the village slowly morphed into suburbia.

Evidence of Bronze Age settlements has been found at nearby Brooklands. Ancient iron-smelting equipment has been found at the Wisley pumping station on the River Wey, showing that the area had been inhabited even earlier, perhaps for thousands of years.

In 727 A.D., a village formed in lands owned by the Chertsey Abbey. Byfleet is listed in the *Domesday Book*—a Middle English spelling of the *Doomsday Book*. This document is a manuscript record of "The Great Survey" of much of England and parts of Wales, completed in 1086 at the behest of William, the Conqueror. The Manor, the mill and the church are mentioned in this historic document. Six acres of Byfleet's meadow and woodland were estimated to be worth 10 hogs. The entire village was valued to produce £4 in taxes a year.

Despite Byfleet's relative obscurity outside of Surrey, you may unknowingly have already visited the village's most notable historic attraction, Byfleet Manor—thanks to ITV's and PBS's television series *Downton Abbey.* The Manor was recently featured on the immensely popular series as the home (Figure 1-2) of the Dowager Countess of Grantham Violet Crawley, played by the venerable actress Dame Maggie Smith.

Figure 1-2. Byfleet Manor—on TV, the home of Dowager Countess of Grantham Violet Crawley,

played by actress Dame Maggie Smith.

Photo: © Mark Percy 2013
(geograph 3492825) license CC BY-SA 2.0

The Manor—originally a hunting lodge visited by various kings and queens—came into crown ownership in 1307. In the 14th Century, it was frequented by the poet Geoffrey Chaucer (who stayed there as part of his job, Clerk of the Works.) In 1616, James I granted the Manor to Queen Anne. A year later, Anne began the construction of a new Manor house, part of which is incorporated into the present building. The Manor House was rebuilt yet again in 1886, just in time for the subject of this volume—a gruesome and mysterious murder that occurred in West Byfleet in January of 1888.

Byfleet boasts at least nine historical landmarks. All nine of these sites were in existence in 1888; and all nine will eventually prove to be of more than passing interest to us in the course of my murder investigation. Although I am not a local resident of Byfleet, or even a Brit for that matter, I will act as your tour guide.

1. **Byfleet Manor Estate** (Figures 1-2 and 1-7) is the village's major historical attraction throughout the year. It is currently maintained in impeccable condition. Various kings and queens have either owned, visited, or temporarily granted the Manor to others.

i. One former resident, **Henry de Leybourne,** was arrested at the manor by Edward I (reign:1272-1307). Edward I was annoyed at de Leybourne for leaving the King's service in Scotland. De Leybourne had journeyed to Byfleet with his paramour for an armored jousting tournament.

ii. **Edward II** (reign: 1307-1327) gave the manor to his courtier **Piers Gaveston**. Edward II's wife, **Queen Isabella** (often called the "She-Wolf of France" due to her French extraction) regarded the Manor as hers. A frequent visitor to the Manor, she later refused to stay there after Edward II gifted it to Piers.

iii. The Byfleet Manor was the favorite country retreat of **Edward of Woodstock** (b. 1330-d. 1376), the son of **Edward III** (reign: 1327-1377), known to history as **The Black Prince.** This celebrated warrior-prince bred horses on the estate.

iv. **Queen Elizabeth I** (reign: 1558-1603)—who needs no introduction—visited the Manor in 1576.

v. **Charles II,** who ruled England, Scotland and Ireland from 1660 to 1665, gave the Manor to his favorite mistress **Barbara, the Countess of Castlemaine,** known for her fiery temperament. Two years after that gift, Charles II took it back and granted it to his new wife, **Catherine of Braganza.** Barbara could not have been pleased.

vi. **Henry VIII** (reign 1509-1547) acquired the Manor in 1509, upon inheriting it from his father, **Henry VII**. In 1529-1530, Henry VIII (**Figure 1-3**) enlarged the Manor House with the addition of a sitting room, two great chambers, a kitchen with a chamber above it, a cellar with two chambers over it, a little chamber over the kitchen, plus other new buildings. He granted the Manor to **Catherine of Aragon** (**Figure 1-4**) upon their bitter divorce litigation and infamous separation in 1533.

Figures 1-3 & 1-4. Henry VIII and Catherine of Aragon;

Figure 1-3. Portrait in oil, 1537, after Hans Holbein, the Younger.
(Photo and portrait; Public Domain in US)
Figure 1-4. Portrait in oil, 1523-1531; English School.
(Photo and portrait; Public Domain in US)

Of his six wives, **Henry VIII** directly coerced a compliant judicial system into executing two: **Anne Boleyn**, Figure 1-5 (while he was wooing **Jane Seymour;**) and **Catherine Howard,** Figure 1-6 (on trumped-up charges of treason.) According to the FBI's recently modified definition of serial murder, Henry VIII now qualifies as a serial killer. In 2005, the FBI convoked a symposium of 135 experts on serial murder. This group of criminologists and law enforcement officers settled on a definition of serial murder as "a series of two-or-more murders, committed as separate events, usually, but not always, by one offender acting alone."

This basic definition does not consider motivation for killing, nor define a cooling-off period. Psychological gratification is typically the motive for serial murders. Serial murder is a distinct classification of homicide that differs from mass murder and spree killings. Before this symposium took place, the FBI had defined a serial killer typically as a person who murders *three-or-more* victims. Now two victims are sufficient if the murders are "ordered."

Incidentally, I note here that both victim-wives of Henry VIII were decapitated. Henry accused Anne of adultery. Anne, Henry's first wife, was convicted and beheaded on May 19, 1536. Of course, Henry's true motive for having her executed was that Anne had not given birth to a male heir. Henry baselessly accused Catherine Howard, his fifth wife of a scandalous past. She was found guilty of adultery and treason, and was beheaded at the Tower of London in 1542.

Figures 1-5 & 1-6. Anne Boleyn; and Young Woman Assumed to be Catherine Howard.

Figure 1-5. Oil Portrait. 1550. Artist Unknown.
(Photo and portrait; Public Domain in US)

Figure 1-6. Portrait miniature, ca 1540; by Hans Holbein the Younger
(Photo and portrait; Public Domain in US)

It has been estimated by historians that up to 57,000 people were executed or murdered at the behest of Henry VIII during his 36 years of ruthless rule over England. Many of his victims were either members of the clergy or ordinary citizens and nobles. They had taken part in uprisings and protests throughout the country. For those victims accused of heresy, witchcraft and treason, the forms of execution included being burned at the stake, hanged, drawn and quartered, or of course beheaded. However, only commoners could be tortured in detention.

vii. In 1616-1617, as mentioned earlier, the wife of **James I** (reign: 1603-1625), **Queen Anne** (of Danish extraction,) rebuilt Byfleet Manor in luxurious style. In subsequent remodeling, however, many of Anne's additions were removed—with the exception of the impressive gateway leading to the courtyard.

Also, Anne's two large chimney stacks remain in place today.

Figure 1-7; **Byfleet Manor Estate in the 21st Century**

(Photo: photographer unknown; Surrey Live)

The 19-acre manor estate dates back to the 7th Century. In 2015, it was placed on the real estate market for sale at £6 million.

2. **The Mill Compound at Coxes Lock (Figure 1-8)** is a charming compound of three brick buildings that extends in part over a photogenic pond on the River Wey at Addlestone, near Byfleet. The three closely grouped structures were originally named the Alexander Raby Mill, the Daniel Lambert Mill and the John Bunn Mill. Built in 1776, the complex gradually became the most significant cluster of mills on the River Wey. The mill compound was rebuilt in 1901 and extended

in 1906. It ceased its operations in 1983. The buildings still stand today. Following the mill's closure in 1983, the old brick buildings were converted into residential use.

Today, the mill compound is usually called the John Bunn Mill, or sometimes Coxes Lock Mill. It is located about 2.5 miles from the center of Byfleet. This lovely locale draws many tourists to the area all year round. Coxes Lock Mill is listed for preservation under a Grade II category.

Figure 1-8; The Mill at Coxes Lock, at Addlestone.

(Photo by Andy Stephenson, 2008; CC BY-SA 2.0)

3. Coxes Lock (Figure 1-9) opens and closes the short navigational canal that leads from the River

Wey into the mill pond. A footbridge crosses the navigational canal above the lock's sluice gate. Coxes Lock regulates the flow of water through the navigational canal into the Mill Pond. Water also flows into the Mill Pond via a slide. Coxes Lock is located about 25 yards from one of the three brick buildings generally known today collectively as the John Bunn Mill.

Figure 1-9. An aerial view of the John Bunn Mill compound (*i.e.,* all three large buildings in the center.) Coxes Lock is located near the top/center of this photo, where the Wey Navigational Canal meets the Mill Pond.

(Aerial Photo © 2016 Google Map; Fair Use.)

4. St. Mary's Church (Figure 1-10) is a small, beautiful, Anglican church near the center of

Byfleet. Its nave and chancel go back to circa 1310. Before that, a church stood on this site, but it may not have been the same structure as St. Mary's. The present nave is 42 feet in length, and the chancel is 20 feet long. The stone walls are made of flint and puddingstone. The belfry is a simple but very tall wooden structure that contains three bells, dated 1853. The church is surrounded by graveyards. There are wall paintings that date from the late 14th Century. Underneath a Medieval engraved brass plate dated 1481—the plate marks a tomb monument—lies the remains of Thomas Teylar, "rector of the parish church of Biflete, and one of the canons of the cathedral church of Lincoln."

Figure 1-10; **Church of St. Mary, the Virgin; Rectory Lane; Byfleet, Surrey. This view shows the rear entrance facing South.**

(Photo by Hassocks5489; 2015; CC 1.0)

5. The Old Fire Station (Figures 11 & 12) in Byfleet is a rare surviving example of a Victorian village fire station. It was built in 1885 (shortly before the Byfleet Murder) at the west end of High Road by the MP (and a former Lord Mayor of London) Sir John Ellis. It served Byfleet's Volunteer Fire Brigade, founded in 1871. In 1963, the fire station's operations were terminated, but the two attached structures still stand today in their

original locations. In 2009, the interiors of the rooms were renovated. The old interior plaster walls were torn out or repainted. In 2014, the large front doors were repainted a glossy fire-engine red. The exterior color photo shown below was taken in 2007 before the doors were completely repainted bright red. The Fire Station is listed as a Grade 2 historical structure.

Figure 1-11; The Old Byfleet Fire Station—built in 1885.
(Photo by Kevin Hale; used with permission.)

Figure 1-12; Byfleet Fire Department in the late 19th Century

(Photographer unknown; Photo: Public Domain in U.S.)

6. **Hoods Field** (**Figure 1-13**) is a 16th Century timber-framed house still in use as a private residence.

Figure 1-13; Hoods Field

(Photo courtesy of the Byfleet Historical Newsletter)

7. **The Blue Anchor** (**Figure 1-14**) is a local inn and pub in continuous business on High Road for more than a century. It has been rebuilt and expanded over the years. Here, below, is the Blue Anchor as it appeared in the late 20th Century.

Figure 1-14; The Blue Anchor in West Byfleet as it appeared in the late 20th Century

(Photo © Colin Smith; CC 2.0 BY-SA)

8. **The Queen's Head Pub and Inn** (**Figures 1-15**) is a local inn and pub in continuous business on High Road for more than a century. It, too, has been rebuilt and expanded over the years.

Figure 1-15; The Queen's Head in 2022

Photo source; whatpub.com

9. **The West Byfleet Train Station** (**Figure 1-16**) was built and opened in 1887 when the Southwestern Main Line was extended from Woking—just months before the occurrence of the Byfleet Murder. The line and the station introduced Byfleet to commuter train travel in Surrey and beyond. In 1887 and thereafter, it was possible to travel from West Byfleet to Waterloo Station in London in less than an hour. Today, this station on Claremont Road is named the West Byfleet Train Station, to distinguish it from the Byfleet & New Haw Railway Station near Brooklands, which opened in 1927.

Figure 1-16; West Byfleet Train Station (photographed in 1962)

(Photo by Ben Brooksbank; CC SA 2.0)

All this historical information about the village of Byfleet, detailed at length above, may seem now like an irksome distraction—apparently irrelevant to the subject of this book: that is, a ghastly murder in January of 1888. By the end of Volume 2 of *A Trail of Blood; The Byfleet Murder & Mutilation (Continued,)* however, a reader may well wonder about this mysterious murder: why was the tiny, obscure village of Byfleet selected for its location? Perhaps the answer to that intriguing question lies hidden deep in the village's historical past. Was the perpetrator (or the perpetrators) of the Byfleet Murder & Mutilation possibly inspired by the beheadings of Henry VIII? Was Byfleet chosen as the location for this still-unsolved 19th Century crime because so many of its historic structures had survived in 1888—and are still standing now? Hmmmm, I wondered. Could these historic sites yet be hiding some undiscovered forensic evidence pertaining to the Byfleet Murder & Mutilation—'new' evidence that still survives, even today?

"What bloody man is that?"

William Shakespeare; *Macbeth* (Act I, Scene ii)

Chapter 2; The Murder and Mutilation of George Chuter

On the morning of January 13, 1888, a Friday, the peaceful, bucolic village of Byfleet was shattered by shocking news, spread by word-of-mouth among the residents, about a savage murder that had occurred during the previous evening. From the presence of a multitude of police officers at the crime scene on Chertsey Road, the residents learned that an elderly man, well-known in Byfleet, had been murdered during the late evening hours of January 12, 1888.

As more news filtered out in the neighborhood, it was subsequently learned that the victim had been found brutally battered while inside his cottage. More precisely, the victim's residence was located between West Byfleet and neighboring Addlestone.

Earliest News Reports.

Byfleet was so isolated and so small that printed news coverage of the murder was initially slow and very sparse—especially in the County of Surrey. I could not find any printed document of the event recorded in a local newspaper published in Byfleet, or in any of the surrounding villages in Surrey, which appeared on January 13, 1888, the day following the murder. Local news would have to wait until Saturday, January 14, the day the county weekly paper, the *Surrey Advertiser*, published its regular edition.

On the evening of January 13, a brief newspaper account appeared in the Lancashire *Evening Post.* Lancashire (Figure 2-1) is a county in northwest England, quite far from Surrey and London in the Southeast.

Figure 2-1. Lancashire County, in North-West England, is marked on the map in red.

The identical item was also published that same evening by the Sheffield *Evening Telegraph.* Sheffield (Figure 2-2) is located near the center of England, still quite far away from Surrey and London.

Figure 2-2; **Map of England showing the location of Sheffield (indicated with a green arrow.)**

Evidently, this tiny news announcement was transmitted on January 13 throughout England by telegraph, sent by one of the wire service news agencies that were based in London. It was subsequently picked up on the evening of January 13, 1888 by the Lancashire *Evening Post* and the Sheffield *Evening Telegraph.* These two identical accounts were the earliest published news reports of the Byfleet Murder that I found in my research. There may have been other accounts published even earlier—that is, published on the morning of January 13—that have yet to turn up.

The news agency wire service's account, as published in these two newspapers, was not only very brief, it was also incomplete with respect to some basic information expected in any news report about a murder. And, as we will soon see, the report was also somewhat inaccurate. However, despite the report's brevity, the agency's anonymous journalist had used some of its limited space to introduce a theory of the crime. "It is supposed that…" one sentence began. "Supposed" by whom? No attribution for the supposition was given. Evidently, it was supposed by the local police (who were never credited, nor even mentioned in this story, other than to say indirectly: "No arrests have been made.")

Here is the news agency wire service item, in full:

> **BRUTAL MURDER OF AN OLD MAN IN SURREY**
> **An old, retired carpenter named Charter *[sic,]* aged between 60 and 70, who lived in a small cottage between Byfleet and Addlestone, was brutally murdered last night. The deceased lived near his son, who, however, was absent last night. It is supposed that this fact becoming known, some person or persons broke into his house, and battered the skull of the old man. No arrests have been made.**

[Quoted texts of all documents are indented and set in a sans serif type font, in boldface, throughout this series of books. I do not use quotation marks for each quoted document.]

Inaccuracies Abound.

First, a major correction, and then two additional, indispensable facts: the victim's correct last name was spelled Chuter, not Charter. His first name was George. His age at the time of his death was 67.

The article correctly reported that "some person or persons broke into his house," although the reporter's careless use of the words "broke into" misleadingly implied that the perpetrator (or perpetrators) had broken down a door, or possibly smashed a window, in order to gain entrance into the house. This was not the case. As we will learn in subsequent news reports, there was no sign anywhere about the house of forced entry. The kitchen door—the sole entrance into George Chuter's residence—had, evidently, been locked.

The brief news report stated that "some person or persons broke into his house and battered the skull of the old man." As subsequent news reports will make starkly evident, "battered the skull of the old man" does not even begin to suggest the full extent of the mutilations inflicted upon the body of George Chuter. He was both brutally battered *and* mutilated.

Lastly, the report states: "The deceased lived near his son, who, however, was absent last night." Not quite so. The deceased did not live "near" his son. In fact, George Chuter shared his cottage with his son, James. Not only did father and son live together in the residential portion of the cottage, the son operated a small grocery store in the front room of the cottage facing Chertsey Road. George's son was indeed absent from the cottage that evening. The grocery had closed early. As we will soon discover, the son's whereabouts were well-known all that evening—and so, the son had an air-tight alibi for the time of the crime. All these details will assume greater significance as I proceed with my investigation.

Person (or Persons)?

At this preliminary stage in the police's investigation, it was not immediately apparent whether the murder had been committed by a sole killer, or by two-or-more killers at the crime scene, all acting in concert. Consequently, the London news service report, published in the Lancashire *Evening Post* and Sheffield *Evening Telegraph,* had quite properly employed an awkward but necessary legal locution—"some person or persons." This vague expression avoids specifying the exact number of murderers when that number is not yet known; and thus, this expression does not prejudice the reader into jumping to unwarranted conclusions about the crime scene evidence on this crucial issue.

Moreover, by using "person or persons" instead of "man or men," the locution does not prejudice the reader into believing that a violent crime like this one could have been committed only by a man, or only by men. But, to be frank, the gender of the killer (or killers) will not prove to be a significant issue in this investigation of the Byfleet Murder. There was never a scintilla of evidence to suggest that a woman (or women) might have been responsible for this horrendous crime. The number of killers, however, will prove to be one of the central issues throughout my investigation.

My Dilemma.

I, too, will avoid using nouns that specify number with respect to the perpetrator (or perpetrators)—that is, until that question is clearly resolved with crime scene evidence. This issue must be credibly documented before I can refer to either one perpetrator or to several perpetrators. When the preponderance of the evidence indicates that this murder was committed either by a lone killer or by more-than-one killer acting in concert, then I will employ nouns that specify either the singular or the plural. Pronouns that refer to the "person or persons" responsible for the perpetration of the crime must also avoid specifying the singular or plural, as long as that number remains unknown.

Awkward Circumlocutions.

The consistent use of nouns and pronouns of indeterminate number is a cumbersome process for any writer. Numerous repetitions of awkward expressions—such as 'the killer (or killers)' and 'the perpetrator (or perpetrators)'—can quickly become tiresome to read. In my first draft of *The Byfleet Murder*, I employed "the killer (or killers)" and similar expressions that are non-specific about number. I used 'the perpetrator (or perpetrators)' and 'the murderer (or murderers') innumerable times. I soon found there were so many instances of these cumbersome expressions in my text, the frequent repetition of these boilerplate phrases had become not merely annoying to read, but utterly oppressive. The problem grew worse when I was forced to employ compound pronouns (such as himself/themselves) to match the common nouns of indeterminate number.

So, as a compromise, I reluctantly decided to substitute yet another type of locution—but a much shorter one—to indicate simultaneously both the singular and the plural of common nouns: e.g. killer(s); or murderer(s.) Even that makeshift workaround has its annoying grammatical problems—such as where to place an apostrophe to indicate a possessive. The agreement of indeterminate nouns and verbs is still a nightmare. Nevertheless, maintaining an indeterminate number of killers until an analysis of crime scene evidence can credibly establish the actual number of perpetrators is an important issue in any murder investigation. An impartial investigation rests on an objective examination of the evidence, not assumptions based on past experiences in somewhat similar murder investigations. So, I ask readers' indulgence for the clumsy word-twisting.

The Chuters' Living Arrangements.

I've already mentioned the erroneous statement: "The deceased lived near his son…" The evidence that this statement was in error can be found in a news article published later in *Lloyd's Weekly Newspaper* (London.) I will examine this article in detail in another chapter. But for now, it is sufficient to quote this sentence: "It appears that an old man named Chutor *[sic]* lived with his son at a small house in Byfleet, the son keeping a portion of the house as a grocer's shop." Thus, the true relationship between George Chuter and his son is made clear in *Lloyd's* report. George Chuter's son—whose full name was James Chuter—lived in the same small cottage with his father, not "near" him. They lived together in the same part of the house, not in separate quarters. Moreover, part of their cottage—the front room—had been converted into a tiny grocery store. In other words, the living quarters of two grown men plus a grocery shop were all part of one house—which was described not only as a "cottage," but furthermore as a "small cottage."

However, as subsequent articles and photographs will later elucidate, the cottage was actually a double tenement—that is, the structure contained two separate residential units, plus James' grocery store, all under rather complex roofs. The two living quarters were divided by a common internal wall. James did not reside in the second unit. The family of bootmaker Simon Choate and his wife lived in the adjacent unit. George and James Chuter's portion of the cottage was indeed quite small in the back. James' tiny grocery store—located in the front, facing Chertsey Road—was separated from the Chuters' residence by the Choates' larger portion of the double tenement.

Clarifying the Date and Place of the Crime.

On the evening of January 13, the two identical reports published in the Lancashire *Evening Post* and the Sheffield *Evening Telegraph* stated that George had been murdered "last night." Since the word "night" when used in a general sense, can encompass the very late hours of one day and the very early hours of the following day, "last evening," or "the evening hours of January 12, 1888" would have been a more precise, unambiguous statement.

The exact time of the murder will be discussed at considerable length later. It is a key element in the investigation. In fact, the murder occurred well before midnight. Thus, it is now accurate to say that George Chuter was murdered on the evening of January 12, 1888. Circumstances surrounding the body made it plain that the murder could not possibly have occurred after midnight, or at any other location at an earlier time. There was no suggestion in any later news report that the body had been moved to-or-from the spot in which it was found by James.

James' Absence and No Forced Entry.

The initial wire service report published in the Lancashire *Evening Post* and the Sheffield *Evening Telegraph* indicated that George was murdered inside his house. Moreover, the articles noted that George's son had been absent from the house at the time the murder occurred. The news agency's reporter (and apparently also the local police) had already developed a theory based upon the fact that George's son was, without any doubt, absent from home when George was attacked inside the cottage. "This fact becoming known," the reporter stated, "some person or persons broke into his house, and battered the skull of the old man." That is an interesting theory; but it raises many unanswered questions.

First, did the killer(s) know in advance precisely when James would be absent from the house that evening, and when he would return? Did the killer(s) plan in advance to murder George in his cottage at that time in order to take advantage of James' absence? Or was the time-range of James' absence merely a fortuitous coincidence with a pre-arranged plan to murder George in his residence that evening? [Fortuitous for the killer(s,) that is.]

And second, in later reports, the police indicated there was no sign about the house of any forced entry. So, how did the killer(s) enter George's locked residence? Did

George let him/them inside—indicating that the killer(s) might have been a person (or persons) whom George knew and trusted? Or did George go out that evening without securely locking his house? Did the killer(s) manage to enter the cottage during George's absence by jimmying the door lock—and then lying-in-wait inside the kitchen for George to return?

The Victim Alone.

It would have been of great advantage for the killer(s) to confront George while he was alone inside his house—where the murder would be unobserved by eyewitnesses. If the killer(s) had managed to enter the house while George was away, then he/they could have surprised George in the dark upon his return. Indeed, if that had been the plan, then the killer(s) would have faced greatly reduced risk—compared to attacking George outside the house upon his return home.

Moreover, assaulting a lone, old, retired carpenter would have been far less risky than attacking both father and son simultaneously. We don't know yet James' age or his physical strength. Nevertheless, we can safely assume that a working man joining his 67-year-old father in a fight could have put up much more of a struggle than just "old" George acting alone. If James had been present at the scene, the killer(s) would have had to face two combatants instead of one; and would have had to murder two victims in order to escape unidentified. Two things the killer(s) must have feared most were a scream in the night or a loud cry for help—either from George or from James (if James had actually been present.) A scream in the night or a cry for help might have alerted neighbors who, in turn, would have contacted law-enforcement officers. With no eyewitness present inside the house, the killer(s) could murder George without fear of raising an alarm from James or from any nearby neighbors.

To prevent George from screaming or yelling for help, the killer(s) would have had to surprise him, preferably in the dark, immediately knocking him unconscious upon entry, or murdering him in the dark before he could react. Killing George quickly, before he could scream, was undoubtedly a key element in the murder plan. Moreover, it is already clear that James' absence was crucial to the success of the attack. The Surrey police appear to have been correct in their deduction.

That the murder was committed during the absence from the cottage of George's son did not appear to the agency reporter of this news article to be mere coincidence. This theory of the crime rests on the "supposition" that James' absence was previously scheduled, and that the time-range of his scheduled absence had become known to the killer(s) prior to the murder. This knowledge aforethought enabled the perpetrator(s) to formulate a low-risk plan to surprise George when he was alone inside his cottage.

A Local Report.

On January 14, the *Surrey Advertiser and County Times* published its own account. Not surprisingly for a local newspaper, a considerable portion of this article was devoted to descriptions of the dramatic impact this savage murder and mutilation had on the local population of Byfleet. This newspaper spelled George's family name correctly. The article ran as follows:

> **Byfleet, early on Friday morning, was thrown into a state of alarm and consternation on its becoming known that a most brutal and cold-blooded murder had been committed right in the midst of one of the most frequented parts, and no more than 50 yards from the King's Head Inn. To add to the feeling, the victim proved to be an old and much esteemed resident, who had been done to death just within the threshold of his own doorway in the quiet little Surrey Village he had made his home and haven of rest after retiring from the active pursuits of life.**
>
> **The murdered man was Mr. George Chuter, aged 67, a retired builder, who was living with his son, James Chuter, grocer, in the Chertsey-road, near the King's Head Inn; and the facts of the case are very few and terribly shocking in their character, so much so that the inhabitants seemed awestruck by the event. The women and villagers generally stood about in groups discussing the**

painful occurrence in its details, and strangers in the village were regarded with eager and scrutinizing looks, whilst the school children were subdued in their play, and regarded with wonderment and fear the large number of police present, who were busy making inquiries in all directions. The details appeared to be that about twenty minutes to 7 on Thursday evening, James Chuter, the son, left home to attend a band practice with the village band, leaving his father at home in the dwelling- house portion of the premises. He returned home at about 10:30, and on letting himself in with the latch-key, fell over the prostrate body of his father. Thinking him ill, he ran to a neighbor near, Mr. Choate, and the light having been obtained, the two men returned to the house, and upon entering were horrified to find the body of Mr. Chuter lying on the floor in a pool of blood; and an examination disclosed the awful fact that his throat was cut almost from ear to ear, whilst his head had been battered terribly by some blunt instruments, which had cut the nose through, and also the left ear.

There was not the slightest evidence of a struggle having taken place, but a cash-box belonging to the deceased, and used by himself only, had been stolen from the bedroom. The alarm was given, and the police communicated with, and Super-intendent Bungard, accompanied by Inspector Barker, were within a very short time on the spot, and a large force of police soon organized to scour the country and make inquiries. The Superintendent carefully examined the premises, but there was no indication of the house having been broken into. The police tried the latch-lock, which being a common one, was easily opened by a piece of bent wire.

At about twenty past 7, that deceased man, who was of robust constitution and a cheery disposition, was seen at the Queen's Head, where he had been to take a glass of beer, and a left about the time named for his home. It is supposed that on going indoors, the deceased must have alarmed the robbers or robber already in the house, and, that he was struck down with the kitchen poker, and afterwards his throat brutally cut whilst lying insensible on the ground. Dr. Seeley was sent for in the morning, but his assistance was of course unnecessary.

On the son of the deceased being questioned by our representative, he said he left his father about twenty minutes to seven, and went with a young man friend to the band practice. He returned home himself about 10:30, and on letting himself in with his latchkey, he fell over the body of his father lying on the floor. This fact greatly alarmed him, and without striking a light, he ran to Mr. Choate next-door and asked him to come back with him as he could feel his father was on the floor. He came with him and they lit a light, when they found this father in a tremendous pool of blood. His poor head was dreadfully battered, and Mr. Choate suggested that he had fallen down and broken a blood vessel, but on closer examination they saw at once a terrible gash in his throat. On the kitchen table near was a large poker, and their own carving knife covered with blood. He then realized too truly that his father had been foully murdered. The police were at once sent for, and the matter placed in their hands. The deceased had a quantity of house property in Byfleet, where he at one time carried on the business of a carpenter, and also kept the Queen's Head Inn. The greatest sympathy is felt for the family in their trial. It is a singular circumstance that some eight or nine months ago, the same house was broken into, and some properties stolen.

Since writing the above, we learn that Mr. Deputy-Chief Constable Barker has visited Byfleet, and although unable to glean any further important particular's that are narrated above, he states that on the deceased leaving the Queen's Head, he remarked to the landlady, "you will not see me again." It is also somewhat remarkable that the next-door neighbor, Mrs. Choate – the house being a double tenement one – was sitting in the front room all the evening, but never heard a sound; whilst, in consequence of a magic lantern entertainment at the National Schools, there was

an unusually large number of people out in the village on the evening of the tragedy. Mr. Barker also states that a watch and chain, with some money, belonging to the deceased's son was found lying on the dressing table in his bedroom untouched.

It is a melancholy coincidence that about a year ago, the deceased's wife died suddenly at Byfleet, and an inquest was held on the body.

How did the Killer(s) Learn When James Would Be Absent from the Cottage?

For the plan to murder George to proceed smoothly, the killer(s) had to have known in advance exactly when James would leave the cottage, and when he would return. As we will learn when I examine reports of the Coroner's Inquest (scheduled for January 16, 1888,) James played in the village band the night of the murder. He had a regularly scheduled rehearsal on the evening of January 12, which conflicted with the time of the murder. There is no doubt James was playing his clarinet in the band when his father was murdered and mutilated in the family residence. The time and place of this regular band rehearsal were no secret; indeed, this information was public knowledge. It took place in a hall in a park about a mile away.

Moreover, the grocery portion of the cottage had closed early that night to enable James to attend the rehearsal. So, on the evening of the murder, the killer(s) could have hidden himself/themselves somewhere on Chertsey Road and waited for James to exit the cottage and walk to his band rehearsal in a park. Both the commencement and the conclusion of the rehearsal had been scheduled far in advance. So, the killer(s) could have obtained in advance precise knowledge indicating exactly when James would return to the cottage that evening. In this initial glimpse of the murder scene, one can already see several signs of advance planning, preparation, organization, and clever strategies devised by the perpetrator(s.) Thus, the Byfleet Murder was a far more complex crime than first meets the eye.

The Victim and His Son.

George Chuter was described in this account as an "old, retired carpenter." In a later article, he was described as an innkeeper. Evidently, he was both at different times during his long working life. In news reports that subsequently appeared, there was no mention that he kept an inn at the time of the murder. Nor was it reported that he then worked in the grocery store. On the evening of the murder, the grocery store portion of the cottage was closed—likely because of James' absence.

Thus., the grocery store was apparently run by the son alone, not by the father—who, as mentioned earlier, had been described in the news account as "retired." It is possible, however, that George had invested in the grocery store, at least in part, since subsequent evidence showed he had sufficient means to live in retirement comfortably, although very modestly.

Murder Most Foul.

The brief article published in both the Lancashire *Evening Post* and Sheffield *Evening Express* mentioned that George had died after his skull was brutally battered. Subsequent reports, including a forensic medical examination by a local doctor, would eventually reveal that his wounds were far more extensive and brutal than just a battered skull. There was never a doubt in anyone's mind that the attack on George was murder most foul—not an accident, nor a suicide. We will examine the nature of George's wounds after his body was examined by the medical doctor—who would testify at the Coroner's Inquest on January 16,1888.

Following the discovery of George's body, the police made no arrests; nor did they name any possible suspects—or even any "persons of interest." They were baffled. Utterly baffled. And they remained so. Never any suspects. Never any eyewitnesses. Never any arrests. Above all, the Surrey Constabulary could not find any physical evidence at the crime scene that would establish a credible motive for this savage attack—despite floating nothing more than a hunch.

The victim's son, with whom George shared his cottage, was absent from the crime scene when George was murdered. Thus, the son had an unshakeable alibi for the time of the murder. Upon his return home, the son discovered his father's savagely mutilated body. George's corpse lay on the floor of his kitchen, covered in blood, next to the entrance door. As James entered through the doorway, he stumbled over his father's body in the dark. At no time was James ever considered a suspect by the police or by the press.

Piecing Together the Police's Theory of the Crime.

Following James' discovery of his father's body, the police were soon notified by a neighbor. The Surrey Constabulary quickly arrived at the scene. The Byfleet Murder appeared to them to be a conundrum *sui generis.* The police had never before seen anything quite like this murder scene; and they had no idea what to make of the mutilations on George's body. After they determined there had been no forced entry into the Chuters' residence, and they had eliminated James as a possible suspect, they were bewildered to come up with any <u>credible</u> motive. So they turned to the 'usual suspects.' In some ways, the murder of George Chuter may have vaguely resembled some 'run-of-the mill' murders of the past. And so, the police pushed forward in a traditional direction. They repeatedly suggested that the murder of George Chuter was probably a robbery-gone-sour by a local burglar.

As a robbery-gone-sour, the evidence—when considered in its entirety—makes no sense to me. A burglar might assault a homeowner in order to escape being captured. A burglar might even kill a homeowner to prevent being later identified. But why would a burglar methodically *mutilate* a homeowner during the course of a robbery? As we will see from medical testimony at the inquest, the multiple mutilations inflicted on George's body were not the result of a momentary slip by a panicked burglar. The wounds indicated methodical, precisely administered mutilations. And the principal mutilation was administered after the victim had been savagely battered and was likely dying (or was already dead.) In this crime, burglary is not a credible motive for methodical mutilations.

As every detective (both amateur and professional) knows: when some physical evidence in a murder makes no sense, there must be a reason for it—no matter how outrageous or outlandish that reason may, at first, seem to appear. Sir Arthur Conan Doyle famously expressed this idea in the following oft-quoted manner:

> **"Once you eliminate the impossible, whatever remains, no matter how improbable, must be the truth."**

Thus, one must never sweep inconsistencies under the rug. One cannot ignore them—which is precisely what the authorities in Byfleet did in their clueless investigation. After 136 years, this mysterious murder and mutilation of an old man alone in his locked kitchen still remains officially unsolved.

Also, oft-quoted is the Chinese proverb attributed to Laozi: "A journey of a thousand miles begins with a single step." Of course, if you take that first step in the wrong direction, you will never reach your destination. From the vantage point of 2024, it is now clear to me that the Surrey Constabulary never recovered from that initial misstep.

The Number of Killers.

The Surrey Constabulary never came to a definite conclusion, based on crime scene evidence, about another central question: the number of killers at the crime scene. They ignored critical evidence deliberately left in plain sight—or they never comprehended the true significance of what they actually saw. Had they understood the evidentiary significance of certain clues that I will soon discuss, they might have pursued a different, more fruitful line of inquiry. But, in 1888, such a line of inquiry was not yet conceivable.

Instead, the Surrey Constabulary immediately focused on a virtually groundless theory that may have served them well in some past murders; *i.e.,* a robbery-gone-sour by a lone burglar. But, as we will soon see from a detailed examination of the crime scene evidence, this murder and mutilation was unlike anything the Surrey Police had ever encountered before. In hindsight, I believe it was this failure to perceive the number of killers from the crime scene evidence that, in all likelihood, was the principal reason why the Surrey Constabulary never solved the case.

My Opinions are My Own.

In the course of my investigation into the Byfleet Murder, my conclusion about the number of killers is solely my opinion. We know today that the theory of the authorities in Surrey led them nowhere toward a solution in 1888—so there is no need to rehash this flawed theory in great detail. Throughout this and future volumes of *A Trail of Blood,* my opinions are always independent. They are based solely on documented evidence, as I have found it in preserved records. My conclusions are not necessarily the judgments of the police; nor the jury of a Coroner's Inquest; nor the opinions of the Coroner, newspaper reporters, historical writers, profilers or criminologists. They are based mostly on the crime scene evidence presented at the inquest by the medical examiner. They will also be based on 'new' evidence that I recently uncovered, and on old evidence that was documented at the time, but never considered by the Coroner or the police.

I will back up all of my conclusions with factual evidence—including 'new' crime scene evidence that still exists today; 'new' evidence that I uncovered during the course of my investigation; 'new' evidence that still survives in Byfleet—and thus can be corroborated. You can evaluate my conclusions for yourselves, based on the evidence. And you can also evaluate my "new" evidence for yourselves. It still survives. It is preserved in archives. Or it is physical evidence that can still be viewed in Byfleet. We will see where all this "new" evidence will lead us soon enough. However, I can assure my readers now that we will not end up where the Surrey Constabulary abandoned the case in 1888. They eventually gave up pursuing any credible proof based on verifiable crime scene evidence. Instead, they fabricated an unconvincing supposition based merely on a hunch, stemming from their years of past experience in run-of-the-mill murders.

Who-dunnit?—but first, *Why*-He-or-They-Dunnit?

What we have in Byfleet are all the ingredients required for a classic whodunnit! However, the most important question posed by this mysterious mutilation and murder is not the *who*, but the *why*. The true identity/identities of the killer(s) will make no sense until we can crack—with hard crime scene evidence, not with empty speculations—the elusive question of motive.

The murder of George Chuter was a mutilation *and* murder with no *apparent* motives for either crime. Nothing has changed in this regard for 136 years. We do not know yet who killed George. And we have no idea yet why he was murdered *and mutilated.*

Yes, it would be satisfying to know right now the name (or names) of the perpetrator (or perpetrators) who killed

George Chuter. But, for the charge to stick to a culprit (or more-than-one culprit,) we must also find a credible motive—*i.e.,* one backed up by documented, verifiable evidence. Until we know the motive—*i.e.,* why anyone would go to such devious, intricate and malicious lengths to murder *and mutilate* an ordinary bloke like George Chuter—this unsolved crime will remain a gnawing mystery. Moreover, it is conceivable that a credible, documented solution to the Byfleet Murder and Mutilation might blaze a new, convincing trail that leads us to solutions of other yet-unsolved crimes. Such possibly related, unsolved murders and mutilations might have occurred both after and before Jan. 12, 1888.

Chapter 3. The Investigation by the Surrey Constabulary

The plays the thing,
To catch the conscience of the King.

Hamlet (Act 2, Scene 2)
William Shakespeare

On the morning of January 14—a Saturday—the same short news article that had appeared on January 13 in the Lancashire *Evening Post* and Sheffield *Evening Telegraph* was printed yet again in several more newspapers elsewhere in England. For example, the Manchester *Courier* ran this same short article on the Byfleet Murder in which George's last name was now misspelled as Chayter. The following day, the news coverage became more serious.

Lloyd's Weekly Newspaper (London.)

On Sunday, January 15, *Lloyd's Weekly Newspaper,* a major newsweekly in London, published a detailed factual account. But once again, the victim's name was misspelled, this time as Chutor. This detailed, fact-filled article is clearly the product of independent, on-the-scene reporting—although there was no byline in *Lloyd's* story, as was common journalistic practice in those days. *Lloyd's* report contained several judgments; but it is not clear, at least not to me, who made these judgments—the nameless reporter or the Surrey Constabulary.

SHOCKING MURDER NEAR BYFLEET

Between half-past seven and half-past eight o'clock on Thursday night, a murder was committed at Byfleet, a small village some three miles from Chertsey, in Surrey. It appears that an old man named Chutor *[sic]* lived with his son at a small house in Byfleet, the son keeping a portion of the house as a grocer's shop. The son had occasion to leave at about seven o'clock, and on returning at half-past 10, a horrible scene presented itself. Lying inside the back door was the dead body of his father with his head battered in, and the whole apartment bearing the appearance of a slaughter-house. A further examination of the body disclosed the fact that the throat was cut from ear to ear, so much force having been used that a cravat worn by the murdered man was completely severed.

Near the body lay a poker, which had been taken from an adjoining room, and not far away was a carving-knife, which had been last seen in the kitchen drawer, whence the murderer had apparently taken it. Upon the alarm being given, a search was made of the house, and it was found that a sum of money, the exact amount of which

> **is not known, had been taken from a wardrobe upstairs. It is surmised that Chutor, who was 67 years of age, had gone to fetch some beer, and on his return was met by the murderer, who was descending the stairs with his plunder. It has transpired that an entry was made into the house about 12 months ago, and some 20*l* stolen. Chutor was a man of considerable means, and had a large amount of cottage property in the district.**

Slowly, critical facts about this ghastly crime were beginning to come into focus. In this detailed news report, the anonymous reporter provided answers to four of the five classic journalistic "W's"—*i.e., What* happened? *Who* did it happen to? *Where* did it happen? *When* did it happen? And *Why* did it happen? It was *Lloyd's* answer to this last "W," the *Why,* that was mere unsupported speculation on someone's part.

Moreover, there were in this article some uncorroborated claims and factual exaggerations. No evidence was cited to back up the unsupported claim that Chuter was a man of "considerable means," vague as that description may be. I was never able to find any evidence of his ownership of "a large amount of cottage property in the district." As my investigation proceeds, it will become increasingly apparent that, in retirement, George lived simply and comfortably, but very modestly, if not quite cheaply, in a small portion of the cottage, with a tiny grocery store run by his son in the front room. Indeed, I was never able to find any evidence that George owned anything at the time of his death other than the small cottage in which he and his son resided. If he did own another cottage at the time of his death, other than the one in which he resided, it was never named and documented in the press. Nor did any such evidence come to light at the Coroner's Inquest. So, this statement in *Lloyd's* looks to me like grasping at straws, planted by the police, desperate to concoct a motive, any motive at all, even one with no factual basis. Nevertheless, there is also much accurate factual information of great significance in *Lloyds'* article.

Determining a Sequence of Events and a Timetable.

Lloyd's report set the possible time-range in which George Chuter's murder and mutilation could have occurred: between 7:30 pm and 8:30 pm on Thursday, January 12, 1888. This information must have come from the Surrey police working the case—even though the officers were not specifically named or credited with the deduction in *Lloyd's* article. However, the closing of this window-of-time was inaccurate. It was 10:10-10:15 pm when James returned home from his band rehearsal and discovered the body of his father, lying dead on the kitchen floor. Thus, it was not known at what time the killer(s) had departed the scene. It is theoretically possible that the killer(s) remained in the house until shortly before James' return. The killer(s) could have departed at any time over a more than two and one-half hour period. It is also possible: the killer(s) may have pursued other activities inside George's cottage for nearly three hours after murdering and mutilating the victim. Hmmm, I wondered. What other activities might the killer(s) have pursued for several hours in George's residence alone with the corpse? It appears to me that the police never considered that possibility—and so, the police may not have looked for any evidence of deliberately hidden activities in the cottage that may have followed the murder and mutilation.

Significantly, the reporter added: "It is surmised that Chutor *[sic]*, who was 67 years of age, had gone to fetch some beer, and on his return was met by the murderer..." *Lloyd's* reporter obviously succumbed to laziness and sloppiness when he wrote "was met by the murderer"—instead of writing 'was met by the murderer or murderers.' Also, the reporter did not indicate who did this *surmising*—so once again, I will assume it was the local police officers investigating the murder—or perhaps the *surmiser* was actually Superintendent Bungard himself. There is no mention in *Lloyd's Weekly* report of any factual evidence (such as the testimony of local eyewitnesses) on which this *surmising* was based. We will have to wait until the Coroner's Inquest—scheduled for January 16, 1888—for direct testimony on this important matter.

According to my email exchanges with Surrey police historian Robert Bartlett, the Surrey Constabulary did not have any dedicated homicide detectives on its force in 1888. Murder cases in Surrey were then exceedingly rare. The investigation of the Byfleet Murder must have been directed by Superintendent Alfred Bungard, head of the Chertsey Division, and Deputy-Chief Constable Charles Barker—neither of whom was a trained homicide detective. Nor did the Surrey Constabulary employ crime scene photography in its investigation at the time. According to Bartlett (a former Surrey policeman himself,) crime scene photography did not begin in the Surrey Constabulary until the 1930s.

Momentarily jumping ahead in my story, I will now inform my readers that, in fact, it was true that George had briefly stepped out of his cottage to drink a beer in a nearby pub only minutes before he was murdered in his kitchen. Shortly after he returned home, he was immediately slain the moment he stepped inside his cottage. This *surmisal* would be confirmed later by eyewitnesses at the Coroner's Inquest (on which I will report, beginning in Chapter 4, in minute detail.)

Locations of the Murder Weapons.

Lloyd's reporter gave us valuable information about the previous locations of the two murder weapons (that is, before they were used to kill and mutilate George.)

> **Near the body lay a poker, which had been taken from an adjoining room, and not far away was a**

> **carving-knife, which had been last seen in the kitchen drawer, whence the murderer had apparently taken it.**

So, according to *Lloyd's* reporter, the "murderer" found a poker in an adjoining room and brought it to the kitchen to bludgeon George's head and face. The location of this adjoining room was not specified. However, *Lloyd's* statement is in direct conflict with a sentence in the report published by the *Surrey Advertiser*, which stated:

> **He [George] was struck down with the kitchen poker.**

Which one was it?: a kitchen poker, or a fireplace poker that belonged to another room adjoining the kitchen (where the murder took place.) Where did the poker normally belong? There is no way now to know for sure. Nevertheless, the information in the report by *Lloyd's Weekly Newspaper*—that the poker was normally placed in an adjoining room—could only have come from James Chuter. Thus, it seems to me *Lloyd's* evidence is authentic; while the statement in the *Surrey Advertiser* appears to me to have been an early observation by that paper's reporter, based on his viewing of the bloody poker lying on top of the kitchen table, next to the carving knife. The statement in *Lloyd's* was published the day after the *Surrey Advertiser* published its article; so, the report in *Lloyd's* appears to me to be a later correction. And consequently, the statement in *Lloyd's* seems to me more credible. We will also learn that a determination of the normal location of the poker is not quibbling over irrelevant details.

From the evidence reported in *Lloyd's* about the two murder weapons, we can now make several observations. The two murder weapons were apparently found by the killer(s) in two separate rooms. The carving knife was found in the kitchen; while the poker was found in an adjoining room. Moreover, the carving knife was normally placed out of view in the drawer of the kitchen table. If George had left his house darkened during his brief absence at the King's Head, then how did the killer(s) know where to find the two murder weapons quickly—particularly, in the dark? The killer(s) did not dare light a lamp during George's absence. Had George seen a lamp burning in his kitchen window upon his return, he would have known that his residence had been entered by an intruder (or by intruders.) The plan to attack George the moment he entered his kitchen might have failed then and there.

Both Murder Weapons Belonged to the Chuter Household.

The two murder weapons belonged to George and James Chuter. They were not brought to the scene by the killer(s.) We also know this from the report in the *Surrey Advertiser:*

On the kitchen table near was a large poker, and their own carving knife covered with blood.

Thus, it is evident: after killing and mutilating George, but before departing the scene, the killer(s) carefully set the two bloody murder weapons on top of the kitchen table—where they knew the weapons would inevitably be seen by the police. The placement of the two bloody murder weapons on top of the kitchen table next to the victim unequivocally establishes this carving knife and this poker as the two weapons that murdered and mutilated George Chuter. So, the two weapons were placed by the killer(s) at a location where they must have been seen by Surrey policemen investigating the crime. It is already obvious to me: the killer(s) deliberately intended for both these murder weapons to be seen together, next to the victim's mutilated body. It is also clear to me that the deliberate, highly visible, careful placement of both weapons together on the kitchen table was intended by the killer(s) to send the police a message. But the Surrey Constabulary never got the message.

The Surrey Constabulary.

In 1888, the Surrey Constabulary was a relatively small rural police force. It began policing the county on January 1, 1851, with a total of 70 officers, the youngest of whom was 14 years old. Byfleet was protected by the Chertsey Division, which in the 1880s apparently consisted of 28 constables and three administrators—at least, according to the 28 badges on helmets and the three administrators' hats on display in the 1880 group photograph, shown below, (see **Figure 3-1**.)

This remarkable photograph was graciously provided to me by Robert Bartlett, who currently maintains a website dedicated to the history of the Surrey Police. Bartlett wrote to me that he had no doubt the man in the top hat was Superintendent Bungard. A local news article mentions that Superintendent Bungard retired from the force in 1890, having served in the Surrey Constabulary for 39 years, 18 of which as the head of the Chertsey Division. Possibly, Deputy Chief Constable Barker was also visible in this photo—in which case he could have been one of the two officials seated on either side of Superintendent Bungard. (Barker was misspelled as Baker in at least one press report.) But that latter identification is merely my guess.

Although there are no names attached to this 1880 photograph, it would seem logical that the three men in the center of the middle row wearing distinctive hats (instead of uniform police helmets) were the top brass in the department; and that Superintendent Bungard of the Chertsey Division was the man in the center, wearing a stove-pipe top hat.

Figure 3-1: The Surrey Constabulary, Chertsey Division in the 1880s. Photo graciously provided to me by local Surrey police historian Robert Bartlett.

(Photographer unknown; photo predates 1929: public domain in US.)

Here, below, in Figure 3-2, is an enlargement of the top brass in the Surrey Constabulary, circa 1880. If the man in the top hat was indeed Superintendent Bungard, then either the man on his left or right may well have been Chief Inspector Barker. Additional information to make an accurate identification of all three officials would be most welcome.

Figure 3-2: **According to Surrey Police historian Robert Bartlett, the man in the top hat in the center of this photo is very likely Superintendent Bungard, who directed the investigation.**

(Photographer unknown; photo predates 1929: public domain in US.)

According to Bartlett, Barker's official title in the Surrey Constabulary was, at one time, Superintendent and Deputy-Chief Constable; and thus, he was *primus inter pares* among all the regional superintendents, including Superintendent Bungard. Evidently, the Chuter Murder was of such critical significance to the Surrey Constabulary that both Deputy-Chief Constable Barker and Chertsey-Division Superintendent Bungard later ventured from Surrey Police Headquarters in Guildford, to attend the Coroner's Inquest at the Queen's Head in Byfleet. But neither Barker nor Bungard got any joy from these official proceedings.

In the 19th Century, the Surrey Constabulary had no separate criminal investigations division, similar to Scotland Yard's famed CID. Serious crimes like murders were investigated primarily by the regional Superintendent with the assistance of some inspectors and constables. Apparently, Superintendent Bungard personally directed the investigation into George Chuter's murder, with the assistance of Deputy-Chief Constable Barker.

What the Constables Found.

During the Coroner's Inquest on January 16, two constables testified: PC Thomas Mears (**Figure 3-3**, below) and PC Dearlove. Here is a preview of their inquest testimony—which I will analyze in Chapter 5. PC Mears deposed that his examination of the scene revealed no indications of a struggle anywhere. He also testified: "Deceased was fully dressed, with the exception of a hat; his overcoat was fully buttoned." When George's hat was pointed out to him, PC Mears picked it up and said: "There was a mark, as if made by the poker, on the deceased's soft felt hat."

Sgt. Thomas Mears, sergeant in charge of Camberley police station in 1906.

Figure 3-3. PC Thomas Mears (1860-1934,) who would Later become Superintendent Mears. Photo graciously provided to me by Robert Bartlett, Surrey Police historian.

Photographer unknown; Photo: public domain in U.S.

PC Mears' testimony contains important evidence—the full significance of which would subsequently be missed by the Coroner at the inquest. The blow that struck George on the back of his head had landed on his hat. Evidently, George had no time to unbutton his 'greatcoat' when he walked through his kitchen door, upon returning from the King's Head. Also, he did not have sufficient time to remove his hat from his head. The first blow from the poker struck George's hat—indicating that George was first attacked with the poker the instant he entered his kitchen. Evidently, the killer (or killers) was/were lying in wait, hidden inside the kitchen, behind the kitchen door—ready to strike, as soon as George stepped inside the doorway.

PC Mears also testified that he found George's gloves and house key in a pocket of George's overcoat. So, when George arrived outside his kitchen door from the King's Head, he removed his gloves and put them into his coat pocket. Then, he used his house key to unlock the kitchen door. He returned the key to his coat pocket. These actions support the conclusion that the lock on the kitchen door was indeed closed when George stepped out for a beer at the pub. Apparently, George did not forget to lock his door when he stepped out for a beer. The lock was not later found smashed and the door was not broken into. In other words, when George opened the door lock with his key and stepped into his kitchen, he had no reason to suspect that an intruder (or intruders) had entered his house during his brief absence.

PC Mears' testimony is clear and convincing evidence that George was attacked immediately upon entry into his kitchen—that is, before he had an opportunity to remove his hat and coat. Moreover, recalling now the reporting in the *Surrey Advertiser,* George's body was found on the floor of his kitchen "within the threshold of his own doorway."

PC Mears also stated that he had searched the deceased and found George's "watch with the chain around the neck." A watch and chain are valuable items. Yet George's watch and chain were not removed from the scene of the crime by the killer(s) upon departure. In other words, these valuable items were not stolen. So, according to the Surrey Constabulary, after a reputed "burglar" had murdered George and mutilated his body with two different weapons, this "lone burglar" did not remove a watch and chain from George's neck—despite the fact that this "burglar," potentially, had many hours of free time in the house, alone with the corpse. This supposed "burglar" had more than two and one-half hours alone with George's dead body, plenty of time to steal whatever valuables that he wanted to take.

Moreover, recalling now a statement by Inspector Barker that was recorded in the *Surrey Advertiser:* another watch and chain, along with some money, all belonging to the deceased's son, was found lying in plain view on the dressing table in James' bedroom, untouched. Add to that, we will soon learn that some of James' rings, also left in plain view, were not stolen. We will hear from James that he saw evidence that the killer (or killers) had searched his room but had taken nothing.

Similarly, 20 shillings left in George's lockbox were not stolen. What sort of burglar does not steal George's watch and chain, 20 shillings in coins, James' watch and chain, his rings, and some more cash? Remember: there was no need to rush following the murder. Thus, the evidence suggests that the killer(s) was/were not intent on robbing George and looting his residence. Apparently, loot was not the primary goal of the killer(s.)

Even though it is still early days, it now looks to me like the unknown loot that reportedly was taken from the house was incidental to the plot to murder and mutilate George. It already appears that murder and mutilation were the primary purposes of the crime. And, as I will show later, whatever loot may have been taken by the killer(s,) it may not have been stolen for its monetary value. The stolen items could have had some intrinsic, non-monetary value to the killer(s)--other than the amount of cash the items might bring in a pawn shop. Pawning stolen items in a pawn shop carried its own risks. Once again, this alternate possibility was, apparently, never entertained by the Surrey Constabulary—who never wavered from their uncorroborated robbery-gone-sour theory.

How Did the Killer(s) Gain Entrance to George's Kitchen?

PC Dearlove stated that he had examined the back door (*i.e.*, the kitchen door—the *only* ground floor entrance into the Chuters' portion of the cottage, according to James.) The constable found it was fastened only by a simple catch lock that was easily opened by a piece of bent wire. PC Dearlove did not find anywhere on the premises a bent wire with which the killer(s) may have opened the lock on the door. If the killer (or killers) had indeed employed a bent wire to open the lock on the kitchen door, then evidently the killer(s) must also have taken that bent wire with him/them upon departure.

PC Dearlove's revelation about the ease with which the lock on the kitchen door could have been easily opened with a bent wire provides us with a credible, possible explanation how the killer(s) entered the kitchen without leaving any sign of forcible entry while George went out for a beer. But how did the killer(s) know in advance that it would be possible to gain entry into George's kitchen easily without a key, simply with a bent wire?

The King's Head.

The pub in which George had imbibed his final beer was the King's Head. This Byfleet landmark—in continuous business operation at the same location from the mid-19th Century until 2010 (when it closed its doors for good)—was located at 59 Chertsey Road. Here, below in Figure 4, is a photo of the King's Head taken in 2010, about the time the King's Head ceased its operations. The King's Head had been remodeled and expanded since 1888.

Figure 3-4. **The King's Head pub in West Byfleet at 59 Chertsey Road. This photo was taken in 2010, before the establishment ceased its operations.**

(photographer unknown)

And here, below in **Figure 3-5,** is a photo of the bar inside the King's Head, in 2010. It is possible that George Chuter drank his final beer in this very room, on the evening of January 12, 1888, just minutes before he was mutilated and murdered inside his cottage.

Figure 3-5; The bar at the King's Head pub in 2010.

(photographer unknown)

After imbibing one beer over a period of five-to-six minutes, George then returned to his cottage within the possible time-range of the murder, as established by the police. All these facts would eventually come out at the Coroner's Inquest on January 16. Forgive me for jumping the gun in the timeline of my story, but it is important to know now that some (but not all) of the unconfirmed speculation and uncredited evidence in *Lloyds'* article would later be corroborated by witness testimony at the inquest.

James' Absence.

Lloyd's reporter noted the time-range in which George's son, James, was absent from the cottage. "The son had occasion to leave at about seven o'clock, and on returning at half-past 10, a horrible scene presented itself," *Lloyd's* reported. The time-range of James' absence was undoubtedly established by Surrey police officers—who remained unidentified in this article. As we will learn at the Coroner's Inquest, the police later refined the time of James' departure to twenty minutes before seven. The inquest also determined that when James returned home around 10:05-to-10:15, he was accompanied by some friends. Simon Choate (James' neighbor) returned home at the same time. Thus, no possibility exists that James murdered and mutilated his father with two murder weapons when he (James) opened the kitchen door. Up until that moment, James was in the company of others.

Already, it is evident that the only opportunity the killer(s) had to enter the cottage unseen and then hide inside was during George's brief absence from his cottage, when George stepped out for 5-6 minutes to the King's Head for a beer. Somehow, yet to be established, the killer(s) had managed to enter the house without making any signs of forcible entry during that small window-of-time. The entrance might have been made by jimmying the kitchen door lock with a bent wire—or it might have been by some other means, still unknown.

The killer(s) laid in wait in the dark, inside the kitchen. Soon, George returned from the King's Head. The moment George opened his kitchen door and stepped inside, the killer(s) pounced on him in the dark. James testified at the inquest: when he returned home after his band rehearsal, he (James) had used his key to open the lock on the kitchen door. Thus, the killer(s) had thoughtfully closed the kitchen door behind when he/they departed the crime scene. The latch must have locked automatically when the killer(s) closed the door upon leaving the residence.

How Did the Killer(s) Know Precisely When George Would Step Out of His Cottage for a Beer?

In order for the plan to murder and mutilate George to work smoothly, the killer(s) had to have known reliably in advance precisely when George would step out of his cottage for a beer at the King's Head pub. The killer(s) had only a brief window-of-time, perhaps 5-to-6 minutes, in which to enter the cottage and hide himself/themselves in the kitchen during George's absence. As we will soon learn in reports of the Coroner's Inquest, hiding was not the only task the killer(s) must have accomplished in those critical 5-to-6 minutes prior to the murder.

In order to observe George's exit from his cottage to the King's Head, the killer(s) must have waited outside, hidden near the cottage, ready to act on a moment's notice once they saw George depart for the pub. To play the devil's advocate, I can also propose an alternate scenario, although not a credible one. The killer(s) could have waited inside the pub and then followed George home. But as we will see from information to be revealed at the Coroner's Inquest—that scenario does not quite fit the facts. Eyewitness testimony at the Coroner's Inquest will make it clear that no one followed George into the pub, nor exited the pub after George left. Moreover, police officers' testimony made it plain: George was murdered inside his kitchen immediately after he entered his cottage from the outside, through the kitchen door. His body was found on the kitchen floor in a huge pool of blood, near the closed entrance door—"done to death just within the threshold of his own doorway," as the *Surrey Advertiser* put it. No doubt, the killer(s) was/were already inside the kitchen when George returned from the King's Head and entered through that door (the sole entrance into the Chuters' residence.).

Stalking Over Time.

Now, to confront directly two key questions: how could the killer(s) have known beforehand precisely when George would step out of his cottage for a quick beer at the King's Head pub? And how could the killer(s) have known beforehand precisely when James would depart the cottage to walk to his village band rehearsal at The Pavilion in a park field, less than 1 mile away?

George may have had a daily routine that included stepping out after dinner every evening for a beer at the nearby King's Head pub. He may have regularly walked to the pub, less than 50 yards away, at the same time, after finishing his dinner. That routine could easily have been observed by the killer(s)—who may have gathered intelligence about George's daily routine through clandestine surveillance over a few days' time—an activity otherwise known as *stalking.* The killer(s) may have hidden in the street, watching the cottage from a short distance away, over a length of time, such as days or even weeks. Or perhaps even longer.

Every Thursday evening, he/they may have observed James exit the cottage to attend his regularly scheduled village band rehearsal. On the Thursday evening of January 12, the killer(s) may have waited for James to depart the cottage, and then waited a bit longer for George to step out for his regular evening beer at the King's Head pub.

All these *surmisals* assume that the killer(s) took time, perhaps days or even weeks before the murder, to learn about the daily activities of both George and his son, James. That assumption will become more plausible when we evaluate additional evidence that reveals the full extent of preparations made over time by the killer(s) prior to the murder. When all the evidence that I have found pertaining to the Byfleet Murder is eventually revealed in two volumes of the series *A Trail of Blood,* it will become clear: the advance preparations for this mysterious crime extended back not days, not weeks, not months, but years.

It is already apparent: George must have been stalked by the killer(s) in order to learn about his daily routine. And so, James must also have been stalked. This murder was not a spur-of-the-moment crime of opportunity. Every detail had been carefully thought out and revised to perfection. Even before George had opened the door to his kitchen on the way home from the pub, he was already a marked man. This murder was an intricately planned assassination by ambush. George was a chosen victim.

In the words of Shakespeare, George's killer(s) were **"as vigilant as a cat to steal cream."** *(Henry IV, Part I.)*

George Chuter's Supposed Wealth.

Lloyd's reporter identified the murder victim (although he misspelled the victim's last name, and he neglected to give Chuter's first name.) He described George Chuter first as an "old man," and later as "67 years" of age. At the end of the report, the reporter added: "Chutor *[sic]* was a man of considerable means and had a large amount of cottage property in the district."

Upon reading that last statement, a big red flag popped up in my mind. I am highly skeptical of the validity of that last statement in *Lloyd's* article. In view of all the information that I have learned in my research, I did not see how it could possibly be true that "Chutor [sic] was a man of considerable means." There was no evidence in any report that I saw—including accounts of the Coroner's

Inquest—that indicated George owned anything at the time of his death except the small cottage which he shared with his son. If *Lloyd's* claim about George's "large amount of cottage properties" were even partly true, then he certainly lived with his son like a miser in meager circumstances.

George had some money (and possibly some small gold items) stored in a toolbox that he used as a lockbox for cash. According to James, some of the valuable items in this lockbox were taken by the killer(s) upon departure—but significantly, not all of them. As we will read in later news reports, the Surrey police found a relatively modest amount of silver coins in the lockbox. The claim of missing gold items came solely from George's son, James. But James had no idea of these gold items' intrinsic value, or how many items had been taken, or even what exactly these items were. More about the allegedly stolen gold items later, when we review James' testimony at the inquest.

Most importantly, if George had been a wealthy owner of numerous properties in the district, that fact would surely have become known to the Surrey police. Ownership of real properties is public knowledge and easily documented. Immediately, George's ownership of numerous cottage properties, if it had indeed been true, would have changed the character and the direction of the police's murder investigation. Inevitably, James would have become the police's prime suspect, despite his air-tight alibi for the time of the murder. Could this crime have been a murder-for-hire, paid for by the son, so that he could quickly inherit his father's "considerable" wealth in local real estate? It wasn't.

Had George been the wealthy owner of numerous cottage properties, the police at the outset would have suspected James of becoming too impatient to wait for his 67-year-old father to die a natural death—whereby James would inherit his father's alleged extensive real estate holdings. In such circumstances, the police would surely have investigated any possibility that James had hired an assassin to murder his father during James' regularly scheduled band rehearsal at The Pavilion. However, there is not even a hint in any news report at any time, or in police testimony at the Coroner's Inquest, that James ever became a suspect, or even a person of interest. Nor was any mention of these supposed local real estate holdings ever broached by any witness at the Coroner's inquest.

Parenthetically, whenever considering any possible murder suspects, we must also ask ourselves the pivotal question: why the *mutilations*? No one ever suggested that James—or anyone else--might have had reason to mutilate George. The savagery of the mutilations would have indicated unbridled hatred between James and his father—and no one ever suggested that might have been the case.

No Suspects. No Arrests. No 'Considerable Means.'

The article in the *Surrey Advertiser and County Times* contained some additional pertinent information: Superintendent Bungard, of the Surrey Constabulary, had taken charge of the case. But thus far, he had not succeeded in effecting an arrest—or even naming a suspect. The highly doubtful claim about George's "considerable means" at the end of the report in *Lloyd's Weekly Newspaper* appears to me to have been merely a baseless rumor overheard in the village—a rumor with no factual evidence to support it. Or perhaps this claim was actually a trial balloon floated by Superintendent Bungard and by the Surrey Constabulary, in a transparent attempt to create a credible motive of robbery to explain George's murder. However, no motive—that is, no motive supported by credible, documented evidence—was then apparent.

Cold Water Poured on Speculation About George's Supposed Extensive Property Holdings.

On January 17, 1888, the Leighton Buzzard *Observer* published an article on the Byfleet Murder. In addition to restating much of the factual narrative already covered here, the article brought up the matter of George Chuter's supposed wealth, but from a different perspective. The *Observer* stated: "In the belief that the deceased had in his possession a considerable sum of money that he had saved, some person or persons, it is supposed, entered the house and battered in the skull of the only occupant." Thus, according to the Leighton Buzzard *Observer*, it was only a conjectured "belief" that the killer(s) had "supposed" that George had stored a considerable sum of money in his house. Apparently, the police's claim that George was the wealthy proprietor of an array of local cottages smelled as fishy to the journalist of the Leighton Buzzard *Observer* as it now smells to me. In other words, there was no confirmed evidence to support the existence of this "supposed" wealth. Indeed, there was no evidence to support the existence of a "belief" attributed to the killer(s) that George had stashed a substantial sum of money inside his house. These sorts of *beliefs* and *suppositions* are what usually is called *groundless speculation.*

No Apparent Motive for Murder and Mutilation Supported by Documented Evidence.

No one knew the motive for George's murder—except, of course, the killer(s). The entire matter of George's "supposed" wealth and the cache of money (or gold) "believed" to have been hidden inside the cottage was pure conjecture, based—at best—on rumor; and—at the very worst—on nothing more than an anonymous, groundless hunch. If the police were trying to establish grounds for a credible motive of robbery for the murder and mutilation of George Chuter, they would have to come up with some substantial well-documented facts to support that conclusion. They never did.

George Chuter, a Likable Bloke.

For the following information about George's life, I am indebted to the article "Murderous Times in Byfleet in 1888" posted on wokinghistory.org.

George Chuter was born on July 5, 1820. He was baptized on July 30, 1820 at St. Mary's Church in West Byfleet

On November 3, 1844, George Chuter married Lucy Dollery at Shepperton Parish Church. Lucy died in February, 1887.

In 1851, George Chuter was recorded in a directory as "carpenter and victualler" at the Leather Bottle, a local pub. In another directory, he was listed as employed at the Queen's Head.

"Victualler" is a dated British term for a person who is licensed to sell alcoholic beverages.

By 1851, George and Lucy were the parents of four children. George, Lucy, and their children then lived together with George's father, John, and a niece.

In his double *métier*—carpenter and innkeeper—George followed in the footsteps of his father, John, who, in 1841 was listed as the occupier of a beer house on Woking Road, later Old Woking Road. This pub was located nearby the future site of the Queen's Head on High Road. John Chuter was also a carpenter. He lived with his wife, Sarah

(George's mother.) George had a brother, John Jr., who was 5 years younger than George. There is no mention of John Chuter Jr. in any article that I found about George's murder.

In 1861, George Chuter was listed as keeping the Queen's Head public house. He declared himself a "carpenter employing two men." In the 1871 Census, he described himself as "a builder and contractor" now living in Chertsey Road, Byfleet; and he stated he was then employing nine men and one boy. George and Lucy were then living with three of their children and a 10-month-old "niece" (actually their grand-daughter, Annie Carpenter.)

The Queen's Head was now run by Richard Minett. So, apparently, George had left his employment at the Queen's Head to devote himself entirely to his building and contracting business.

On September 29, 1877, George officially retired from trade—according to an announcement that he placed in the *Surrey Advertiser.* The announcement was signed: George Chuter, Juniper Cottages, Byfleet. In 1881, George and Lucy were residing at 26 Royal Avenue, Chelsea—but apparently he also then kept Juniper Cottages in West Byfleet. George and Lucy at that time were recorded as living with two of their children and a boarder.

George Chuter, Formerly an Innkeeper at the Queen's Head Pub.

On January 21, 1888, the Dudley *Mercury* published an article entitled "A Village Murder," in which yet more details were provided about George's life in Byfleet. It stated:

> **The deceased was one of the oldest and most respected inhabitants of the place. He was formerly in business as a builder, and also kept the Queen's Head Inn; but at the time he was murdered, he was living with his son, having retired from trade.**

Thus, George was innkeeper at the Queen's Head early in his working life. This inn was then and still is located at 2 High Road, less than a mile distance from the location on Chertsey Road where George resided at the time of his death. The Queen's Head (Figure 5, below) is still in operation today at its original location—although the building has been expanded and rebuilt over the decades. Ironically, on January 16, 1888, the Queen's Head was also the location of the Coroner's Inquest into George's murder and mutilation. And a year before that, it was the location of a Coroner's Inquest into the sudden, mysterious death, later attributed to an unexpected heart attack, of George's wife, Lucy.

The Queen's Head Pub and Inn.

Here, below, in **Figure 3-6,** is a photo of the Queen's Head, as the pub and inn appeared in the 20th Century.

Figure 3-6. 20th C. photo of The Queen's Head. Located at 2 High Road, the Queen's Head Inn is a pub and inn where George Chuter was innkeeper many years before he retired from work as a building contractor. The photo, above, shows the inn many decades after expansions had added two large sections on the right of the original building. In the 19th Century, the inn included only the section of the Main building with three big windows on the upper floor. The original building is defined by the location of the two chimneys. The two dormers on the roof between the two chimneys are not original. They must have been added sometime before this photo was shot. Ironically, it was here in the Queen's Head that the Coroner's Inquest on the body of George Chuter was held on January 16, 1888.

(photographer unknown)

The photo below (Figure 3-7) shows the Queen's Head as it appeared in the late 19th Century. This historic photo was made available to me by Surrey historian Iain Wakeford—who obtained it around 1960 from the then-proprietor of the Queen's Head. Wakeford wrote that the photo hung framed on the pub's interior wall.

Figure 3-7. A late 19th C. photograph of the Queen's Head pub and inn, provided to me by Surrey historian Iain Wakeford, reproduced here with his permission. The Queen's Head Inn, as it appeared around the time of the Byfleet murder. Surrey historian Iain Wakeford obtained this photo around 1960 from the then-landlord of the Queen's Head. Evidently, the one-story structure in the front that served as the entrance to the pub was later demolished—while the two-story building behind was remodeled and expanded.

(Photographer unknown; photograph pre-dates 1928, public domain in the US.)

The front entrance of the Queen's Head was a small, squat, ground-floor structure that appears to have been a pub room. Behind that structure stood a two-floor building that looks like an inn. The front pub room may have been the location of the Coroner's Inquest on January 16, 1888.

Friary, Holroyd & Healy's (the name on the roof sign) was a local brewery, developed from 1865-on by Thomas Taunton of the Cannon Brewery. The company was the maker of a beer well-known in Surrey in the late 19th Century. The full name was often used around 1890, when Taunton acquired Healy's—but the full name of the company was not registered until 1895. G. B. Holroyd would become active in the local campaign to raise money for a reward for information leading to the arrest of George Chuter's killer(s.)

Comparing the two photos of the Queen's Head, it can be seen that the front room was demolished; but the two chimneys, the three upper-floor windows, the ground floor window and the entrance door were retained (although modified) in a subsequent remodeling.

Where, Exactly, in Byfleet did George and James Chuter Reside?

According to the 1881 Census, George had already retired from the building trade and was then living in Chelsea. However, at that time, he 'retained' a cottage in Byfleet, 'Rose Cottage'—according to Leonard Steven's book, *Byfleet – A Village in England.* However, 'Rose Cottage' was in another part of town, a considerable distance from Chertsey Road. 'Rose Cottage' was not the cottage in which George was murdered.

Juniper Cottages, the Murder site.

In 1888, George was reported to be living in 'Juniper Cottages.' But which house on Chertsey Road was named 'Juniper Cottages'? Official records could not answer this question for me. My inquiries prompted no answers. Nor could I find any documents with a numerical address on Chertsey Road for 'Juniper Cottages.' After contacting Surrey Heritage at the Surrey County Council, I received the following reply from the Surrey History Centre in Woking, informing me:

> **"By looking at the censuses for 1881 and 1891, and the Electoral Register for 1887, there is no doubt whatsoever that George (and, presumably, James) Chuter did, indeed, live at Juniper Cottage, on Chertsey Road, in Byfleet. The newspaper reports seem to suggest that George was living with James; but actually it seems to have been the other way around—since George is listed on the Register, but James isn't, which would have meant that George was the householder at the cottage, not James." (signed: Duncan Mirylees, for Public Services and Engagement Manager)**

But Which House on Chertsey Road was—or Still is—Named 'Juniper Cottages'?

Even though the public records did not show an exact street address on Chertsey Road for George's residence at

Juniper Cottages, I think we can hone in on George's house, if indeed it still there today, using clues in the news articles, and by utilizing the assistance of Google Maps Street View.

Locating the Street Address of "Juniper Cottages" on Chertsey Road.

The *Surrey Advertiser* stated that George's home was "no more than 50 yards from the King's Head Inn." The address of the King's Head Inn was 59 Chertsey Road (that is, until 2010, when the inn ceased its operations. This inn, constructed in mid-19th Century, was demolished in 2013.)

Moreover, the *Surrey Advertiser* stated that George "was living with his son, James Chuter, grocer, in the Chertsey-road." Thus, it appears that "Juniper Cottages" was located on Chertsey Road, about 50 yards from the former location of the King's Head Inn at 59 Chertsey Road. And in other news accounts, it was reported that James' grocery was located in a small, somewhat isolated room in the front part of the house.

In the *Surrey Advertiser,* it was mentioned that George's cottage was a "double tenement"—that is, it comprised two separate family units joined together by a common wall, with both units under one split-level roof. Using Google Maps Street View, I examined all of the houses now on Chertsey Road within 100 yards distance of King's Terrace (formerly the King's Head Inn.) Today, there are several old double tenement houses roughly within this range, still standing on Chertsey Road. So, I was not quite there, yet.

Getting Closer.

I had to determine whether any of these old houses were specifically named "Juniper Cottages." To do that, I turned to the Byfleet Heritage Society, whose *Newsletter* has been edited by Secretary Tessa Westlake since the inception of the society decades ago. In Issue 26 of November 2004, members of the society discussed precisely the relevant question: *i.e.,* the street address number of Juniper Cottages on Chertsey Road. (Evidently, this location had been the starting point in January 1911 of an historic funeral procession to St. Mary's Church for PC Walter Choate, a Metropolitan Policeman killed in action in the "Sidney Street Siege," a notorious gun battle in Houndsditch, in London's East End.)

Two members of the Byfleet Heritage Society, Pam Starling and Maurice Alder, had communicated with Ms. Westlake to settle the matter about the location of 'Juniper Cottages.' "It is in fact number 65 Chertsey Road," states the newsletter. "A plaque with the name Juniper Cottages is set into the house." (I should add that the similarity of the family name of PC Choate, who had lived there, and George's neighbor, the bootmaker Simon Choate, only strengthens my belief that 65 Chertsey Road was indeed George Chuter's "Juniper Cottages" in January 1888.)

Google Maps Street View to the Rescue.

I now turned to Google Maps Street View to see what 65 Chertsey Road in West Byfleet looks like today. Unsurprisingly, I saw an old, slightly dilapidated house part of which contained an upper floor. Was this "Juniper Cottages" in 1888? In the front, facing Chertsey Road, I saw an isolated brick-walled room jutting out toward Chertsey Road (where two cars were then parked.) In every detail, this house matched the descriptions in the 19th Century news reports of George's cottage with James' tiny grocery store out front. Evidently, the original 19th Century crime scene building had survived. It is located about fifty yards from King's Terrace on Chertsey Road. King's Terrace now occupies the former location of the King's Head Pub at 59 Chertsey Road (where George drank his final beer.). The tiny brick-walled room facing Chertsey Road could easily have served as James Chuter's grocery store. The much larger white building behind the former grocery looked big enough to enclose a second family unit under its large square roof. I must note now that the white structure is not the separate part of the double tenement in which George and James resided. The second tenement—*i.e.* George's and James' residence—is located in back of the the white structure. The Chuters' residence is not visible in the photo shown below, in **Figure 3-8.**

Figure 3-8. "Juniper Cottages," 65 Chertsey Road, Byfleet, Surrey, in 2017. This is the front of the house in which George and James Chuter resided in January, 1888—as seen from Chertsey Road. George and James lived in a residential unit in the back of this building. Their small residential unit is not visible in this photo. The large, white portion was occupied by the Choate family. The location of James' grocery store is the small brick building visible in front, here facing the cars on Chertsey Road. On the front wall of the white house, just under the chimney, one can see a mounted plaque (unfortunately the inscription on the plaque is not legible in this photo.) This is the plaque mentioned by members of the Byfleet Heritage Society, identifying this double tenement building as 'Juniper Cottages.' Note the plural in the name 'Juniper Cottages,' indicating the building was a double tenement in which two families resided.

What Was George Chuter's Actual Net Worth at the Time of His Death?

Before I investigate the Chuters' residence, as it appears today, let's take another quick look at the question of George Chuter's supposed wealth. The matter of George's *actual* wealth, versus his *supposed* wealth attributed to him in the form of alleged local real estate holdings, is a significant issue in this murder investigation. The source of the highly doubtful claims in the press about George's "considerable means" appears to me to have been the Surrey Constabulary—who persisted in attempting to establish a motive of robbery-gone-sour for the brutal murder and mutilation of a supposedly wealthy victim, despite all the mounting evidence to the contrary. The police never provided at the Coroner's Inquest on January 16, any documentary evidence of extensive local real estate holdings owned by George at the time of his death.

As I noted earlier, I found documentary evidence showing that George owned the residence in which he and James lived. As attested to earlier by Duncan Mirylees, Public Services Manager in Surrey, George was listed in the register as the householder—not James. However, whether George owned the entire building—including the much larger Choate family's residence—or just his own small residence in the back and the tiny grocery store facing the Chertsey Road, I could not determine from the response I received from the Surrey History Centre in Woking. Nor could I locate any records of other buildings owned George Chuter at the time of his death.

Consequently, I decided to determine for myself what, in fact, was George's real wealth at the time of his death. I was able to track down a record of his last will in the Principal Registry at Surrey, which was probated on February 3, 1888 (**Figure 3-9**.) George's entire probated estate totaled 48 pounds 17 shillings. This sum represents George's total accumulation of wealth at the end of his life, including any real estate holdings that he left to be inherited by his children. This document conclusively proves that George's total net worth was very modest, even by the standards of the times. In modern American terms, 48 pounds 17 shillings in 1888 Britain is roughly equivalent to the range of $2,000 to $3000 in the US today. That sum represents George's entire retirement savings at the age of 67. It includes any local real estate, which of course was not liquid cash (and thus could not be stolen in a residential robbery-gone-sour.) This modest estate is clear evidence that George Chuter's means were not "considerable," even by 1888 standards.

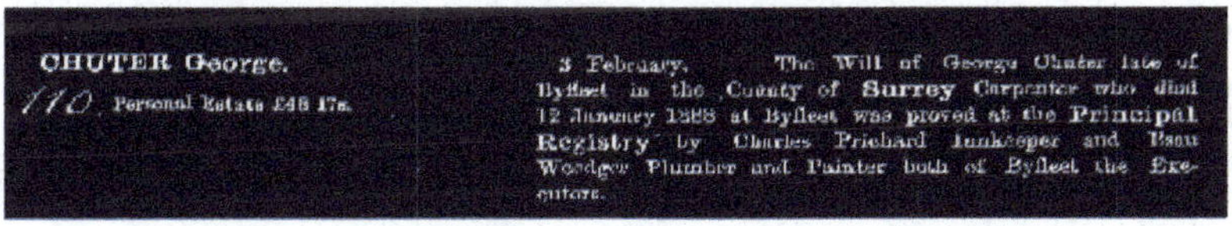

CHUTER George.
110 Personal Estate £48 17s.

3 February. The Will of George Chuter late of Byfleet in the County of Surrey Carpenter who died 12 January 1888 at Byfleet was proved at the Principal Registry by Charles Prichard Innkeeper and Esau Woodger Plumber and Painter both of Byfleet the Executors.

Figure 3-9; microfilm of official record
Registry of Probate of the Will of George Chuter

Here, below, is a legible transcript of the document reproduced above:

> **CHUTER, George.**
> **110. Personal Estate £48 17s.**
> **3 February [1888] The will of George Chuter, late of Byfleet in the County of Surrey, Carpenter, who died 12 January 1888 at Byfleet, was proved at the Principal Registry by Charles Priebaud, landscaper, and Tlanu Woodger, plumber and painter, both of Byfleet, the Executors.**

Thus, the premise upon which the police's conjectured motive was based—that George was wealthy man who owned an array of local cottages and had stashed a fortune in gold and cash in a toolbox in his closet—was without any factual basis. George was not a major real estate developer. He was a carpenter and a small time building contractor of cottages. George was not the owner of a profitable inn. In his youth, he worked as an employee at the Leather Bottle. Then, later, he kept the Queen's Head in Byfleet. At the Coroner's Inquest on January 16, 1888, there would be no testimony by anyone—including any officer in the Surrey Constabulary—that asserted George held any important properties at the time of his death, other than the small cottage in which he then lived with his son James. Indeed, neither Superintendent Bungard nor Deputy Chief Superintendent Barker ever said a word at the Coroner's Inquest—which they both attended.

A Preliminary Peek at the Ghastly Wounds Inflicted on George Chuter's Body.

The article in the Leighton Buzzard *Observer* also gave us some valuable information about the extent of the mutilations observed on George's body: "The old man, who was between sixty and seventy, must have been most savagely ill-treated, his features when he was found being almost unrecognizable." So, George's head and face were bashed in so violently with a poker, the reporter could not distinguish the victim's features—such as his nose, eyes, and mouth. In other words, the killer(s) had repeatedly beaten George's skull and face to a pulp.

We have yet to hear any medical testimony from a qualified doctor about the full extent of the mutilations on George's body. And when we do, at the Coroner's Inquest—which was scheduled to be held on January 16, 1888—we will see that the Leighton Buzzard *Observer* gave us only mere hints about the full extent of the wounds administered with the poker. Moreover, that newspaper gave us virtually nothing about the shocking wound administered to George's throat with a carving knife.

"BRUTAL MURDER," screamed the headlines of the Lancashire *Evening Post* and Sheffield *Evening Express*, in all-caps. "SHOCKING MURDER" shouted the headlines of *Lloyd's Weekly Newspaper* and several other newspapers. The Leighton Buzzard *Observer* stated that George's body "must have been savagely ill-treated." Slowly, an idea began to emerge in the press that the murder of George Chuter was no 'run-of-the-mill' murder, but rather a gruesome mutilation and murder with no apparent motive. The full extent of the mutilations had jarred the senses of everyone who had seen them. However, despite the shocked headlines, traditional British reserve, family values, and norms of good taste restrained the family-oriented press from describing all the gory details. Despite mounting evidence to the contrary, the Surrey police still refused to accept the possibility that this crime could be anything other than a traditional robbery-gone-sour. Anything more complex and more mysterious was, for them, inconceivable—literally *inconceivable!*

A Robbery-Gone-Sour, or a Mutilation/Murder?

With regard to motive, the reporter for the Leighton Buzzard *Observer* went out on a limb (and so, apparently, did his obvious source, the local police.) "There can be no doubt that robbery was the motive of the murderer," wrote the reporter for the *Observer*—while offering no credible evidence to back up that blind assertion. Two assumptions were conflated in that one sentence. First, that robbery was the motive; and second, that a lone robber had committed the murder and the mutilations. No evidence had yet been uncovered to support either of those assumptions as proven fact.

One small technical correction now to the statement that appeared in the Leighton Buzzard *Observer*: the reporter for that newspaper should have claimed that *burglary*, not robbery, was the alleged motive for the murder. Under British Common Law, a robbery in a house at night is termed a burglary, not a robbery. Night-time is a key legal distinction between a burglary and a robbery. The British Common Law definition of burglary is:

> **The breaking and entering the house of another in the night- time, with intent to commit a felony therein, whether the felony be actually committed or not. *Breaking* can be either actual, such as by forcing open a door, or constructive, such as by fraud or threats. Breaking does not require that anything be 'broken' in terms of physical damage occurring.**

The legal penalties for robbery and burglary are not the same.

George's Bedroom Wardrobe.

Following the discovery of George's mutilated body in the kitchen, the Surrey police searched the rest of the Chuters' cottage. In the wardrobe of George's bedroom on the upper story, they discovered a lockbox that had been forced open. According to James, a sum of money was missing—the amount of which was not known by James. James said he knew where his father kept his money—but he had no idea how much money was stolen. Thus, there was some confusion over the contents of the lockbox. Later reports claimed there were some gold items inside—but once again, the exact items and their value were unknown to James. I will have much more to say about this lockbox and its alleged contents later when I explore in depth the conjectured motive of robbery (*i.e.* burglary) gone sour. The police repeatedly floated this conjectured motive.

For now, it is significant to note that the discovery of the forced-open toolbox establishes that the killer(s) had searched George's bedroom and its wardrobe—and taken time to force open the lock on the toolbox. We already know from comments by Deputy-Chief Superintendent Barker, recorded in the Surrey *Advertiser*, that the killer(s) also searched James' bedroom (taking nothing.) The killer(s) could hardly have accomplished all these searches in the few minutes he/they awaited George's return from the King's Head. When George returned from the pub, the killer(s) were waiting behind the kitchen door, ready to attack the instant George entered. Thus, it appears to me that these bedroom searches could only have occurred after the killer(s) had murdered and mutilated George, not before. As we will read in the following chapter, reporting on the Coroner's Inquest, that was also the conclusion of the medical examiner, Dr. Sealy.

Two Bloody Murder Weapons at the Scene of the Crime,

Aside from the victim's mutilated body lying in a "huge" pool of blood, the most striking and significant evidence found at the crime scene was undoubtedly the presence of two different, bloody murder weapons. Both weapons were found lying in plain sight, near the mutilated body. "Near the body lay a poker," stated *Lloyd's Weekly Newspaper.* The poker had been used to bash in George Chuter's skull and face. "And not far away was a carving-knife," *Lloyd's* reporter added. The carving knife had been used to slash George throat from ear-to-ear. As previously noted by the *Surrey Advertiser,* the victim's "throat was cut from ear to ear, so much force having been used that a cravat worn by the murdered man was completely severed." In later reports, we will learn that the carving knife had gone far deeper and severed much more than merely George's cravat. But the slashing of the cravat was nonetheless significant as evidence—for reasons that will later become vividly apparent. We will also learn that both weapons were covered in blood (and, in the case of the poker, with some hair, as well.)

Lloyd's reporter stated vaguely that the poker was "near" the body, and the carving knife was "not far away." As we will learn at the Coroner's Inquest, the body was found lying in a huge pool of blood on the floor of the kitchen, next to the entrance door. The poker and knife were both set close by, on top of the kitchen table, next to the body. There was never a doubt in anyone's mind that these items were, in fact, the two weapons used to murder and mutilate George—and they could only have been placed atop the kitchen table by the killer(s.)

What the Killer(s) Did Not Do.

Significant evidence is also revealed by what the killer(s) did not do. After bashing in George's skull and face, and slashing his throat from ear-to-ear, the killer(s) did not take any of the following actions:

i. the killer(s) did not take the two murder weapons with him/them upon departure;
ii. the killer(s) did not attempt to hide these two weapons at the crime scene;
iii. the killer(s) did not wash the two weapons clean of blood, in order to prevent the police from connecting these two household items to the murder and mutilation;
iv. the killer(s) did not hastily toss the two weapons outside in his/their excitement to escape.

Any of these four actions might seem reasonable for an alleged, panicked lone burglar who had just committed a desperate act of murder during a robbery-gone-sour. But instead, the killer(s) cooly placed both murder weapons on top of the kitchen table, next to the mutilated body. This was a *display.*

A Deliberate Display.

Evidently, the killer(s) deliberately displayed the two murder weapons on the kitchen table, next to George's body—where he/they knew the weapons would inevitably be seen by investigating officers. Undoubtedly, the killer(s) wanted the police to connect the kitchen carving knife and the fireplace poker to the murder and mutilation. The question for us to confront is: *why* did the killer(s) want these bloody murder weapons to be seen by the police and directly connected to George's murder and mutilation? Why did they deliberately leave for the police and the press this obvious clue?

Here was a deliberate act of defiance by the killer(s), aimed straight at the Surrey Constabulary. The killer(s) could easily have taken any of the above-mentioned evasive actions, and thereby reduced the risk of being apprehended holding crime scene evidence. But the killer(s) did not do so—deliberately. There was no time pressure while the killers were in the kitchen. The killer(s) knew that James would not return home from his band rehearsal before 10 p.m., at the earliest. The obvious fact that the killer(s) had made no attempt to hide or remove the two weapons from the crime scene indicates that the killer(s) wanted the police to find both murder weapons; wanted the police to connect these two weapons with George's murder and mutilation; and wanted the police and the press to give credit for what was so brilliantly accomplished with these two bloody weapons. Evidently, the person (or persons) who committed this atrocity were proud of what they had done.

There was no sign of remorse—as might have been the case with a panicked burglar who had just murdered an elderly homeowner in a confused act of desperation. Apparently, following the mutilation, the killer(s) had calmly and carefully placed both bloody murder weapons on top of the kitchen table, near each other, and near the body. The proximity of the two bloody weapons to the body and to each other was obviously a *Deliberately Placed Big Clue*, maliciously planted at the scene by the killer(s.) Here was a visual message sent directly to the police, expressing the killer(s') utter contempt for the intelligence and crime-solving abilities of the Surrey Constabulary. The message was: Catch Us If You Can! (Yes, *Us!*). Their symbolic message flew over the heads of the clueless Surrey Constabulary, un-intercepted.

Staging the Crime Scene.

The deliberate altering of a crime scene by a killer after a murder has been committed—but before the arrival of the police—is known in criminology as 'staging the crime scene.' The obvious placement of the two murder weapons on the kitchen table was but the first example of staging the crime scene that we will encounter here. It is so significant a clue that we can now reasonably inquire: for what ulterior purpose did the killer(s) stage the crime scene?

The killer(s) may have had *multiple* reasons for staging the crime scene with the brazen placement of the two bloody murder weapons at center stage. At least one of these reasons is self-evident. As just noted, the placement of the two bloody weapons on display next to the body was a sign of bemused contempt by the killer(s) for the anticipated, befuddled incompetence of the police. The obvious placement of the two weapons of murder and mutilation indicated the belief of the killer(s) that the police were so foolish, so blind, and so stupid, they would prove incapable of solving this crime—despite the *Deliberately Placed Big Clue* set "rite before yer eyes" (as he/they would write later.) However, the placement of the two weapons on the kitchen table next to the body was, I believe, intended to convey multiple messages. Another critical, symbolic message, sent by the killer(s) would soon emerge at the Coroner's Inquest.

The Two Bloody Weapons Set on Top of the Kitchen Table.

An iron poker (**Figure 3-10**) was a common murder weapon in 19th Century England, and a weapon of choice in countless Victorian mystery novels. In a country in which most homes were heated by coal-burning stoves or wood-burning fireplaces, a poker was a ubiquitous tool. Because of its considerable weight and great strength, a poker made for an effective and easily accessible tool as a bludgeon. Many pokers have a hook at one end to roll logs, but some do not. A hook increases its lethality when used as a murder weapon. There was no report of the Byfleet Murder indicating whether or not the Chuters' poker had a hook at the end. Here, below, is an image of an iron poker with a hook, typical of pokers that were popular in 19th Century England.

Figure 3-10; A typical 19th Century iron poker with a hook at one end.

(photographer unknown)

A carving knife (Figure 3-11) is an unusually long knife with a fixed blade, as compared to a shorter, foldable pocketknife. Thus, a carving knife is not easily portable. In fact, the particular carving knife used to slash George's throat was a permanent fixture of the Chuters' domestic arrangements. *Lloyd's* reporter noted: "it had been last seen in the kitchen drawer, whence the murderer had apparently taken it." (The first part of that observation could only have come from James Chuter, who—as a resident of the cottage together with his father—must have been familiar with the contents of the kitchen drawer.) Here, below, in Figure 3-11, is a photo of an elegant 19th Century carving knife from Sheffield (whose carving knives were renowned throughout England.) With its long, sturdy blade and its large, thick handle, a strong carving knife like this one can sustain far greater force than, let's say, a pocketknife—whose short, folding blade might break off if too great a force were applied by an assassin.

Figure 3-11; A 19th Century Sheffield carving knife, about 12-inches long, typically used for carving fowl or slicing roast beef.

(photographer unknown)

The Murder Weapons Were Not Brought to the Crime Scene by the Killer(s).

Significantly, the carving knife and the poker used to kill and mutilate George were not brought to the cottage by the killer(s). The criminal(s) may have carried additional weapons—in the event that suitable murder weapons could not be found quickly inside the cottage. But evidently, he/they had previously decided to utilize two of George's personal possessions to mutilate and kill him. And somehow, he/they knew *a priori* where those suitable weapons could be found. And found quickly. It was not a spur-of-the-moment, desperate decision to use the victim's own weapons to murder and mutilate him. That is another of the multiple messages to the police contained in the careful placement of the two weapons on the kitchen table, next to the mutilated corpse.

The evidence indicates that the killer(s) knew where these two murder weapons could be found quickly—even before they entered George's cottage while he was out. He/they must have known the exact location where both weapons could readily be found. Aside from George's wardrobe, the police found no signs of a search about the house. Moreover, the kitchen was shrouded in total darkness. The killer(s) did not dare light a lamp. Even a lighted 'bullseye' might have tipped off George upon his return. To find these weapons in darkness in the few minutes that George drank his beer at the Kings Head, the killer(s) must have visited George's kitchen on an earlier occasion—and cased the residence.

The use of two murder weapons, both of which belonged to the victim—rather than employing two murder weapons that belonged to the killer(s)—might seem an odd and precarious *modus operandi* for anyone planning to assassinate a chosen victim. How could a killer (or killers) possibly know beforehand that suitable lethal weapons were in fact waiting and quickly accessible inside the cottage? How did the killer(s) know beforehand there was a carving knife in the kitchen drawer? Not every kitchen drawer contains a carving knife. How did the killer(s) know beforehand that a poker was readily accessible in a room adjoining the kitchen?

To leave to chance such a crucial matter as murder weapons in a planned assassination would have been foolhardy. Any rational plan that counted on using weapons already located at the crime scene would depend on certain knowledge aforethought that these weapons were in fact easily accessible at the scene. The killer (or killers) was/were rational in every respect. Thus, the killer(s) must have known beforehand that a carving knife and a poker were indeed already present inside the cottage, and that they were quickly accessible. But how—and when—was such critical knowledge obtained? One wonders: had the killer(s) entered George's kitchen on a previous occasion and noted the presence of these two weapons then? Moreover, had the killer(s) on a previous occasion also noted that the latch-lock on George's kitchen door could be easily opened with a bent wire?

An Earlier Robbery at the Cottage.

Lloyd's reporter mentioned—almost in passing: "It has transpired that an entry was made into the house about 12 months ago, and some 20*l* stolen." The intended implication of this seemingly irrelevant fact in *Lloyd's* report is that the illegal forced entry into George's cottage a year earlier by a burglar may have been connected in some way to the illegal unforced entry in 1888 that resulted in George's death.

It appears that either *Lloyd's* reporter or the Surrey police were suggesting that George's murder in 1888 was just another home robbery, similar to the successful home robbery in George's cottage in 1887, in which 20 pounds were stolen. Thus, it was hypothesized: the 1888 robbery was interrupted, went sour, and then spiraled wildly out of control—resulting in George's unplanned murder. According to this theory, the robbery in 1888 supposedly went sour when George unexpectedly confronted a robber descending the stairs leading up to George's upstairs bedroom.

I must again interject here to ask rhetorically: if that theory were indeed true, then why the *mutilations* of George's body? Why the use of two murder weapons by a lone robber? It would have been sufficient for a lone robber to use only one murder weapon to kill George, who was unarmed. No mutilations would have been necessary for a lone robber to kill George and escape unidentified. One murder weapon would have been sufficient to kill George and escape. At the inquest, Dr. Sealy would confirm this last conclusion.

Lloyd's reporter (or the Surrey police) implied that the robbery in 1888 was merely a return visit of the same lone robber who had stolen 20 pounds from the Chuter's household in 1887. Of course, there was no evidence that directly connected the perpetrators in these two events, separated by nearly a year. According to this unsubstantiated theory, this same robber had returned to the Chuter residence for yet more plunder. While this speculation by *Lloyd's* reporter is not impossible, the inverse could also be true.

An Inverse Theory.

Perhaps the true purpose of the burglary in 1887 was the murder and mutilation of George Chuter—and the theft of 20 pounds sterling on that occasion was merely an incidental crime of opportunity. The cash had been carelessly left downstairs, sitting on top a table, left out in plain view. So, the killer(s) may have grabbed the cash upon entering the residence through an open window. Possibly, the intruder(s) in 1887 noted the poker next to a fireplace in an adjoining room, and the carving knife in the kitchen drawer. There's no reason to believe that George's killer(s) would leave behind 20 pounds left on top of a table because theft was somehow beneath them.

In this 1887 intrusion, some unforeseen event may have forced the killers to flee before he/they could mount the stairs and murder George asleep in his upstairs bedroom, Perhaps the killer(s) suddenly abandoned in mid-stream their plan to murder and mutilate George on that occasion. Possibly, some passersby walked down the alley, near the Chuters' kitchen door; or voices could be heard on Chertsey Road. To avoid being identified in 1887, he/they may have aborted the murder plan after the theft downstairs, but before the murder upstairs. The murder plan depended on absolute secrecy.

And then, in January 1888, the killer(s) returned to 'Juniper Cottages' to finish the murder and mutilation of George Chuter, started earlier in 1887. This hypothetical scenario also fits all the known facts.

Evidence of Meticulous Planning.

The murder of George Chuter in 1888 was the successful fruition of meticulous advance planning. Nothing was left to chance by the killer(s.) Moreover, everything in the murder plan had been calculated and prepared over a considerable length of time—not at the last moment. We have already seen evidence that the killer(s) must have obtained knowledge of the daily routines of George and his son, likely gathered by the stalking of both Chuters over a considerable period prior to the murder.

Later, I will reveal additional evidence that shows the advance preparations in the Byfleet Murder were even more extensive than just the stalking of the victim and his son. As we will see in Volume 2 of *A Trail of Blood,* the preparations for the Byfleet Murder & Mutilation apparently went back much earlier than January 12, 1888, and even earlier than 1887.

A Perfect Crime.

In the 1888 attack, there were no slip-ups in the execution of this intricate assassination plot. Every element in the murder functioned smoothly like the movements in a Swiss watch. As police would report later at the inquest, there was no sign of a violent struggle found anywhere inside or outside the cottage. The only clue at the scene noted by the police was a huge pool of George's blood surrounding the body on the kitchen floor.

The Byfleet Murder/Mutilation is still an unsolved crime. Significantly, it is also a *perfect* crime. The perpetrator(s) encountered no resistance from the victim. No one ever observed any part of the crime—from the formation of the plot, to the stalking, to the successful execution of the murder and mutilation, to the mysterious escape of the killer(s,) to the search by the police in Byfleet for the perpetrator(s.) The killer(s) successfully murdered George and mutilated his body, and then made a clean escape without leaving any trace for the police to follow. Neighbors heard no sounds of violence to alert them that George was being attacked. Upon departure, the killer(s) left no clues behind as to the identity of anyone involved. The gold items, whatever they were, allegedly stolen by the killer(s,) were never found.

As we will soon observe in reports of the Coroner's Inquest on Jan. 16, 1888, the police investigation uncovered no trail of physical evidence to track down the perpetrator(s) after the getaway. Despite the huge pool of George's blood on the kitchen floor, there were no bloody footprints to be seen anywhere. There were no known witnesses to the murder. The police found no trail of blood on the ground to follow outside the cottage. The killer(s') means of escape was unknown. The police had no suspects—and in fact, the Surrey Constabulary would never charge anyone with George's murder.

Most importantly, there was no visible evidence at the crime scene that established a credible motive. The police's conjectured robbery-gone-sour theory is not convincingly supported by substantial physical evidence at the crime scene. It is not a credible motive for murder and the mutilation of the victim. Indeed. the evidence against the police's theory is, I believe, overwhelming. More evidence—'new' evidence—will soon be forthcoming. But first, I will present some modern analysis of all the evidence that we have seen thus far.

Disordered vs. Ordered Murders.

In the 1970s in the US, the FBI's Behavioral Science Unit began a program of classification of murders, based on a theory that homicidal crime scenes could be categorized as either *disordered* or *ordered.* The theory, credited to FBI agent Roy Hazelwood, is based on prison interviews with convicted murderers, conducted by FBI agents John Douglas and Robert Ressler. A long history of successful results in murder investigations, including successful prosecutions, from the 1970s to the present day, has firmly established this theory as useful, among many criminologists.

This disordered/ordered categorization eventually became the basis for the Crime Classification Manual: A Standard System for Investigating and Classifying Violent Crimes (1992,) a text on the classification of violent crimes by John E. Douglas, Ann W. Burgess, Allen G. Burgess and Robert K. Ressler—currently in use by the FBI and by many law enforcement organizations throughout the world.

The place of a murder crime scene on the scale of order vs. disorder is determined by a number of factors. According to the order/disorder dichotomy described in the FBI's *Classified Crimes Manual,* ordered murders are premeditated and carefully planned. At an ordered crime scene, little if any evidence can normally be found that reveals the identity of the killer (or killers.) Ordered killers are likely to be above average to average intelligence, attractive, married or living with a domestic partner, employed, educated, skilled, orderly, cunning, and controlled. They have some degree of social grace, may even be charming. Above all, they are highly organized. Organized criminals are typically antisocial and often psychopathic. However, they know right from wrong, and are not insane. Significantly, they show no remorse for their crimes. They feel entitled to do whatever they do—as if they were granted the right to kill by some inner need or by a higher power.

Disorganized crimes, in contrast, are typically not planned in advance. Disordered criminals typically leave incriminating evidence at the scene of the murder—such as fingerprints, their own blood, DNA, or even their personal belongings. Disorganized criminals may be young, under the influence of alcohol or drugs, or mentally ill. They often have deficient communication and social skills and may be below average in intelligence.

The Robbery-Gone-Sour Theory: a Disordered Murder.

A robbery-gone-sour resulting in murder by a lone burglar is the archetype of a disordered murder. According to the theory of the crime held by the Surrey Constabulary in 1888, a lone burglar was confronted by George Chuter on the staircase leading to George's upstairs bedroom. At the time, the burglar was allegedly descending the staircase with some money and perhaps some gold items taken from George's lockbox in his bedroom closet. Supposedly, a fight between the two men broke out in the stairwell (although no evidence of a struggle anywhere in the house was ever revealed.) Supposedly, this hypothetical burglar chased George to the kitchen. Now panicked, the burglar decided to kill George—to prevent him from later identifying the thief to the police. The burglar then supposedly grabbed the poker from an adjoining room and bashed George on the back of his head—either knocking him unconscious or killing him. The police conjectured that this burglar, now hysterical, continued to wield the poker—bashing and mutilating George's face until the features were unrecognizable. As George lay unconscious and dying on the floor of the kitchen, the lone burglar supposedly then put down the poker and searched the drawer in the kitchen table for a knife. Allegedly, in the dark kitchen, he found the carving knife in the kitchen table drawer. Supposedly, the burglar then slashed George's throat from ear-to-ear.

Lastly, according to the Lone Burglar Theory: before departing the scene, the lone burglar then set the two murder weapons on top of the kitchen table, next to the dead body—where the police would be sure to see them. The apparent contradictions in the Lone Burglar/Robbery-Gone-Sour Theory make no sense—at least, none to me.

A hypothetical lone burglar's panic—and his sudden, improvised change of murder weapons in mid-stream—are clearly elements of confusion and desperation. The Lone Burglar Theory does not describe an ordered murder. Quite the contrary, it describes a disordered murder. According to the Lone-Burglar-Theory, the crime was originally planned as a simple house burglary, to be committed while the homeowner was out. The switch from a common household burglary to an unplanned murder and gruesome mutilation—committed with two murder weapons—cannot be reconciled with the Lone Burglar Theory.

On the contrary, the murder and mutilation of George Chuter was evidently an *ordered* murder. Indeed, it was a highly ordered murder. It is accurate, I think, to describe it as a 'perfect, ordered murder.' The killer(s) accomplished precisely what he/they had set out to do. There were no unexpected glitches in the execution. They made a clean escape. The crime has remained unsolved for 136 years.

The Byfleet Murder: An Intricately Ordered Crime—Planned Long In Advance.

As my examination of the crime scene evidence has consistently shown throughout this chapter, the murder of George Chuter was meticulously planned in advance. It was not a spontaneous crime committed in panic. On the evening of January 12, 1888, an intricate murder plan was scrupulously executed. No mistakes were made by the killer(s.) Preparations for the murder—such as stalking the routines of George and James Chuter; waiting for James to depart for his band rehearsal; lying in wait in the kitchen for George's return from the King's Head; securing murder weapons that belonged to the Chuter household—all of these preparations certainly began long before the actual perpetration of the murder on the evening of January 12, 1888. All this meticulous planning paid off handsomely for the killer(s.) There was no sign of a struggle anywhere in the residence when the police arrived. There was no trace of a forcible break-in anywhere about the cottage. There was no trail of blood to follow—either in the kitchen or on the ground outside. There were no bloody footprints to compare. All of George's leaking blood was contained in a large pool on the kitchen floor surrounding his mutilated corpse—and nowhere else. You don't get perfect results like these in a murder without careful advanced planning.

The *mutilations* were not an unexpected act of violence. The *mutilations* were, in fact, the goal of the murder. Was the purpose of the attack to torture and to punish George? I don't think so. As Dr. Sealy will affirm in Chapter 5, George was already unconscious and dying from the first blow oi the poker. George never knew what hit him. He was out cold instantaneously. The sole purpose of the murder was to release George's blood from his body. The mutilations were symbolic wounds. But symbolic of what? The "tremendous pool of blood" in which George's body lay, and the lack of any bloody footprints, are evidence that the mutilation with the carving knife was, in fact, exactly what the killer(s) had planned to accomplish. Nothing had stopped them. Evidently, George's blood was shed to make a symbolic statement. But, to whom was this statement addressed? And what did it mean?

George Chuter Was Murdered and Mutilated by Two-or-More Persons Unknown, All Acting in Concert.

Now, it is abundantly clear to me: the crime scene evidence indicates that George Chuter was murdered and mutilated by two-or-more persons unknown, who acted in concert. Here are the reasons for my conclusion—and the evidence that supports them.

The body of George Chuter was found by his son, James, on the floor of the kitchen, lying in a huge pool of blood, next to the entrance door. *Lloyd's Weekly Newspaper* wrote: "Lying inside the back door was the dead body of his [James'] father." The *Surrey Advertiser* observed that George "had been done to death just within the threshold of his own doorway." *Lloyd's Weekly Newspaper* added:

"The evidence of police officers showed that the deceased's greatcoat was buttoned all the way down, as though he was attacked as soon as he entered the house."

At the inquest on Jan. 16, 1888, PC Mears would depose that his examination of the crime scene revealed no indications of a struggle anywhere in the house. In other words, George Chuter was murdered and mutilated quickly, immediately, but a moment after he stepped inside his kitchen doorway. He was not murdered by a lone burglar descending the stairwell to George's bedroom. He was murdered and mutilated within the threshold of his kitchen entrance by two assailants who were lying-in-wait, hidden behind the kitchen door, both already armed and ready to spring. One of his assailants wielded a poker; the other, a carving knife.

George was slain and mutilated at the location on the kitchen floor where his body was later found by his son, near the threshold. There was no indication that George had confronted a lone robber on the stairwell leading up to his bedroom. There was no indication of a struggle anywhere else in the house. There was no indication that the body had been moved next to the kitchen door after George had been murdered elsewhere. George was murdered and mutilated within a matter of seconds after he entered his kitchen door.

Two different weapons were used to mutilate and murder George Chuter: a bloody poker and a bloody carving knife. In other words, George's head was bashed in with the poker, and his throat was slashed from ear-to-ear with the carving knife. Both the bashing with the poker and the slashing with the carving knife occurred at that same location just inside the kitchen door. Otherwise, there would have been splashes of blood all about the kitchen, and perhaps elsewhere in the house. But there were none—outside the huge pool of blood under George's body on the floor. Two killers murdered and mutilated George in concert.

The evidence gathered by the police confirms that George was attacked the moment he entered the house (as shown by the mark on George's hat made by the poker and the fact that his overcoat was still "buttoned-down.") Medical evidence introduced at the Coroner's Inquest will confirm that the bashing of George's head and the slashing of his neck occurred in quick succession. The bashing of George's skull with the poker occurred first. Once the attack on George began with the first blow of the poker, there was no time—and above all no need—to stop the attack and fetch a second weapon: the carving knife from the kitchen table drawer. The poker was more than sufficiently lethal to bludgeon George to death. As medical testimony at the inquest will make clear: George was undoubtedly unconscious and inevitably dying, or perhaps even already dead, from the *first blow alone*, administered to the back of his skull. The rest of the attack was overkill with two weapons—which is clear evidence of murder and mutilation by at least two killers working in concert.

Moreover, these two (or more) killers were proud of what they had accomplished. They brazenly displayed the two murder weapons on top of the kitchen table, next to the victim's body. There, the weapons would be certain to be seen by the investigators and directly connected to the crime. This was a deliberate display. These two pitiless killers showed no remorse. They showed their utter contempt for the police. There is, I believe, no credible explanation why a lone burglar would murder George multiple times with two weapons, thereby mutilating the victim's body for no reason that might enhance his chances of escape, unidentified. Thus, it is now clear to me: one killer administered multiple blows to George's head with the poker; and, immediately after that, a second killer slashed George's throat with the carving knife. At present, the motives for the actions of these killers still remain a mystery. More evidence is still required to uncover suitable motives that explain both the murder and the mutilations.

Overkill.

It is the stroke of the carving knife across George's throat, from ear-to-ear, that conclusively establishes the participation of a second killer, working in concert with the poker-wielding killer. The slashing of George's throat from ear-to-ear with the carving knife, after George's head had been bashed to a pulp with the poker, was *overkill.* Overkill is the infliction of death more than once on the same victim. Overkill is also lethal mutilation of a body that is *unnecessary for the perpetration of murder.* Here we have both. This mutilation with the carving knife was unnecessary for a lone burglar's primary purpose: *i.e.,* to escape the crime scene without being identified by the victim to the police. A lone burglar intent on killing George to avoid identification would have continued to bludgeon him with the poker until death was absolutely certain. Switching from the poker to the carving knife to slash George's throat would have served no useful purpose for a lone burglar. The purpose of the carving knife was to release virtually all of George's blood upon the kitchen floor.

Immediately after the first blow, George was—according to the medical examiner at the Coroner's Inquest—certainly unconscious, probably already dying, or perhaps already dead. That was merely the first blow with the poker. The doctor will testify at the Coroner's Inquest that there were at least two lethal blows with the poker. Thus, George was apparently killed thrice: twice with the poker; and then, killed yet again, with the carving knife.

The Leader of a Team of Killers Emerges.

The slashing of George's throat with the carving knife was the final, symbolic act: the *coup de grâce.* Not only does the slashing of George's throat with the carving knife indicate the participation of a second killer, but it also indicates that the knife-wielding killer was the leader of the team. He was a symbolic executioner. As we will learn at the Inquest, the knife-wielding killer had evidently attempted to decapitate George—and he almost succeeded in this attempt. Shades of Henry VIII.

The Message of The Two Bloody Murder Weapons.

The two murder weapons carefully placed together on top of the kitchen table, next to the victim, were a message of defiance, explicitly sent to the Surrey Constabulary by the killer who led the team. This crime was committed by two killers working in concert. The police would never figure out why George Chuter was murdered *and* mutilated—or whodunnit. For 136 years, that's been so.

The Killer(s) Now Become the Killers.

Now that I am convinced by crime scene evidence that the Byfleet Murder & Mutilation was indeed perpetrated by two-or-more killers who worked in concert, I have already begun to refer to the killers in the plural. And I have removed the parentheses surrounding the 's.' Thankfully, I will continue to do so from here on.

\

**"I am ill at these numbers.
I have not art to reckon my groans."**

William Shakespeare; *Hamlet* (Act II, Scene ii)

Chapter 4. The Coroner's Inquest

On January 16, 1888, a Monday, Mr. G. F. Roumieu, Coroner of West Surrey, held an inquest on the body of George Chuter at the Queen's Head Inn in Byfleet. The Queen's Head was the same pub and inn where, many years earlier, George had worked as innkeeper.

On January 17, 1888, the London *Daily News* published a truncated report of the Coroner's Court proceedings. Evidently, the source of this account was a wire service dispatch, since the identical account was later published in numerous other newspapers throughout Britain, and even abroad. On January 21, the *Illustrated Police News* published a more extended account from the same wire service report. However, it, too, skipped coverage of some significant issues discussed during the inquest (but not the same issues skipped over by the London *Daily News.*) Consequently, I have combined these two reports in the transcription below, to give us fuller coverage of the proceedings. I begin with the report published in the *Illustrated Police News* on January 21:

THE MURDER AT BYFLEET

Mr. G. F. Roumieu, Coroner for West Surrey, held an inquest yesterday at the Queen's Head Inn, Byfleet, on the body of Mr. George Chuter, aged 67, retired builder and innkeeper, who was murdered at his house in the village on

Thursday evening last. Deputy Chief Superintendent Barker and Super-intendent Bungard, of the County Constabulary, watched the proceedings.

James Chuter, grocer, Byfleet, the son of the deceased, said his father had lived with him. About twenty minutes to seven on Thursday evening, witness left home to attend a band practice at the pavilion in the cricket field, and was absent till half-past ten. He let himself into the house by opening the back door with a key, and, in the darkness, fell over the prostrate body of his father in the kitchen. Without waiting to get a light, witness ran to Mr. Choate, a next-door neighbor, with whom he returned to the house, and found the deceased was dead. The body was lying in a quantity of blood, and a poker and a carving knife, which were on the table in the same apartment, also had marks of blood on them, the blade of the knife being quite covered with it. A box, in which deceased had kept his money, was found open on his bed, and the contents, with the exception of a packet containing 20 shillings, the appearance of which might have deceived the murderer, had been abstracted. Witness could not say how much money the box had contained, but he was sure there had been gold. The box had been removed from a wardrobe in the bedroom, and the lock had been forced. Nothing else was missed. The house was broken into some time ago, and on that occasion, some money belonging to the witness was stolen.

Simon Choate, boot maker, said he went to Purford *(sic)* on the evening in question, and did not return until about the same time as deceased's son. He, however, had been told by his wife that nothing unusual was heard in the next house during the evening.

Charlotte Slaymaker, of the King's Head public-house, a few doors from deceased's residence, said the man [George Chuter] came there about quarter past seven, and had a glass of beer, only remaining five or six minutes. He wished her "Good night" when he left. About a quarter of an hour later, she sent a messenger to the son's shop, but it was an early closing night and the place was shut. The messenger, however, said there was a light in the living room. While deceased was at the King's Head, he stood in front of the bar alone. There were several persons in the tap room, but no strangers.

The evidence of police officers showed that the deceased's greatcoat was buttoned all the way down, as though he was attacked as soon as he entered the house. There were no indications of a struggle. On the back door, there was a single catch lock, which could be worked by a piece of bent wire.

Dr. Sealy, of Weybridge, said he saw deceased about half-past two on Friday morning and found that life had been extinct for several hours. The head and face presented evidence of being severely battered, while all the structures about the throat had been divided almost down to the bones of the spine.

> **Witness had no doubt that any one of the blows which caused the injury to the head would have been sufficient to render the deceased insensible; and he thought it very probable that the man would have died had his throat not been cut.**

At this point in the wire service report of the inquest, the account published in the *Illustrated Police News* skipped a critical paragraph of Dr. Sealy's inquest testimony, and part of the summation by the Coroner. The missing paragraphs from Dr. Sealey's testimony and the Coroner's summation were published earlier, on January 17, in an otherwise truncated wire service report published in the London *Daily News.* I insert now these two paragraphs, beginning with Dr. Sealy's testimony:

> **On both cheeks, there were severe contusions, caused, in witness's [Dr. Sealy's] opinion, by a poker or some similar instrument. On the bridge of the nose, there was a very deep wound, everything being separated down to the bone.**
>
> **There was a similar wound on the point of the chin, a bad one on the back of the head, and another on the left knee, while all the structures about the throat had been divided almost down to the bones of the spine.**
>
> **The Coroner, in summing up, described the crime as the most diabolical in his experience; and he expressed the hope that the Home Office would offer a large reward for**

information that would bring the murderer to justice.

Returning now to the wire service account published in the *Illustrated Police News* on January 21:]

> **[The Coroner] regretted the fact that at present, the police had no clue to guide them, but said he did not think there would be anything gained by an adjournment of the inquiry; and, by his advice, the jury at once returned a verdict of wilfull murder against some person or persons unknown.**

Figure 4-1. The King's Head Inn in the 21st Century, where George Chuter drank a beer just minutes before he was murdered and mutilated in his cottage on the evening of January 12, 1888.

Photo published in the Byfleet Heritage Society Newsletter. Photographer unknown. Photo reproduced here with permission of BHS.

Dr. Sealy's Medical Evidence.

Unquestionably, the most revealing and significant testimony to come out of the inquest was the medical evidence and opinions of Dr. George John Sealy. He had examined George Chuter's body in the cottage kitchen six or seven hours following the murder. It was Dr. Sealy's conclusion—about which he was certain—that any of the blows that had battered George's head would have been sufficient to have immediately knocked him unconscious. This observation was followed by another important opinion from the doctor. He "thought it very probable that the man [*i.e.*, George Chuter] would have died [even] had his throat not been cut." Dr. Sealy added: "I should think it quite likely that death would ultimately have resulted from either of the [two major] blows upon the head."

In other words, George probably would have died from either of the two major blows to his head *alone,* even without the subsequent slashing of his throat with the carving knife. Evidently, each of these two major blows to the head, administered with the poker, was very powerful. Dr. Sealy added that if he had removed George's scalp in an autopsy, he would undoubtedly have found George's skull crushed into fragments in the areas where the poker had struck. The first blow, in particular, was likely delivered to the back of George's head by a strong man while George was still standing upright inside the kitchen doorway.

Following this first blow—which had certainly rendered George unconscious—George must have fallen to the kitchen floor "insensible." Inevitably, George would have died from that first blow alone. Nevertheless, the poker-wielding killer administered yet more blows to George's face and head as the victim lay upon the kitchen floor. At least one of these subsequent blows to the face would also have inevitably proven fatal—even if George's throat had not subsequently been slashed from ear-to-ear. Dr. Sealy described the wound to the bridge of the nose thus: "Just above the bridge of the nose, leading to the forehead, there was a deep wound dividing everything down to the bone."

"This was the most unkindest cut of all."
(William Shakespeare *(Julius Caesar, Act 3, Scene 2)*

In addition, the doctor testified that "all the structures about the throat had been divided almost down to the bones of the spine." By that, he meant that George's throat had been slashed almost down to the spinal vertebrae, thus severing George's esophagus and all his blood vessels leading to and from the brain—including the Carotid Artery and the Jugular Vein. The slash divided the Pharyngeal Plexus: that receives branches of the Vagus Nerve, the Glossopharyngeal Nerve and Maxillary Nerve. It divided the three Pharyngeal Constrictor Muscles, and the three Longitudinal Muscles.

The slashing of George's neck from ear-to-ear, down to the vertebrae, was undoubtedly sufficient to kill him. Moreover, the doctor ruled the cause of death was "the immense loss of blood caused by the division of the large arteries in the throat." Thus, George Chuter was, in effect, *murdered thrice*—at least twice with the poker, and then soon after, yet a third time, with the carving knife. Apparently, the slash was a symbolic *coup de grâce.*

The Doctor Could Not Tell at which of the Two Blows on the Head or the Slash of the Throat George Had Actually Expired.

As we have read in a direct transcript of the Coroner's Inquest testimony, it was the opinion of the medical examiner that George was *first attacked with the poker.* From the initial blow to the back of his head, George was immediately knocked unconscious. Indeed, that first blow may even have killed him momentarily after he was struck. The doctor could not determine exactly when George expired—although he indicated that George would have died eventually, if not instantly, from that first blow alone. It was also the opinion of the doctor that *either* of the two most severe blows from the poker would eventually have killed George, even if his neck had not been slashed down to the vertebrae. So, George was subjected to attempted murder multiple times with the poker alone—even before the *coup de grâce* was administered with the carving knife, probably upon a corpse on the floor, Here is the very definition of *overkill.*

Dr. Sealy's Medical Testimony Supports My Earlier Conclusion About Two Killers Acting in Concert.

Here, in the doctor's testimony, medical evidence can be found that supports my earlier conclusion: that George was mutilated and murdered by two killers who acted in concert. Dr. Sealy's medical evidence drives a stake into the heart of the Lone Burglar/Robber-Gone-Sour Theory. Ask yourself: why would a lone burglar mutilate and murder George *twice or thrice?* Why would a lone burglar put down the poker in the midst of an attack, and then search in darkness in a drawer for a carving knife in order to kill George yet a second or third time? The doctor's medical evidence renders the Lone Burglar/Robbery-Gone-Sour Theory absurd on its face.

Remember: the police testified that "there were no indications of a struggle" anywhere about the cottage. So, evidently George had offered no resistance. He never had an opportunity to offer any resistance or start a fight. George was attacked in his darkened doorway the moment he entered his kitchen. Following the first blow to the back of his head, George lay unconscious on the kitchen floor—possibly then dying or already dead. In order to kill George straight away with absolutely no possibility of the victim's survival, all that the poker-wielding burglar would have had to do: *continue bludgeoning George's skull with the poker until death was certain.* After all, George was immediately unconscious on the floor after the first blow.

He could not put up a fight after he fell to the ground "insensible." He could not get up and flee. And indeed, the poker-wielding killer then administered a second major blow again to his head—which, according to Dr. Sealy, was also lethal.

A lone burglar would have had no need and no reason to switch murder weapons, from the poker to the carving knife, while killing George. To slash George's throat with the carving knife, the lone burglar would first have had to put down the poker, go to the kitchen table, open the drawer, search for and extract the carving knife, and then resume mutilating George's body with the carving knife. All for no purpose. George was already dying or dead. And supposedly, a lone burglar did all that in total darkness.

Killing George multiple times would hardly enhance the killers' chances of escaping unidentified. In answer to a question posed by the Coroner, Dr. Sealy stated: "any of the blows on the head were enough to cause unconsciousness quite sufficient to allow anybody there to get away in perfect security."

Consequently, based on Dr. Sealy's medical testimony at the inquest, I now reassert that no explanation for the use of two weapons can be made credible by invoking the Lone Burglar Theory. Why would a lone burglar suddenly put down his poker in the midst of an attack, and then search for a carving knife to slash George's throat—only to murder him a second or third time? The idea is not credible on its face. It is unsupported by any medical evidence. As far as I am concerned, the Lone Burglar/Robbery-Gone-Sour Theory is now exploded by Dr. Sealy's medical testimony.

The Coroner Suspected that a Killer Had Visited George's House at an Earlier Time.

The Coroner, Mr. Roumieu, was evidently troubled by the self-evident fact that a killer had obtained the carving knife from the drawer of the kitchen table. The Coroner stated: "As to how the perpetrator of the deed got hold of the knife, there was no evidence to show. The knife was usually kept in a draw in the room, and there was no evidence that Chuter had the knife out; and so they [the jury] must presume that the man [the assassin] got it out, and this, added to the fact that he [the assassin] went up and got the cash box, leads one to suspect that the individual knew something about the house, but they [the police] had no suspicion at the present time to rest on anyone."

Deliberately Shared Participation in the Murder and Mutilation by Two Killers Wielding Two Weapons.

Moreover, here in the doctor's testimony lies convincing evidence of deliberately shared participation in both the mutilation and the murder, by two killers who worked in concert. Evidently, each of these two killers felt compelled—for motives that are still unknown—to participate directly, *i.e. hands-on*, in the mutilation and the murder of the victim. The second killer, the knife-wielder, delivered the *coup de grâce*—a symbolic, final death stroke. This idea—that both killers felt compelled, for reasons yet unknown, to participate directly in the murder and mutilation—will assume even greater importance in subsequent chapters. The concept is critical to the establishment of a credible, new motive for two killers in this crime. Curiously, as we will soon see, this new motive was momentarily suggested in passing by the Coroner himself during his summation at the inquest—but then ignored by one and all.

Determining the Sequence of Events—Yet Again.

Dr. Sealy's testimony indicated that George's head had been battered *before* his throat was cut—not the other way around. Referring to the injuries on George's battered skull and face, the doctor stated: "The injuries were certainly inflicted before death. Death, of course, was the result of the immense loss of blood caused by the division of the large arteries in the throat." Note well the doctor's use of the word "certainly."

George's neck was deeply slashed down to his spinal vertebrae. Apparently, only by striking by chance a particularly tough cartilage—or perhaps a bony vertebra—was the carving knife prevented from severing George's head entirely from his body. Decapitation was clearly the intention of the knife-wielding killer. Obviously, the slashing of George's neck down to the vertebrae was the instantaneous cause of George's death. No one could possibly survive such a deeply slashed neck for more than a few seconds. That a decapitation was the true intention of the slash explains why the knife-wielder had chosen a lengthy, sturdy carving knife to sever George's throat.

The Bruise on George's Left Knee and the Fractured Skull.

Dr. Sealy also testified that he found a bad bruise on George's left knee. Thus, medical evidence indicates that after the first blow with the poker to the back of George's head, George fell unconscious onto his knees, incurring a bad bruise on his left knee. More about George's bruised left knee in a moment.

Dr. Sealy had "no doubt that deceased was insensible before his throat was cut." He added that either of the two most serious blows to the victim's head "would cause immediate insensibility. And no doubt, if the scalp would be taken off, extensive fractures would be found."

George's Beard.

In reply to further questions from the Coroner, the doctor stated: "probably after the deceased had been stunned, they might have held up his beard, and then inflicted the terrible wound in the throat." The Coroner, Mr. Roumieu, then stated that the lifting of George's beard, while George lay on his back, before his neck was slashed, must indeed have been the case. George's beard had not been cut by the carving knife. Evidently, the Coroner had determined that fact for himself during his own examination of George's body at the crime scene. Thus, we learn that George had a substantial beard, and that it was not slashed. This seemingly innocuous detail will become highly relevant in a subsequent chapter.

Dr. Sealy's Telling Use of the Plural Pronoun "They."

I cannot let pass without comment the highly significant fact that Dr. Sealy used the plural pronoun "they" when he referred in his testimony, quoted above, to those persons who "might have held up his [George's] beard, and then inflicted the terrible wound in the throat." This statement was recorded in a direct quote from the doctor's testimony, as published in the *Surrey Advertiser* on Jan. 21. Moreover, the accuracy of Dr. Sealy's statement was confirmed by the Coroner, Mr. Roumieu—who offered no objection to the Doctor's testimony.

Dr. Sealy's use of the plural pronoun "they" indicates that the doctor thought two-or-more killers working in concert had mutilated and murdered George—although Dr. Sealy never specifically testified in detail, pro or con, on that particular issue. The idea that this remark was a slip of the tongue is absurd in medical testimony by the examining doctor in a Coroner's Inquest. Every word spoken by Dr. Sealy was carefully chosen by him—and he never corrected or contradicted himself. The direct implications of Dr. Sealy's use of the plural pronoun "they" are that one killer lifted George's beard, away from his throat, while a second killer then slashed George's neck down to the vertebrae with the carving knife. Each killer co-operated with the other.

George's Body Was Rolled Over by the Killers onto his Back on the Kitchen Floor.

Following the line of thought opened by the doctor's testimony, it is now clear to me: George's beard could have been lifted up by the knife-wielding killer only when George lay flat on his back, *face up.* The slashing of George's neck by a second killer—through George's cravat; through his skin; through his windpipe; through the sturdy masses of cartilage in his throat; through all the many blood vessels in his neck, down to the spinal vertebrae—could only have occurred when George's unconscious body lay on his back, on the kitchen floor, *face-up.* However, those apparent facts also reveal to me: there is still an important event unaccounted for in the sequence of events thus far documented in reports of the Coroner's Inquest.

The bruise on George's left knee mentioned earlier by Dr. Sealy is evidence that George fell onto his knees after he received the first blow with the poker administered to the back of his head. Indeed, the doctor stated: "deceased on receiving the first blow probably fell on his knees." If

George fell unconscious onto his knees immediately after he was bludgeoned with the first blow of the poker, then surely he would have fallen *forward* onto the kitchen floor. Falling *forward,* he would have fallen onto his belly, lying *face-down or face-sideways.* He could not have fallen from his knees to a position flat on his back, *face-up.* To have landed on his back, George would have had to twist his body 180 degrees. But he was then unconscious. Yet, *w*hen George's beard was lifted up, and his throat was deeply slashed down to the spinal vertebrae, he must have been lying on his back, *face-up.* And when the poker-wielding killer subsequently smashed the bridge of George's nose, the victim's body also must have been lying flat on his back, *face-up.*

As noted in a previous chapter, when some factual evidence makes no sense in a murder investigation, there must be a real explanation for it—even if that explanation seems, at first, improbable. Contradictions must never be swept under the rug. Some necessary event is clearly missing from the sequence of events thus far described.

The documented evidence indicates that George's body must have been deliberately rolled over by the two killers, from a position on his belly or on his side to a position flat on his back, *face-up.* The rollover must have occurred sometime before George's beard was lifted by one killer; before the bridge of George's nose was smashed with the poker; and before George's throat was slashed down to the spinal vertebrae by the knife-wielding killer. Why would the killers bother to roll over George's body on the floor if he was already unconscious, dead or dying? Kneeling over George's body *face-up* on the floor, the knife-wielder could then add his body weight to his arm's strength in his attempt to sever George's head from his body with the carving knife. The rollover was part of the killers' plan to decapitate George's head from his body.

I will return in a later chapter to George's position flat on his back, or on his side, lying on the kitchen floor, face up. It has more than passing relevance to ultimate revelations about what really happened in George's kitchen on that fateful evening.

More on that First Blow with the Poker.

Of the several blows to George's head cited by Dr. Sealy, there was only one blow—the initial blow—that was administered to a fragile part of the skull that directly encases the brain: "a bad one on the back of the head." The doctor described the wound from this blow in these words: "There was a wound about an inch and a half in length at the back of the head."

We must keep in mind: the first blow was delivered to the back of George's head in a dark kitchen only a moment after he opened his kitchen door. It must have been very difficult for the poker-wielding killer to hit that exact spot on the back George's head in the dark in only a moment's time. Hitting that exact, vulnerable spot on George's skull could hardly have been accidental. The blow was carefully aimed by the poker-wielder. But don't forget: George was then wearing his felt hat that covered the top of his head. As we will learn later, the darkness in the unilluminated kitchen was nearly total that evening.

The mark found on George's felt hat is evidence that the poker-wielding killer had cooly and specifically aimed for the most vulnerable spot on the top-back part of the skull: *i.e.*, the area that covers the Great Cerebral Vein of Galen. Evidently, the poker-wielding killer's purpose was not merely aiming to kill George, but also to spill his blood. Perhaps the poker-wielding killer had some knowledge of human anatomy. Though the wound was only one and a half inches long, George's blood undoubtedly gushed from his fractured skull—even before his throat was cut. From the outset, the release of George's blood was the goal of the attack with the poker. Dr. Sealy also noted: "the face presented evidence of having been seriously battered." He added: "Just above the bridge of the nose, leading to the forehead, there was a deep wound dividing everything down to the bone, and another deep wound on the chin."

The doctor also cited some contusions. These are bruises that do not break the skin and draw blood—although they may severely damage the blood vessels and bones under the skin. Said Dr. Sealy: "On both cheeks were severe contusions, formed, in my opinion, by a poker, or some similar instrument, probably the poker which has been produced."

A Messenger Arrives at the Crime Scene.

Charlotte Slaymaker, mistress of the King's Head, testified about a messenger whom she had sent to James' grocery store about 15 minutes after George had departed her pub. The messenger was a little girl. Upon the girl's return to the pub, she told Charlotte that the grocery store was closed—but that she had seen a light burning in the Chuters' "living room."

Did the little girl actually see a light burning in the Chuters' living room, as described? Or was this the room that James Chuter called his "front room" in later testimony? Or was this window in the Choate's portion of the double tenement? The lamp might even have been shining by then in the window of George's kitchen. George's residence was located at the end of a long alley, a considerable distance from James' grocery shop. Whichever room was in fact illuminated, the little girl evidently did not look through the kitchen window to see if George was home. The messenger was sent by Charlotte to deliver an outstanding bill to James, not George.

Had the young messenger peered into the Chuters' kitchen through an illuminated window, she would have seen George's body sprawled on the floor. And if she had seen George's body lying on the kitchen floor in a pool of blood, she would inevitably have screamed and given the alarm. But, as we know, that did not happen. Lucky for this little girl; lucky that she did not see George's bloody body lying on the kitchen floor; lucky that she did not react in panic. If she had screamed, the killers might well have murdered her, too. Potentially, this chilling, unforeseen event could have upset the killers' carefully laid murder plan.

The Kitchen Entrance Was Dark—Very Dark.

We know the kitchen was dark when James returned home from his band rehearsal. James Chuter later testified he stumbled over his father's body on the kitchen floor when he entered the doorway. At first, he did not see that George had been murdered and mutilated. He did not see the blood or the wounds. It was so dark in the kitchen, he first called his neighbor to fetch a lamp. When the neighbor arrived, both James and the neighbor still could not see that George had been murdered and mutilated. At first, James remarked that George must have fallen ill.

In England, there is very little, if any, daylight left between 7:30 p.m. and 10:30 p.m. on every January 12. In fact, Jan. 12, 1888 was the date of a New Moon in England--when absolutely no light was reflected by the moon that evening. The only available light was starlight—that is, if there had been no cloud cover in Surrey that cold January evening.

The evidence indicates that the moment George had entered his kitchen after returning to his residence from the King's Head, he was immediately set upon in virtually total darkness by a killer who wielded a poker, and then by another killer who wielded a carving knife. George never saw anything. He never knew what—or who—had struck him.

One Stroke of the Carving Knife, or Two?

The doctor stated he could not tell whether the assassin "had inflicted the wound in the throat with one stroke of the knife. To go through the whole of the structures of the throat, as in this case, would require considerable force." Evidently, the doctor could not find definitive evidence of two-or-more strokes of the carving knife in the wound on George's neck. One stroke would have required "considerable force."

The doctor did not rule out George's throat being slashed down to the vertebrae with only one stroke. But neither could the doctor rule out multiple strokes with the carving knife. Thus, it appears to me that the doctor was incredulous that the knife-wielding killer could have slashed George's throat down to the vertebrae with normal arm-strength—but the doctor could not rule out that physical possibility. But theoretically, it was possible the knife-wielding killer had administered a second stroke with the carving knife to exactly the same spot on George's throat as the first stroke, just deeper.

It seems to me that in a dark kitchen, the knife-wielding killer could hardly have administered a second slash of the carving knife in *exactly* the same spot as he had previously administered the first. Moreover, Dr. Sealy marveled at the "considerable force" that it would have taken a killer "to go through the whole of the structures of the throat, as in this case." Considerable force, but not impossible force—especially if the knife-wielder had augmented his arm-strength with his body weight while kneeling above George's body. An attempt in one stroke may have been symbolic.

The Cut Cravat.

Interestingly, Dr. Sealy did not mention the cut cravat, about which we learned earlier in a previous news report. On January 15, *Lloyd's Weekly* reported:

> **A further examination of the body disclosed the fact that the throat was cut from ear to ear, so much force having been used that a cravat worn by the murdered man was completely severed.**

Evidently, the knife-wielding assassin had cut through not only "the whole of the structures of the throat," he had also slashed through George's cravat. If the knife-wielding killer had cut through *both*—the cravat and George's neck down to the spinal vertebrae—in a single stroke, then the carving knife must have been exerted with even more than "considerable force." If the knife had done its work in only one stroke, then the knife-wielding killer must have exerted *an exceptionally strong force downward*, using his body weight to add to his strength in one arm. Evidently, the knife-wielding killer was a very powerful man. And he needed a long, fixed, carving knife to make the slash. A short, folding pocketknife would not do.

With George lying on his back, face up, the knife-wielding killer could have added his body weight to his arm strength while kneeling above George's head. This is yet more evidence of a calculated attempt at decapitation. It now seems credible that the unexpected interference of the cravat may have been the sole obstacle that prevented the knife-wielder from attaining his goal of cutting off George's head. The knife wielder may have wanted to decapitate George with only one mighty stroke for symbolic reasons—like famed executioners of old.

A Victorian Cravat.

In Victorian England, men's cravats could be quite elaborate affairs that completely covered a man's neck up to the chin. Here, below, in Figure 4-2, is an example of a 19th Century British cravat that left no skin exposed.

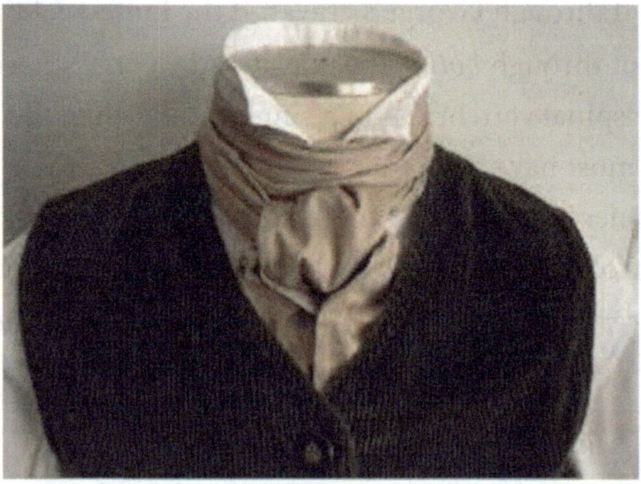

Figure 4-2; A Victorian-Era Cravat

Photographer unknown.

If George was wearing a cravat like this one, it seems to me possible that the cravat could have absorbed some of George's spurting blood when his throat was slashed. The cut cravat may have prevented George's blood from spurting from his neck wound onto the killers' clothes and hands—although the carving knife itself was reported to have been covered with blood when found by police. It probably took only a moment—perhaps 2-3 seconds—to slash George's neck with the carving knife, especially if George's neck had been slashed with only one stroke. So, it seems to me possible that quick use of the carving knife may have avoided getting George's blood on the killers' clothes and shoes.

We know from police testimony that no traces of blood were found about the house, other than on the kitchen floor surrounding George's body. Despite the "tremendous pool of blood" around George's body on the floor near the kitchen door, there was no mention of bloody footprints anywhere. The killers' expertise in murdering George and mutilating his body without getting any blood on the soles of their shoes is extraordinary. Perhaps the killers brought a change of footwear with them.

An Attempted Decapitation.

The reporter for *Lloyd's Weekly Newspaper* noted that George's cravat had been "completely severed." He marveled at "so much force having been used" by the "murderer." According to the reporter for *Lloyd's Weekly Newspaper*—who evidently had viewed George's body on the kitchen floor on Jan. 13 or 14—"the carving knife slashed George's throat from ear-to-ear." Thus, the carving knife not only slashed through all the tissues and cartilage inside George's throat, but it also sliced through the knot in his cravat. Dr. Sealy testified that George's throat had been slashed so deeply, *his head was nearly severed from the rest of his body.*

Cartilage in the neck is thick and sturdy. Thus, the various cartilages are particularly difficult to sever—especially collectively. They include the tough cricoid cartilage, a protective ring of cartilage that surrounds the trachea. The ring functions as an attachment site for muscles, cartilage, and ligaments; and it is quite tough. The neck also houses the thyroid cartilage, the largest of the nine cartilages that make up the laryngeal skeleton—whose function is to protect the larynx. From the doctor's testimony, it is clear: all these cartilages must have been severed by the slash in George's neck—from ear-to-ear, from George's Adam's Apple down to the vertebrae that surrounded his spinal column.

If the slash of the carving knife had not been cushioned somewhat by the knot in George's cravat, the killers might well have succeeded in this obvious attempt to cut off

George's head. That the killers had clearly attempted to decapitate their chosen victim casts the Byfleet Murder in a new light. Intentional decapitation in a murder is always a symbolic act of some kind. The inherent symbolism varies in each murder. So, what did the attempted decapitation of George Chuter mean symbolically? If the killers had succeeded in their attempt to decapitate George, would the Surrey Constabulary have even proposed the Lone Burglar/Robbery-Gone-Sour Theory? Would anyone have believed the police's theory if George's head had been severed? I think not.

A Hierarchy of Killers Can Now Be Determined From the Sequence of Events.

A detailed sequence of events is beginning to emerge from the crime-scene evidence. Dr. Sealey established that first, the poker-wielding killer bludgeoned George's head and face to the point that George was unconscious, dying, or perhaps already dead. So, the poker-wielder laid the groundwork for the murder/mutilation. Then, at the last moment, the knife-wielding killer took over the sacrifice and delivered the symbolic *coup de grâce.* In an instant, the ritual murder/mutilation was over.

It is already clear to me: the poker-wielding killer was the lowly assistant; while the knife-wielding killer was the leader of the pair, the guru, the mastermind who delivered the sacred stroke. Nevertheless, to satisfy the inner compulsions of both killers, it was essential for both men to participate directly in both the murder and the mutilation. It was essential for both killers to release George's blood. Blood was always the goal of the ritualistic mutilations.

This scenario is based on a premise: that only two killers acting in concert perpetrated the murder and mutilation. However, I cannot yet rule out nor confirm yet another possibility: that perhaps more than two killers, all acting in concert, perpetrated the Byfleet Murder & Mutilation. It is still possible that a third killer, serving as an accomplice, may have acted as a lookout, stationed outside the kitchen, watching for James' unexpected return. These meticulous killers left almost nothing to chance. A lookout would have been a prudent precaution for them to have taken. So, we must still search for crime scene evidence of more than two killers.

"Blood hath been shed 'ere now…
Murders have been perform'd
too terrible for the ear."

William Shakespeare, Macbeth (Act III, Sc. iv)

Let's be sacrificers…
Let's carve him as a dish fit for the gods."

William Shakespeare; *Julius Caesar* (Act 3. Sc. 1)

Chapter 5. Direct Testimony by James Chuter

On January 21, 1888, the *Surrey Advertiser* published its own account of the Coroner's Inquest, not a wire news service report like most other newspapers. In contrast to the reporting of testimony deposed mostly by officials that was published earlier by the *London Daily News* and the *Illustrated Police News*, the *Surrey Advertiser* included huge swaths of direct testimony by local witnesses—especially the direct testimony of George's son, James Chuter. In analyzing and commenting upon the evidence introduced in the inquest, I will draw upon much of James' direct testimony—several details of which differ somewhat from the paraphrasing contained in the earlier wire news service reports.

But first, James' biography.

James Chuter's Biography.

James Chuter was born on January 15, 1860. The son of George and Lucy Chuter, he was baptized at St. Mary's Church in West Byfleet. Thus, he was 28 years old at the time of his father's murder. He was then single, a widower. In 1884, James had married Priscilla Mattocks. In 1886, Priscilla died at St. Thomas Hospital in London. The 1891 Census lists James Chuter still living in Chertsey Road, then employed as a butcher. He was single. In 1893 at the age of 33, James married Kate Derisley (sister of Lloyd Derisley, a former boarder at Juniper Cottages.) In 1901, James became a licensed victualer in Byfleet, employed at The Plough—where he lived with his wife Kate and their three children: George Bertram (born in 1894,) Edgar James (born 1896,) and Walter Alfred (born 1898.) On March 12, 1905, James Chuter died. And on March 16, 1905, he was buried at St. Mary's Church in West Byfleet. James had two brothers (both sons of George and Lucy Chuter.) George Jr. died at the age of 5. Alfred Chuter was a builder and a joiner; and later a sanitary inspector. There is no mention of brother Alfred Chuter in any news account of the Byfleet Murder, or at the Coroner's Inquest.

James Chuter's Direct Testimony.

At the Coroner's Inquest on Jan. 16, 1888, James Chuter identified the body of his father; and he testified that his father lived with him on Chertsey Road. In response to questioning, James stated:

> **[My father] "was 67, and was a retired builder. I last saw him alive about twenty minutes to seven last Thursday evening, January 12th. I saw**

him in the kitchen of his house, but he followed my friend [Henry Wattingham] as far as the door.

I was going to the Pavilion in the cricket field. My father was not going anywhere that I am aware of. He knew what time I should be back, a little after 10, but he would in all probability be gone to bed. I went straight to the Pavilion with Henry Wattingham. I went to the Pavilion for band practice, and stayed there till about half-past nine.

When I left, we [James and Henry] came here to the Queens Head. Wattingham came with me. He was with me the whole night, but others with there, of course. We stayed there until ten, when I walked home with Henry Wattingham and another man.

At the gate of my father's house, we stayed about five minutes talking. Mr. Choate and his son passed by while we stood there, and we said "Good night" to them. I then said "Good night" to Wattingham, and went in at the back door.

I let myself in with the latch key, as was my custom. It was dark, and I could not see anything. It was about half-past ten then. I had taken about two steps into the back kitchen, and I fell over something. Before I got off my knees, I put my hand back to feel what I had fallen over, and then I could feel my father's legs.

I got over him again as quickly as I could, and ran round to Mr. Choate's door. I knocked at the door, and said "Will you bring a light and come with me, as there is something the matter with father. He is lying on the floor!"

Mr. Choate brought a light and of course we saw a great quantity of blood. Mr. Choate said, "Why, your father has broken a blood vessel."

I said, "Where does all this blood come from?" And he said: "I suppose it is come out of his mouth."

I said "Wait a moment, I will call Harry," That is my cousin opposite. When I got there, I found Mrs. Choate calling, and he [James' cousin Harry] was just opening the window answering her. He [Harry] said, "I'll be down in a moment."

I ran back to Mrs. Choate before Harry came, and we stood by the back door looking. Harry came a minute or two afterwards, and then we spoke again of his [George] having broken a blood vessel.

Harry stepped over his [George's] legs, and went further into the room, and he [Harry] said: "What is this knife here?" (A large ivory handled carving knife was here produced, horribly stained with blood, which the police had found on the table in the house). At the same time he [Harry] lifted it up. It was on the table. I said, "That is our knife," and he put it on the table again near the inner door. Then he [Harry] took up the poker and said: "Look at this poker." (A poker produced, with which the injuries appeared to have been inflicted, a large instrument with heavy knobs on it.)

And I replied, "that is our poker also."

The poker and knife were lying side-by-side on the table, and we saw some blood and hair on the poker, and the knife was covered with blood as if painted. The knife was usually kept in a draw in a table with other cutlery in the kitchen. The poker is never used, but is kept cleaned every week, and it stands in the kitchen in the corner by the fireplace.

I took hold of my father's hand and found it was very cold. I might say when Harry came, and we were satisfied he [George] was dead, we [James and Harry] made an examination of the house, going all over it.

In my father's bedroom we found his cashbox on the bed with the lid open. It had been forced open, and all the money extracted, with the exception of 20 shillings. I had no knowledge of the amount he kept, but I had knowledge that there was gold there. He [George] was in the habit of keeping his money there. The 20 shillings was roughly done up in a piece of newspaper and put in a very small compartment in the side; and it looked like a small reel of cotton; and has not the appearance of a pound of silver; and that decidedly accounts for it not being taken.

The cashbox was taken from a wardrobe. The key was in the lock of the wardrobe, but the door was wide open. A person would have to open the door to see the cashbox. My father always kept his cashbox there. I should think most likely father left the key in the lock. He might turn it and leave it in when locked. Nothing else in the bedroom was disturbed.

We [James and Harry] came from his [George's] room into the passage of the stairs at the landing, and I saw some books lying on the floor; and they had been removed from an iron or tin box, but nothing was taken. The box had been turned over, and the books thrown out, but nothing was taken.

Then we [James and Harry] went into my room and found one drawer open. It was the top right-hand drawer of the chest that I used. It only contained collars and ties, and nothing was taken from it. I had left this draw closed. My cashbox stood on the top of those drawers; and one watch was lying on the looking glass, which was also on the top of the drawers; and two rings on a ring stand there. Nothing was missing in my room. There was no appearance of anything being disturbed.

We [James and Harry] came downstairs and Harry said, "I will run for the policeman." And Mr.

Choate and I closed the door again and came out; and I went in and sat with him until the police came.

I have no idea what money my father had. I lost some, some little time ago, from the front room downstairs. I am positive that the man got into the house on that occasion through the back kitchen window. The persons were never traced. That took place when we were in bed.

I am sure all the windows were securely closed and had not been pried open on the night of my father's death. They had not been opened either from outside or inside.

The shop door was fastened, and the only way to get into the house was by the back door, which is open from the outside by a latchkey.

I waited in Mr. Choate's house until the police came. This had been done between seven and 10 o'clock. I am sure father had been dead some time, he was so cold. I noticed no signs of a struggle in the kitchen. There was one chair knocked over at the foot of the staircase. My opinion is that this might've been knocked over by a person coming downstairs.

My father was fairly active for a man of 67.

In response to a question posed] by the foreman [Mr. Charles Henry Pritchard]:

I should not think there was a note or check [in George's cashbox,] as my father did not like paper money. He generally gave me the checks. It was not a properly made cashbox, made of iron; it was a work box, but it was what he used to keep his money in.

[In response to a question posed] by Mr. Muggleton:

I saw my father's face looked peculiar, and was injured; but I did not like to touch it. I suggested that we should send for our housekeeper, but Mr. Choate said: "No, I had better lock the door until the police come," which was done.

The Dog Was Not at Home.

In response to a question posed by a juryman, James Chuter stated:

My dog went with me to the practice. Almost the last words my father said to me were: "Your dog knows it is [band] practice night, for he is whining to be let loose," The dog always slept in the house behind the kitchen door. Before the former robbery, he was tied up, where you gentlemen saw him to-day, at the back. After that, we always had him indoors.

The Coroner then said:

If this had been the case on Thursday night, the murder might not have happened.

The killers must have observed from the street that James had taken his dog with him to the band rehearsal when he left the cottage at twenty minutes to seven p.m. The Coroner was, of course, correct in his assessment. A dog in the kitchen, sleeping behind the entrance door, would have upset the killers' plans to murder George. A dog would have barked furiously when the killers had entered the kitchen. A barking dog would have alerted George before he opened his kitchen door. Any dog would have defended its master under attack. The killers would have had to kill a barking dog, lest it rouse the neighbors to fetch the police. Like Conan Doyles' "dog that didn't bark," in *Silver Blaze*, James' dog did not bark. In fact, the dog was not present at the crime scene when George was murdered and mutilated. Lucky dog!

The Darkness in George's Kitchen was Virtually Total.

The initial thing that struck me when I read James' direct testimony for the first time was just how dark it was in George's kitchen that evening. The murder and mutilation were committed in virtually total darkness. James' could not see the wounds and blood on his father's body—even when he fell down upon it. The execution in darkness of the murder and mutilation by two killers working in concert was flawless. That could have happened only with meticulous planning and frequent rehearsals spread over time. Both killers knew their exact roles, like actors in a play. Such precision—in the dark!—can only be achieved through frequent rehearsals.

James' Valuables.

Among the significant pieces of new evidence added by James' direct testimony was his information about valuable items in his bedroom. James' stated that, following his discovery of his father's body, he searched the upstairs bedrooms. In his bedroom, he found that the top right-hand drawer of his chest was now open. He was sure he had left this drawer closed when he departed for his band rehearsal. Thus, the killers must have entered his bedroom and searched it. According to James, the open drawer contained only collars and ties—and nothing had been taken from the drawer. So, the killers had found nothing of value—that is, of value to <u>them</u>—to steal from that chest of drawers.

However, James also noted that his cashbox sat on the top of that chest of drawers. There was no mention in James' testimony whether this cashbox had been locked and was found forced open, like George's lockbox. According to an earlier report by Deputy-Chief Constable Barker, that cashbox had indeed contained some money; and that money was not stolen. Inspector Barker stated: "a watch and chain, with some money, belonging to the deceased's son, was found lying on the dressing table in his bedroom, untouched."

Moreover, James testified at the inquest: "Nothing was missing from my room." Thus, in addition to the 20 shillings that the killers had left untouched inside George's lockbox, here is another example of visible cash left behind, untouched by the killers.

James' watch, chain, two rings and cash were all clearly accessible to the killers when they searched James' bedroom. James stated that "one watch was lying on the looking glass," which was set on top of the chest of drawers. Also, two rings on a ring stand were set upon his chest of drawers. Evidently, these two rings were not stolen by the killers, either.

The watch, chain and the two rings were of unknown value; but they undoubtedly had some monetary value. One can also say that the watch and the two rings were small items, and thus they were easily transportable. Placed in plain view on top of James' chest of drawers, these items could readily have been stolen by the two killers, had the killers wanted to take them. Here is physical evidence that clearly indicates that George's killers were not primarily burglars focused on stealing cash and jewelry—at least nothing owned by James. The killers must have seen these valuable items, but they did not want to steal them for reasons of their own.

The Theft.

One cannot deny that a limited burglary of some sort did indeed occur during the course of the evening of January 12, 1888. But the central question for us to confront is whether that burglary was merely incidental to the murder and mutilation of George Chuter; or whether burglary was in fact the principal motive for the break-in on January 12, 1888.

Some questions related to the theft from George's lockbox still remain unanswered.

i. Besides an unknown sum of George's cash, what exactly were the gold items that the killers allegedly stole from George's lockbox—and how much were they worth?

ii. Why did the killers leave untouched some items of value in George's and James' bedrooms—and how much were they worth?

iii. Did the killers say to themselves after the attack "Now George won't be needing these gold items in his lockbox anymore—we might as well steal them to cover our operating expenses?"

iv. Or did the killers say to themselves "these gold items in the lockbox had special sentimental or personal significance to our chosen victim—so let's steal them, not for their monetary value (which we don't need;) but rather to use them symbolically for our own secret purposes?"

I am perplexed that James never gave any detailed description of the gold items that he claimed were stolen. If these gold items had been worth a fortune, then how come James had no idea what they were? If these gold items were George's personal items, like jewelry, the police would have circulated descriptions to local pawnshops and jewelers, to be on the lookout for anyone attempting to exchange similar items for cash. If they were gold coins, the police would have transmitted detailed information to coin dealers and collectors; but that did not happen. If the items were pure gold ingots, the police would have transmitted the items' weights to banks and precious metals exchanges in Surrey and in London. There was no mention of any such notifications to pawn shops, jewelers, coin dealers or banks—either at the inquest or in the press. Indeed, no trace of the allegedly stolen gold items was ever found.

It looks to me that the allegedly stolen items must have been small to fit into an old toolbox. Stored in a bedroom wardrobe, and apparently not even hidden there, it also seems to me the allegedly stolen items were not likely to be worth a fortune. But that is merely my impression.

Let's recall now that the two killers had apparently planned long in advance to use George's own household possessions—the poker and the carving knife—to murder and mutilate him. That was no spur of the moment decision. Why did they do that? Use of the victim's own possessions to murder and mutilate George may have had hidden symbolic significance for them in a ritual murder. Similarly, the stolen gold items may have had some special intimate personal significance for the victim—such as a wedding ring. And that intimate connection with the victim may have made these gold items especially valuable to the killers, as sacred symbols to be used as religious artifacts in an occult ritualistic murder.

More a bit later about possible ritualistic purposes for the allegedly stolen gold items stored in George's lockbox.

Twenty Shillings.

James testified that some unknown sum of money and some unspecified gold items belonging to George had been taken from a lockbox in George's bedroom by the killers. However, news reports of the inquest noted that one item in the lockbox was not stolen. These accounts stated that "a box, in which deceased had kept his money, was found open on his bed, and the contents, with the exception of a packet containing 20 shillings, the appearance of which might have deceived the murderer, had been abstracted." I think we can summarily discount the unsupported speculation, apparently originating from James, that a burglar would have been fooled by the appearance of 20 shillings in silver in a lockbox, wrapped in a piece of newspaper.

In 1888, twenty shillings was not a negligible sum. According to measuringworth.com's online historical Currency Converter, twenty shillings (or one pound) in

1888 is now worth (*i.e.*, in March 2023) around **£118.50** (the real wage or the real wealth value of that income today.) In American currency in 2023, £118.50 equates to **$141US.** Whatever the exact value of 20 shillings (or 1 pound) was to George Chuter in 1888, the sum was not a small amount of spare change likely to be left behind by a burglar.

Besides, 20 shillings in coins were not very heavy or bulky. Twenty shillings could easily have been transported in one pocket, or divided into one pocket in each of two killers' jackets. So, the 20 shillings left behind in George's lockbox are powerful physical evidence that the burglary of valuables was not the principal motive for the crime.

Why would burglars leave behind James' watch, chain and two rings? Why would burglars leave untouched James' cash sitting on top of his dresser? In addition to these items, the killers also left behind twenty shillings wrapped in a piece of newspaper in George's lockbox in his bedroom. And they left behind a watch and chain that George wore around his neck, under his greatcoat, when he was murdered and mutilated. The killers lifted up George's beard when they slashed his throat, nearly decapitating him. They could have unbuttoned George's overcoat to steal his watch and chain. But they did not. Thus, the crime scene evidence does not support the police's shaky theory of a robbery-gone-sour. Evidently, the burglary was incidental to the murder and mutilation—which were paramount. The killers were intent upon taking only certain specific items—but not all of the valuable items that were easily available to them inside George's residence.

A Timetable.

James' band rehearsal concluded around 9:30 p.m. Then, he and his friend Henry Wattingham walked to the Queen's Head, where they remained until 10 p.m. The Queen's Head was—and still is—located at 2 High Road in West Byfleet, about a 15-minutes' walk from George's cottage.

Here, below, in **Figure 5-1**, is the 19th C. photo of the Queen's Head that I displayed earlier in Chapter 1. It shows the original Queen's Head Inn—before its many renovations and expansions. The pub room is the small room in the front where James Chuter, Henry Wattingham and an unidentified friend went for drinks after their band rehearsal. The Queen's Head was the location where George once worked as an innkeeper. It was the location where the Coroner's Inquest into the mysterious death of George's wife, Lucy, had taken place around a year earlier. And it was the location where the Coroner's Inquest on George's body was held on Jan. 16, 1888. As we will learn in a later chapter, this undated 19th Century photo may have been taken around the time of the Byfleet Murder.

Figure 5-1; An undated 19th Century photo of the Queen's Head Inn in Byfleet. It was here the Coroner's Inquest upon the body of George Chuter was held on Jan. 16, 1888.

(Same photo as Figure 15 in Chapter 1)
Photographer unknown; public domain in US

At 10 p.m., James walked home, from the Queen's Head to the front gate at the head of the alley at 65 Chertsey Road. He was still in the company of Henry Wattingham and another man. The three men remained at the front gate for five minutes to talk. During those five minutes, James saw his neighbor Simon Choate return home from his trip to Pyrford. James said "Good night" to Simon. James then walked down the alley, on the left side of his grocery shop, to the back of the cottage, to enter his residence through the kitchen door. It was at that moment, roughly between 10:10 and 10:20 p.m., that James discovered his father's body on the kitchen floor, just a few feet inside the threshold of the kitchen door.

A Key Witness Who Was Not Present at the Coroner's Inquest.

One of the most significant witnesses about the true nature of this crime was not present at the inquest. Nor was she present inside George's residence at the time of the murder. Yet, she was indeed present inside 'Juniper Cottages' when the murder occurred. That was Mrs. Choate, the wife of George's neighbor, Simon Choate, a bootmaker.

The Choates resided in the other family tenement that was part of Juniper Cottages. Simon Choate was not at home when George was attacked in his kitchen. But Mrs. Choate was in her home (as were her children), spending the evening in the Choate's portion of the double tenement, separated from George's residence only by an internal wall. Simon Choate returned home about the same time that James had returned to his front gate after his return from the Queen's Head —*i.e.* around 10:00-10:05 p.m. Earlier that evening—during the time of the murder—Simon had been in nearby Pyrford. During Simon's absence from his own house, his wife was reportedly sitting in their "middle" room.

No Screams of Terror or Cries for Help Were Heard All Evening by Mrs. Choate.

Simon Choate testified at the inquest that his wife and children had told him they had heard nothing unusual from George's apartment that evening. Simon explained to the Coroner that, because the cottage was a double tenement, they—*i.e.*, his family—could hear very well through the common wall in their "middle room." They could hear the Chuters' clock strike every hour, he added. On the night in question, his wife was in the "middle room," and George's murder had taken place in the "back kitchen"—which was not directly adjacent to their common wall. Mrs. Choate heard nothing that evening from the Chuters' portion of Juniper Cottages, she told Simon later. Though hearsay evidence, Simon testified at the Inquest what his wife had told him.

The Choates' descriptions of that evening might explain why Mrs. Choate had not heard any faint noises from George's kitchen—such as the thud of George falling to his knees and then onto the floor. But it would hardly explain why no one heard any screams of terror, cries of pain, or the yelling "murder!" and "help!"—if, in fact, such loud screams, cries and yelling had also emanated from George's portion of the double tenement during that evening. Evidently, that evening, there were no screams of terror, cries of pain, or yelling of "murder!" and "help!" to be heard by anyone. Had George actually screamed in terror when he was attacked by surprise in his kitchen, then surely Mrs. Choate would have heard something. But she didn't.

The Rest is Silence.

The *absence* of any loud screams or shouts by George, overheard that evening, is also significant evidence. It is clear from Mrs. Choate's testimony to her husband that George Chuter never had a free moment to scream or cry out for help. The instant he stepped through the entrance door into his dark kitchen, he was bashed in back of his skull with the poker. George never uttered a sound. In the darkness, he never knew who or what had hit him. He never cried "Help!"

No Sounds Were Made by the Killers.

Evidently, the killers never shouted commands or instructions to each other, either. The absence of any shouts from the killers indicates:

i. that the killers encountered no resistance from George;
ii. that both killers already knew every detail of their pre-conceived murder plan. They had no need to communicate instructions to each other during the violent attack.

There was no ruckus heard from overturned furniture crashing against the walls, or objects falling onto the floor from kitchen shelves in a violent struggle. As the police had made clear, there was no evidence of a violent struggle, either in the kitchen or anywhere else in the house. James made the same observation in his testimony. Evidently, George's murder and mutilation occurred not only in total darkness but also in total silence.

Here is yet another indication of detailed preparations by the killers prior to the murder. Each killer knew his exact role in advance. Nothing had been left to chance. The plan had evidently been thoroughly rehearsed to perfection.

Was the Evening of Jan. 12, 1888, the First Time the Killers Had Entered George's Kitchen?

The police earlier determined that the poker had been taken from an adjoining room, and the carving knife had been taken from a drawer in the kitchen table. There is some conflicting evidence on the normal location of the poker. James said it belonged to a corner in the kitchen. Nevertheless, what is significant for us: both murder weapons belonged to the Chuter household. The police also stated to the press that there was no evidence of a struggle anywhere in the house. So, how did the killers know there was a poker in an adjoining room (or in a corner of the kitchen) and a carving knife in the kitchen table drawer? There was no evidence of a frantic search in the kitchen or adjoining rooms—such as disheveled contents of the kitchen table drawer, or items strewn elsewhere on the floor, broken dishes, etc.. Remember, the kitchen was dark.

Moreover, it appears from the police's description of the bedroom that the killers knew exactly where in George's wardrobe to find the lockbox. They took out the lockbox, forced it open, and threw it on George's bed—all without disrupting the bedroom or the rest of the house. The killers' intimate knowledge of the inside of George's house opens up a new possibility. Was the murder and mutilation of George Chuter on the evening of January 12, 1888, the first time the killers had entered George's residence? As I pointed out in Chapter 4, Coroner Romieu was highly disturbed by this very question. Is it possible the killers were the same intruders who had broken into George's residence a year earlier and stolen 20 pounds that James had carelessly left on a downstairs tabletop in the "front room." The killers may have planned a murder on that occasion, too—but perhaps they may have been forced to abort that plan in midstream by some unforeseen occurrence—that is, after they had taken 20 pounds from the tabletop. Maybe that was the reason these killers did not murder and mutilate George in 1887.

More Questions Arise.

The killers' brilliant expertise in committing murder and mutilation, and their meticulous advance planning, make me wonder: was the murder and mutilation of George Chuter their first murder? And was it to be their last? Another critical question arises. If the killers departed shortly before James returned home, they would have had at least two hours alone in the kitchen with George's dead body, and possibly even more free time than that. It took only a few minutes for the killers to murder and mutilate George. What else might they have done in the kitchen during all that free time, together with George's bloody corpse, unobserved by anyone?

The Killers Departed the Scene of the Crime, Unobserved by Any Witness.

Lastly, the killers made a successful escape. No one saw them leave George's cottage. They left no trail of blood on the ground for the police to follow. They left no bloody footprints in the kitchen or elsewhere in the cottage. They left no broken door lock and no smashed window. They left no visible clues at all. When did they make their escape? Where did they go when they departed the Chuters' residence? I will explore those issues in detail in a later chapter.

At the Inquest, there was no discussion at all about the killers' means of escape. The police produced no eyewitnesses who had seen suspicious persons leaving Juniper Cottages around the estimated time-range of the murder. The police never picked up any suspicious characters hiding in the area of George's residence that night—despite a massive search in the neighborhood, as reported in the local press. The absence of any eyewitness to the killers' departure is made even more remarkable by the fact—reported in the *Surrey Advertiser*—that the area around the King's Head was somewhat crowded with villagers that evening. Nor did the police find a trail of blood on the ground leading from George's kitchen door up the brick alley that leads to Chertsey Road. The Surrey Constabulary did not employ any bloodhounds. Apparently, there were no scents to track or hounds to track them. The killers had made a clean get-away. They left behind no trace whatsoever for the police to follow. Where did the killers go? Were they local residents, or did they come to Byfleet from elsewhere? They left no hint of that, either. No one knew the answers to these important questions—least of all the Surrey Constabulary.

"Foul deeds will rise, though
all the Earth o'erwelms them to men's eyes."

William Shakespeare; *Hamlet* (Act I, Scene ii)

Chapter 6. More Direct Testimony at the Coroner's Inquest

George's Glass of Beer and his Time of Death.

According to inquest witness Charlotte Slaymaker, mistress of the King's Head, George came into the public house about quarter past 7 p.m. He drank one glass of beer at the bar and remained in the pub for only five or six minutes.

If George left the pub about 7:21 p.m., and it took him only a minute or two to walk home, that means he opened his kitchen door somewhere around 7:22-to-7:23 p.m. Let's say 7:25. According to the police and Dr. Sealy, George was murdered and mutilated in a matter of seconds-to-minutes after he entered his kitchen door. There were no signs of a struggle other than the huge pool of blood on the floor at the spot where his body was later found. Estimating the time of death from this sequence of events, it appears to me that George was murdered and mutilated sometime around 7:23-to-7:28 p.m., estimating conservatively.

Darkness in Surrey in January

In England, in mid-January, there is little or almost no daylight around 7:23 p.m. when George returned home from the King's Head. According to an almanac, sunset occurs in London in mid-January around 4:15 p.m. Moreover, January 12, 1888 was the night of a New Moon—so there was virtually no available moonlight in

England that evening. There was no street lamp anywhere near George's cottage. Thus, the scene of the crime was shrouded in darkness when George returned home to his cottage, walked down the brick alley from Chertsey Road, and entered his residence through the kitchen door. When evaluating the complexity of this murder—and the expertise necessary for two-or-more killers to pull it off successfully—one should always keep in mind that every element of the crime was executed in almost complete darkness.

Two Constables Conduct a Search of the Premises.

During the Coroner's Inquest, two constables testified about their search of the premises. These constables were PC Thomas Mears and PC Dearlove. PC Mears deposed that his examination of the scene revealed "no indications of a struggle." He also testified:

> **"Deceased was fully dressed, with the exception of a hat; his overcoat was fully buttoned."**

When George's hat was pointed out to him, PC Mears picked it up and said:

> **"There was a mark, as if made by the poker, on the deceased's soft felt hat."**

Here are two bits of physical evidence whose true significance to the perpetration of the murder was not fully comprehended at the inquest. The first blow that struck George on the back of his head actually landed on his soft felt hat, not directly on his skull. George had no time to unbutton his greatcoat when he walked through his kitchen door upon returning home from the King's Head. Nor did he have sufficient time to remove his hat—thus proving that George was attacked immediately upon his entry through the doorway. Once again: there goes the Robbery-Gone-Sour Theory!

Moreover, the first blow to the back of George's head was somewhat cushioned by "the deceased soft felt hat"—just as the wound on George's neck made with the carving knife had been somewhat cushioned by George's cravat. The first blow of the poker-wielding killer must indeed have been mighty in order to inflict such terrible damage, through the felt hat, to George's skull—which, as Dr. Sealy testified, was severely fractured beneath his scalp. PC Mears also stated that he searched the deceased's person, and that he had:

> **"found gloves, etc., in his [George's] pocket; and his watch with the chain around the neck."**

So, George's gloves were found by PC Mears in a pocket of George's overcoat. Evidently, George had removed his gloves while standing outside the kitchen door and placed them in a pocket of his overcoat. Then, George employed a bare hand to grab his latchkey in a pocket of his overcoat, to open the lock on his kitchen door. As James testified earlier: "the only way to get into the house was by the back door" [*i.e.*, the doorway that led into the kitchen]—"which is open from the outside by a latchkey."

There were two additional items of potential monetary value--George's watch and its chain--that were not stolen by the killers. They were not taken from the scene of the crime by the killers when they departed. So, the total list of valuable items that were not stolen amounts to: George's watch and chain; James' watch and chain; James' two rings; George's 20 silver shillings; James' cash (the amount unknown.)

PC Dearlove added that he had examined the kitchen door. He found it was fastened by only a simple catch lock that was easily opened with a piece of bent wire. He did not find a bent wire anywhere with which the killers may have opened the lock near the door. The significance of PC Dearlove's revelation about the facility with which the lock could be opened with only a bent wire has already been commented upon. Evidently, upon their departure, the killers kept the bent wire—or whatever implement they might actually have used—to jimmy open the catch lock on the kitchen door.

The Jury's Verdict.

On the advice of Coroner Roumieu, the inquest jury immediately returned a directed verdict of "willful murder against some person or persons unknown." Thus, the murder was left unsolved at the inquest; and it has remained unsolved to this day. However, the verbiage of the verdict of the Coroner's Inquest was not meaningless boilerplate. Let's examine in detail what the legal jargon really meant.

No evidence or testimony presented at the inquest excluded the possibility that two-or-more killers had murdered George Chuter. The jury's verdict did not state that the crime had been committed by a lone burglar. There were no eyewitnesses to the crime, so no one could state positively that he (or she) ever saw one—and only one—person commit the murder. Then, by law, the verdict of the Coroner's jury had to include the possibility of two-or-more unknown persons working in concert had murdered George Chuter.

The police failed to consider seriously the considerable crime scene evidence that indicated the participation of two-or-more killers working in concert. Above all, they never offered at the inquest an official opinion on the use of two different bloody weapons; or the killers' deliberate placement of both weapons, side by side, on the kitchen table next to George's mutilated body. Both Superintendent Bungard and Deputy-Chief Constable Barker reportedly attended the inquest—but inexplicably neither official offered any testimony. Apparently, Coroner Roumieu understood the implications of this evidence somewhat better than the police. But, in my opinion, he did not fully comprehend the significance of some crime scene evidence that, I believe, conclusively establishes that the murder and mutilation were undoubtedly committed by two-or-more killers working in concert—not one.

I have shown that—under the circumstances revealed by the known evidence—one burglar, acting alone, could not have credibly murdered and mutilated George with two dissimilar weapons found in two different locations. The Coroner directed the jury to deliver a verdict "against some person or persons unknown." Yet, in his summation, the Coroner employed a plural noun ("perpetrators") to describe the person or persons unknown who had murdered George. He seems to have been of two minds. Coroner Roumieu said:

> **"I should think that the perpetrators of such a crime as this would be brought to justice."**

The Coroner also used the plural noun "persons" to describe the perpetrators.

> **"It was a very unfortunate thing for Mr. Chuter that the persons had not finished before he came in."**

Thus, no one today should be under the misapprehension that the inquest concluded that George was murdered by one person acting alone—much less, by a robber acting alone. The Coroner left open the possibility of two-or-more killers acting in concert. The official verdict did not mention a robber or burglar.

With respect to the motive for the murder, the Coroner could not free himself from past assumptions about traditional motives for run-of-the-mill murders. Because this crime had no apparent motive commensurate with mutilation, he speculated on a run-of-the-mill murder such as then was all too common. Despite all the evidence to the contrary that I have compiled thus far, Coroner Roumieu fell back on a traditional motive of a possible "robbery-gone sour." But significantly, he called this motive a "presumption." In other words, there was no proven evidence to back it up. It was merely his speculation. Coroner Roumieu ruled:

> **"The presumption was that the perpetrator of the deed had gone to the house to ransack it, and heard the deceased coming, when the dreadful act was committed."**

After further conjecture as to the probable nature of the crime, the Coroner said:

> **"There was no doubt that plunder was the motive, and it was a very unfortunate thing for Mr. Chuter that the persons had not finished before he came in. The case was in an unsatisfactory position at the present moment, because they [the police]**

> **had no one charged with the murder; but I sincerely hope that the Brute would be brought to justice, for a more wicked act one could not imagine. They [the police] have heard of many cases about the country now, and I'm sorry to say they were getting more frequent. Now if men robbed the house, they seem to stand at nothing, but drew revolvers and fired at everything that came out. As to how the perpetrator of the deed got hold of the knife, there was no evidence to show. The knife was usually kept in a draw in the room, and there was no evidence that Chuter had the knife out; and so they [the jury] must presume that the man [the assassin] got it out, and this, added to the fact that he [the assassin] went up and got the cash box, leads one to suspect that the individual knew something about the house, but they [the police] had no suspicion at the present time to rest on anyone. I should think that the perpetrators of such a crime as this would be brought to justice. Beyond a doubt, this poor unfortunate individual [George Chuter] was murdered in his house; and it would be the duty of the jury to return a verdict of wilful murder against some person or persons unknown."**

And then, for a moment—but only for one brief moment at the Inquest—Coroner Roumieu had a flash of insight when he suddenly imagined another possible motive for

George's murder and mutilation, a motive so shocking that no one else dared to propose it at the inquest, lest he be ridiculed and scorned. The Coroner stated:

> **"There was no doubt whatever that this poor man had been diabolically murdered, and as far as his experience went, I do not think that I ever came across a more horrid case than this."**

"*Diabolically* murdered"? Were George's killers *diabolically* inspired?

"Hell is empty and the devils are here."

William Shakespeare; *The Tempest* (Act I, Scene ii)

Chapter 7. Revisiting the Scene of the Crime.

Before considering the critical issue of the Getaway, let's take stock of what we have learned thus far.

The Kitchen Door was Located in the Back of a Long Brick Alley.

At the Coroner's Inquest, James Chuter testified that he had let himself into the kitchen through the "back door" with his latch key when he returned home from his band rehearsal. Thus, the latch on the door must have been locked after the killers had departed from the scene. If James had found the kitchen door unlocked or ajar when he returned home, he would have suspected something was amiss at home, even before he had entered the kitchen. Thus, it seems to me highly likely that the single catch lock had closed by itself, automatically, when the killers had, very considerately and carefully—shut the kitchen door behind them and departed.

The police testified that the back door was fastened with a single catch lock that could easily have been opened by anyone picking it with a piece of bent wire. James testified that the windows and the door in his grocery shop had been securely fastened shut when he left for his band rehearsal. "The only way to get into the house was by the back door," he added. The "back door" was the kitchen door. This last statement by James is quite revealing. It resolves several unexplained elements in the narrative, thus far. If the grocery store in the front of the building was securely locked, the intruders could not have passed from the grocery into the Chuter residence in the back of the building via any communicating hallways. The grocery store and the Chuters' residence were widely separated within Juniper Cottages by the Choates' portion of the double tenement. Two windows lay in between the grocery store and the Chuters' residence. They were not broken. If there was a communicating hallway, it was not open—or broken into.

George's half of the double tenement did not have a front door. The fancy, big white front door that we saw earlier in the photograph of 65 Chertsey Road (in Chapter 3, **Figure 8**) was the front door that led into the Choates' half of the residence. It is set at a 45-degree angle in the corner where the grocery shop met the white front wall of the cottage. George and James resided in the rear of the double tenement structure. James' tiny grocery store was located at the front of Juniper Cottages, far in front of the Choates' front door. The grocery faced Chertsey Road and had very small windows on its front wall. None of those windows had been smashed or forced open.

In the photo of 65 Chertsey Road, shown below in **Figure 7-1**, we can see some of the 2-floor beige brick cube in "the back" of Juniper Cottages. That was the portion of

Juniper Cottages in which George and James resided in 1888.

Figure 7-1: 65 Chertsey Road, a.k.a. "Juniper Cottages." The red brick alley on the left side of George Chuter's residence in Juniper Cottages, at 65 Chertsey Road, Byfleet. In 1888, the beige brick room in front of the double tenement served as James' grocery store. The store's entrance faced south, through the small white. door in the alley. The living quarters of George and James was the brown, two-story unit in the rear of the double tenement. It is only partly visible in this photo. The grocery store in the front and the Chuters' residence in the rear were separated by the white, stucco, two-floor part of Juniper Cottages. This central white apartment was occupied by the Choate family. The entrance to the Choates' tenement (not visible in

this photo) was located on the north side of Juniper Cottages, on a 45-degree angle to the grocery store.

Photo © 2017 Google Maps Street View; photo taken in 2016; fair use

The Chuters lived in the small cubic section of the double tenement, far behind the large white structure that housed the Choate family. The Chuters' portion of the cottage was accessible from Chertsey Road by way of a wide dark brick alley on the left side of the cottages. On the left side of the alley was a brick wall, painted white, now topped by a thick hedge.

Unfortunately, the kitchen door—also known by James as the "back door"—is not visible in this photo from Google Maps Street View. The small, white, side door that is visible in this photo was the entrance into James' grocery store located at the front of Juniper Cottages. Also, as is visible in the photo, this small door had a tiny window. Evidently, that tiny window was dark when the little girl messenger reported to Charlotte Slaymaker that evening "the shop was dark."

In the photo, we can see the sidewalk of Chertsey Road in front of the grocery store. Evidently, that is the spot in front of the red brick alley from which this photo on Google Maps Street View was recently taken. One can see a black, iron gate there. That is the gate at which James Chuter chatted with his friends for a while before walking down the alley, opening the kitchen door with his latch key, and stumbling over the dead, mutilated body of his father on the kitchen floor—all around 10:05-10:15 p.m. on January 12, 1888.

The Killers' Expertise.

As noted in previous chapters, there is powerful evidence in the inquest testimony that the Byfleet Murder was well-planned in advance. But just as important as the advance planning was the killers' expertise in executing the plan. In every detail of the murder and mutilation, their execution was fast and flawless—despite the almost-total darkness in the kitchen at that time. Such expertise could have been accomplished only by gathering essential information by stalking the victim over time; with careful planning begun well before the commission of the crime; and with repeated training. Undoubtedly, the killers had discussed and rehearsed their plan multiple times. The plan to murder and mutilate George Chuter ran smoothly like clockwork. There was nary a hitch. The killers' expertise at murder and mutilation makes me wonder whether the Byfleet Murder was these killers' first crime of this kind.

Interestingly, Coroner Roumieu broached this very subject: *i.e.,* numerous instances of unsolved, violent robberies-gone-sour popping up recently in England. In his summation, he stated:

> **"They [the police] have heard of many cases about the country now, and I'm sorry to say they were getting more frequent. Now if men robbed the house, they**

seem to stand at nothing, but drew revolvers and fired at everything that came out."

At a later time—actually, in Volume 2 of the series *A Trail of Blood*—I will explore some remarkably similar murders and mutilations committed in various locations in England, and elsewhere, prior to the Byfleet Murder. But unlike the examples cited by Coroner Roumieu, all of the bloody and mysterious crimes that I will explore were committed with knives and bludgeons, not revolvers. They all have no apparent motive. And all of them remain unsolved to the present day.

No Conclusive Evidence Pointing to a Lone Robber.

When the inquest concluded, it should have been apparent to the Coroner, I believe, that this murder was no spur-of-the-moment, panicked reaction of a spooked robber. There was no evidence that George had inadvertently discovered a burglar in the act of "descending the stairs with his plunder." There was no blood on the stairs. There was no trail of blood from the stairs to the spot on the kitchen floor where George's mutilated body was later discovered by James. It is sometimes hard for police to break old habits and ingrained preconceptions about murders. It is far easier to blame, without any conclusive evidence, the usual suspects—*i.e.*, robbers—in cases of unsolved murders.

All the evidence that was revealed at the inquest confirms the conclusion that the assailants had lain-in-wait behind the entrance door in the dark kitchen, ready to pounce on George the moment he crossed the threshold. When George entered the kitchen from outside, one killer was already armed with the poker—which he had taken either from a room adjoining the kitchen, or from a corner of the kitchen. When George entered the threshold, a second killer was also laying-in-wait, already armed with the carving knife—which he had been taken earlier from the kitchen table drawer. Certainly, these two killers did not begin to search for these two murder weapons in the dark after George had already entered the kitchen. There had been no time for that. Both the murder and the mutilations were completed in a matter of moments after George stepped into the kitchen doorway.

When George crossed the threshold, he never had time to unbutton his overcoat—much less take it off. Immediately, two killers attacked him the instant he stepped inside. George never had time to remove his soft, felt hat. The poker-wielding killer bashed the back of George's head with the poker, leaving a mark on the hat. The poker-wielding killer knocked George's hat off his head with the first blow. The hat fell on the floor near the body—where PC Thomas Mears later found it. The pool of blood on the floor showed that George's body was not moved to another location after his head was bashed with the poker. The knife-wielding killer slashed George's throat in the same location where the body was found.

The Getaway.

I find it extraordinary that one important aspect of the Byfleet Murder was never mentioned at the inquest by any witness, including by any police officers—that is, the getaway. Nor was this critical subject ever broached by Coroner Roumieu, or even by members of the jury in the form of questions posed to witnesses. Remarkably, Superintendent Bungard never testified at the inquest (although he was reportedly present.) Bungard never described any details of his investigation—I think because he never came up with a means of escape that could be confirmed with hard, physical evidence or eyewitness testimony. All he could have presented were empty speculations and self-congratulations about how hard his officers had searched the neighborhood for a lone burglar.

Thus, there was no discussion about the elephant in the room: *How did the killers make their escape after committing the murder and mutilation—without being seen by anyone, including policemen searching the streets of Byfleet?* And how did the killers make their escape without leaving any physical evidence behind that might have been traceable? These are critical issues, and yet no one brought them up at the inquest. Nor were these questions discussed in articles in the press.

Apparently, discussion of this vital subject was discouraged, or completely ignored, as a result of the police's Lone Burglar Theory. If George had indeed been murdered by a lone burglar in a robbery-gone-sour, then Q.E.D., the burglar must have been a local resident. He had to have been a resident of West Byfleet, or Byfleet, or Addlestone—and he simply walked home after murdering and mutilating George. Of course, now we know there was never any evidence indicating that a local resident (or two-or-more local residents) had murdered and mutilated George Chuter. No local burglar was ever suspected or charged with the crime. None of the allegedly stolen gold items or George's cash was ever found. The possibility that the killer (or killers) might have been strangers was never mentioned by anyone at the inquest. It is as if that idea was too terrible to even contemplate.

Local Residents or Peripatetic Outsiders?

Let's suppose for a moment: what if the killers of George Chuter were not residents of Byfleet—nor of West Byfleet, nor Addlestone—nor of anyplace else in Surrey? What other possibilities exist? What if the killers were outsiders who visited Byfleet only momentarily, specifically to commit the murder and mutilation of someone—anyone—with whom they had no personal connection? What if they had selected George Chuter as their chosen victim precisely because they did not know him, and he did not know them? The lack of any personal connection between the victim and the killers would make them virtually untraceable by the police. Was that the main criterion used by the killers in selecting their murder victim? The ostensible lack of any personal connection between the killers and their victim gave the assassins perfect anonymity.

Apparently, the Surrey Constabulary never considered the possibility that the killers were peripatetic outsiders who had momentarily visited Byfleet only to murder and mutilate a man with whom they had no person connection, or that the killers were sociopaths motivated by an occult ideology of ritualistic sacrifice. Why would the police even think that? From the moment the police were alerted a murder had occurred, they had fixed their sights on a Lone Burglar. In January 1888, thoughts of a Peripatetic Wolf Pack were inconceivable—literally impossible to conceive.

But—as we in the 21st Century know only too well—today, such thoughts are no longer inconceivable. The current roll call of known sociopathic, sacrificial serial killers is horrifically long and varied. It includes some instances of teams of serial killers of varying numbers. The only noticible difference between the murder and mutilation of George Chuter and some of the most famous modern serial murder/mutilations that followed the Byfleet Murder, is the apparent lack of any obvious sexual motivation for the murder in George's kitchen. But is sex the only motivation for serial murders? Are some ritualistic murders motivated by non-sexual compulsion—such as occult beliefs?

A Clean Escape.

Following the murder of George Chuter, the perpetrators vanished into thin air. The police had no idea whether the killer was a local man from Byfleet, or someone from outside the local area. And, of course, the Surrey police still had no idea whether George had been murdered by a lone-wolf, a burglar or by more-than-one killer working in concert. Nevertheless, from the outset, the police had their sights set solely on a lone burglar lurking about on the streets of Byfleet that evening. They were not especially looking for two-or-more men making their escape from Byfleet to a destination yet unknown.

There was no report in the press that any witness ever saw a burglar—or any suspicious strangers—lurking about in Byfleet on the evening of Jan. 12, 1888. The Surrey Constabulary—which, according to the early report in the *Surrey Advertiser*—was out in force late that night searching for a suspect. The police never came up with anyone whom they could charge or even detain. The killers had left no trail of blood near George's kitchen door for policemen to follow. Evidently, the killers had taken pains to avoid stepping in the large pool of blood on the kitchen floor, or they had carefully wiped their shoes clean. No footprints were ever found on the ground around the cottage.

The police never employed bloodhounds in an attempt to trace the killers' tracks. Apparently, the Surrey Constabulary did not have bloodhounds on call—since historically, murderers on the run or escaped convicts were very few and far between in the County of Surrey. There were no reports that I could find indicating that the police had investigated the nearby Byfleet train station and its environs.

The Killers Must Have Departed the Crime Scene Before 10:00 P.M. (at the very latest.)

At the inquest, James testified that, following the conclusion of his band rehearsal at 9:30 p.m., he and his friend Henry Wattingham walked to the Queen's Head and stayed there until 10. p.m. Then, they walked to the gate at the head of the alley at 65 Chertsey Road—where they stopped to talk for about five minutes. According to Google Maps, the Queen's Head, located at 2 High Road, is about .4 miles from 65 Chertsey Road, George's and James' street address. Walking at a leisurely pace (since they were not in a hurry,) it may have taken James and his friend Henry about 8-10 minutes to walk from the Queen's Head to the gate at the head of the alley at 65 Chertsey Road.

James testified:

> **"At the gate of my father's house, we stayed about five minutes talking. Mr. Choate and his son passed by while we stood there, and we said**

> **"Good Night" to them. I then said "Good night" to Wattingham, and went in at the back door."**

At that spot—*i.e.,* the front gate of the brick alley—James had a clear, unobstructed view of the entrance door to his kitchen from around 10:05 P. M. on. He never saw anyone open the door from the inside of his kitchen and then exit. He never saw anyone in the alley during the five minutes when he stood at the gate chatting with Henry and Simon Choate. He never saw anyone rush out of the kitchen when he opened the kitchen door with his latch key. Thus, the killers must have departed some time before James' arrival at the gate around 10:10 P.M. (at the very latest.)

Residents or Strangers?

Were the killers longtime residents of Byfleet? Perhaps, but there was no documented evidence of that. Thankfully, the police's search never resulted in the arrest of the wrong local man, walking about on the streets of Byfleet that night. Had they arrested a hapless, local burglar, violence might have broken out in the village, given the anger that was slowly brewing among the residents—as we will soon see. Apparently, no consideration was given by the police to the possibility that the perpetrators might be peripatetic killers. I could find no mention in press reports that the Surrey Constabulary ever contacted other police departments to inquire about similar homicidal robberies-gone-sour elsewhere in England. According to Coroner Roumieu, there had been quite a few recently. If the killers were not residents of Byfleet or nearby towns like Weybridge and Addlestone, then how did they make their getaway to a destination unknown, possibly far away, without being observed?

There were no reports of a horse-and-buggy that evening on Chertsey Road, much less a horse and rider galloping through the streets of Byfleet. If the killers had come from out-of-town, then logically they would have wanted to depart from Byfleet as quickly as possible. But by what means? Was there any form of transportation nearby that could be used to make a quick getaway from Byfleet? How could the killers have vanished—so quickly and totally—without drawing the attention of any eyewitnesses or the police?

A New Train Station Opens in Byfleet.

Co-incidentally, less than two months before George Chuter's murder and mutilation, West Byfleet was introduced to commuter railroad travel. On December 1, 1887, the London and Southwestern Railway celebrated the grand opening of a new train station on Madeira Road, at Camphill Road, now called the West Byfleet Rail Station. This new train station was, and still is, located less than 2 miles from George's cottage at 65 Chertsey Road. In other words, this new train station, on the line to Waterloo Station in London, was located about a 45 minutes' leisurely walk from George's home. On a cold winter's night, it is likely very few pedestrians were walking the residential streets in West Byfleet between Chertsey Road and Madeira Road. No one reported seeing any suspicious strangers walking about around 10 p.m. to the new train station. I could find no mention in the press that any police officers had visited the station to check the train departures.

The Southwestern line was predominantly a commuter line, with frequent trains arriving and departing in the early morning to take residents of Byfleet and environs to work in London; and in the evening hours, to bring workers back, not only to Byfleet, but also to surrounding towns in the vicinity. Today, this train station is generally called the West Byfleet Station.

More precisely, the station was, and still is, located 1.5 miles from George's cottage. Google Maps estimates that it takes 30 minutes to walk from George's kitchen to the entrance of the train station. It is not yet known, with any documented evidence, how and when the killers departed from Byfleet (if, indeed, they did depart the village following the murder.) But the presence of the new train station so close to George's residence certainly provided them with a possible means of quick escape. By walking to the new train station, they could easily have disappeared almost immediately after perpetrating the crime—especially if they had timed their departure from George's kitchen to precede the scheduled departure of a train around 30 minutes later.

Thus, the killers could have left Byfleet undetected by the police, or unnoticed by residents going about their business in the dark, late evening hours, even before the crime was discovered by James. A commuter ticket on the Southwestern Railway was relatively inexpensive. The killers could easily have purchased tickets far in advance of the commission of the crime to prevent the stationmaster from remembering their faces. The exact schedule of trains stopping at the West Byfleet station every evening was posted. Indeed, the killers may have carefully planned their exit from George's residence to give them adequate time to walk to the station, and then quickly board a train that had just stopped.

The well-publicized opening of the train station in West Byfleet on December 1, 1887 may have made the murder and mutilation of George Chuter possible. Without the inauguration of this safe, dependable, inexpensive, nearby means of escape, the killers might not have selected Byfleet for the location of their crime. There were numerous other villages in Surrey, but most then had no train service.

Here, below, in Figure 7-1, is a photograph of the Byfleet Train Station, as it appeared on an early 20th Century picture postcard, published by the W. H. A. company. The publisher was, in fact, the W. H. Applebee company, located in Ashford, Middlesex. This postcard company was in business between 1912 and 1928.

However, there is no indication exactly when the photo was taken. Postcard companies often purchased photos, and the rights to publish them, from outside submissions. This photo could have been taken years before the company began doing business. Are those multiple telegraph lines on the tall pole on the left-hand edge of the photo?—as shown below, in Figure 7-1. Telegraph service began in England around 1840. Or are those telephone lines? Telephone service began in England in 1878.

Figure 7-1; Photo of the Byfleet Train Station, published on a picture postcard sometime between 1912 and 1928, by the W. H. Applebee Co. in Middlesex.

Photographer unknown; Photo: Public Domain in the U.S.

George Chuter, A Randomly Selected Victim.

From all indications, George appears to me to have been a victim randomly selected for murder and mutilation. There was never any suggestion at the inquest that he had been murdered by someone whom he knew, or who knew him. There was never a hint that his son James was somehow involved. No one proposed a motive of revenge for some past action or for an inappropriate relationship with someone in his circle of acquaintances. No known enemies of George Chuter were ever brought to light.

George was an easy random victim to kill. There was little risk for the killers of ever being caught. And there was a readily available means of escape located nearby: the train to London. To make an unobtrusive getaway, all the killers had to do was take a late evening (or early morning) train out of town. They may have purchased their tickets to-and-from Byfleet days earlier to avoid being noticed by the station master or ticket seller.

It would seem that George Chuter was selected as a victim simply because he was a vulnerable old man, alone in his house, all by himself all that evening, living in an unilluminated, sparsely populated neighborhood with few if any witnesses on the streets. Perhaps the principal reason George was chosen to be murdered: his residence was located near a train station.

The Allegedly Stolen Gold Items and their Potential Significance to the Murder.

Let's examine once again George's lockbox from which James claimed that some gold items were stolen. We don't know exactly what was taken—other than James' vague, unsubstantiated claim that the loot included some cash and some gold items. James did not know how much money had been taken from George's lockbox. At the inquest he stated:

> **"I have no idea what money my father had."**

Nor did James know what gold items were missing, or their value. He testified:

> **"In my father's bedroom we found his cashbox on the bed with the lid open. It had been forced open, and all the money extracted, with the exception of 20 shillings. I had no knowledge of the amount he kept, but I had knowledge that there was gold there."**

A central question of this mystery for us to determine is whether this alleged robbery/burglary was the intended purpose of the intrusion into the Chuters' residence that night. In other words: was the murder/mutilation of George merely an unfortunate incident, an unforeseen result of George's unexpected early return home from the King's Head during a run-of-the-mill residential burglary? Or was the murder/mutilation of George Chuter the sole intended purpose of the intrusion into George's residence that night? To give us an idea of the true significance of the allegedly stolen gold items, it might be helpful to determine when the alleged robbery occurred. Did the burglary occur *after* the murder and mutilation—almost as an afterthought? Dr. Sealy testified that the upstairs were evidently ransacked after the murder and mutilation were perpetrated.

In previous chapters, I have shown in minute detail that the murder and mutilation were carefully planned and prepared, far in advance of the evening of January 12, 1888. Any thoughts that robbery alone was the intended purpose of the break-in are rebutted by evidence of multiple instances of cash and valuable items left in plain sight, which were *not stolen* by the killers. After the murder and mutilation, the killers were not rushed for time; so, they were not forced to depart hurriedly and leave behind all that cash, and all those valuable items (including rings and two watches with chains.)

Why did the killers allegedly steal some gold items from George's lockbox, but they left untouched not only George's 20 shillings in the lockbox, but also James' cash, his two rings, and his watch and chain. Moreover, the killers left behind George's watch and chain on his body, under his overcoat. Some of the items left behind may also have contained gold—such as the two watches and chains, and James' rings.

What Could the Allegedly Stolen Gold Items have Been?

That the killer's would have left behind so many valuable items while taking only a few others that may have contained gold is explicable by either of two hypotheses. The first: the killers were interested only in liquid items like cash. They did not want riskier items like watches, chains and rings—that they would later have to pawn. But then, how can one explain the untouched sum of cash sitting on top of James' chest of drawers, or the 20 shillings that remained in the lockbox?

The second hypothesis is more complicated, but much more interesting to me. Evidently, the killers stole George's cash for monetary reasons alone. Perhaps they figured George could no longer use the cash, and they had operating expenses to cover. But how about those gold items that were allegedly taken from the lockbox? Can we be sure that they too were stolen only for their monetary value? James could not identify exactly what they were, or how much they were worth. It is easy for us to conclude that these items must also have been stolen for their monetary value, that they were subsequently melted down, and that the pure gold was later sold to some dealer, possibly on the black market. But that may not have been the case.

We still have no idea what these gold items were. They were never recovered. So, I must speculate about them on the basis of some other facts known about George. With only 48 pounds to his name at the time of his death, it seems to me highly unlikely that George owned gold ingots, or even gold coins. He was not a wealthy man. Moreover, he lived with his son quite modestly. He had no known source of income at the time of his murder—except possibly rent on the Choate's portion of the double tenement.

George's wife, Lucy, died about a year earlier. It seems likely to me that, after 43 years of marriage, she owned a wedding ring, and it might well have been made of gold. She probably also had other jewelry of modest value—such as rings, lockets, chains and bracelets. Some of them might even have been made of gold—without being worth a fortune. For sentimental reasons, George may have kept Lucy's jewelry in his lockbox following her sudden and unexpected death a year earlier. He may have held on to her gold items as precious souvenirs of their decades of marriage together. The monetary value of her jewelry was of no concern to him. He had no pressing need to pawn them. Lucy's items would have served no practical use for George. But for sentimental reasons, he could not bear to part with them. And so, he may have stored them for a year in his lockbox.

Thus, I am suggesting that George's sentimental attachment to these intimate gold items—such as jewelry that had once belonged to his late wife—may have been the very reason why these items were stolen by the killers. The killers may have used these intimate, sentimental items of gold jewelry as amulets or talismans in an occult, sacrificial ritual.

Why would I think that? Well, for one reason, noted criminologist Jack Levin—in his book *Serial Killers and Sadistic Murderers*—points out that "many serial killers are so thrilled with their murders that they keep mementos or souvenirs from their victims." Levin then documents his observation by citing numerous notorious 20th Century serial killers and the personal items belonging to their victims that these killers stole from the crime scenes. One modern killer, in particular, caught my eye: Joel Rifkin, who "collected the jewelry and underwear of his victims."

A Recent Widower.

As noted in the *Surrey Advertiser* on January 14, 1888, George was a recent widower. According to census data, George's wife Lucy had died in February 1887. Her mysterious death prompted a Coroner's Inquest. Although ostensibly in good health, Lucy's death was ruled probably a heart attack. It is now quite unfortunate for us that James could not account precisely for the gold items that he reported as stolen from George's lockbox. As noted: when Lucy died, George may have held on to her wedding ring—possibly a gold band. Moreover, he may have saved some jewelry that he had given her over their forty-three years of marriage.

In addition to Lucy's jewelry, the stolen items may have included some miscellaneous gold pieces that George wore to church services on Sundays--such as his dress cufflinks or a gold cravat pin. These are just the sort of gold items that a man of modest means might hold on to in a closet cash box—instead of storing them in a bank vault. Remember: James pointed out that this lockbox was actually an old toolbox.

In sum, the gold items mentioned to the police by James may not have been very valuable. There was no mention of any gold ingots in the lockbox. They may have been small items of jewelry whose value in gold was mostly sentimental. If such personal items had indeed been stolen from the lockbox, then this theft might now be seen in a much different light. Its relevance would stem not from the monetary value of the gold, but rather from the items' intimate relation to George's personal life, and the sentimental value of the items to him.

However, the allegedly stolen gold items may have had another, far more sinister significance to the murder and mutilation of George Chuter. Personal items belonging to a murder victim, especially items that were made of gold, could have held symbolic meanings in a ritualistic sacrifice that was part of an occult ceremony.

Murder Trophies.

The theft of personal, intimate items that belong to a victim of a ritualistic murder—such as a wife's gold wedding band—might indicate that these items were stolen as murder trophies. The gold items allegedly taken from George's lockbox may well have been taken by the killers as trophies to commemorate—symbolically—the success of their murder plot. As we will explore in Volume 2 of *A Trail of Blood,* various criminologists have noted: in ritualistic murders that objects intimately connected to the victim can be used later in sacrificial rituals as amulets and fetishes. A ritualistic killer might regard intimate items, especially gold items, as sacred objects with magical powers that could increase the religious intensity of a subsequent human sacrifice.

Trophies, Mementos (or Souvenirs), Talismans, Amulets, Fetishes and Totems

Studies of numerous serial murders in the 20th and 21st centuries have revealed that some serial killers regard such trophies taken from murder victims as talismans or amulets—that is, supernatural charms that ensure good luck in future ritualistic endeavors. Some ritualistic killers believe that murder trophies offer them supernatural protection from capture or death in some future exploits.

Trophies can also enable a killer to relive a murder in his mind at a later date. These trophies are sometimes called mementos. A serial killer can enjoy intense psychopathic pleasure from his reminiscences. Criminologist and author John Douglas wrote relatively recently an article entitled

"Why Killers Take Trophies." By killers, he was mostly referring to ritualistic serial killers. Douglas wrote:

> **Killers like to take trophies and souvenirs from their victims. Keeping some memento — a lock of hair, jewelry, newspaper clips of the crime — helps prolong, even nourish, their fantasy of the crime. In my research, I've seen this happen again and again. Here's what to look for in an investigation: Is there anything missing that belongs to the victim? Often police will mistakenly look for valuable missing items. But I'm not talking about a stereo component—that's an impersonal item. I'm talking about something more personal — a ring, earrings, even costume jewelry — something the victim was wearing at the time of the crime.**

How about a deceased wife's gold wedding band? Might a ritualistic killer consider such a ring to be a personal trophy of a murder? Or a pair of gold cufflinks that a victim may have worn at his wedding or his father's funeral years earlier? Or a gold watch that the victim may have received years ago at his religious confirmation? If items like these had been stolen from a murder victim—especially any items that contained gold—the police might mistakenly conclude that a ritualistic murder was merely a robbery-gone-sour.

The Terminology of Murder Trophies.

In his article "Why Killers Take Trophies," FBI criminologist John Douglas uses several terms of evidence rather loosely. There are some subtle distinctions in the dictionary definitions of the meaning of *trophies, mementos or souvenirs, talismans, amulets, fetishes, personal items* and *totems.* All these terms will be used in the course of my investigations, spread over the span of several volumes of *A Trail of Blood.* It is possible—depending on the circumstances in a particular murder—that a particular object at a crime scene might qualify for more than one of these definitions.

- **i.** A *trophy* is an object that marks a specific achievement—usually a victory. Typically, a large, engraved cup of some monetary value that commemorates a triumph in a sporting contest, the word *trophy* can also be used metaphorically or symbolically to indicate any object that marks a victorious achievement—even a successful murder.
- **ii.** A *memento* is an object kept as a reminder or *souvenir* of a person or a past event. A copy of the newspaper article about the Coroner's Inquest might serve as a *memento* of the Byfleet Murder for residents of Byfleet, years after the event had passed. A *memento* or *souvenir* is not

generally believed to possess supernatural powers. However, for a ritualistic killer, a *memento* might serve as a trigger—unleashing a flood of memories of a past crime and providing intense psychological gratification by re-living those significant memories.

iii. A *talisman* is an object or symbol that is thought to be endowed with occult magical powers. The bearer believes a *talisman* brings good luck. A powerful *talisman,* such a ring with the insignia of an occult group, might be believed by members of this group to offer magical good luck. Millenia before the Nazi era, the swastika was used as a talisman of good fortune in primitive societies when incised on stone implements and prehistoric structures.

iv. An *amulet* is typically a small piece of jewelry believed to be endowed with magical powers that offer the wearer protection against evil, danger or disease. *Amulets* are somewhat different from talismans in that talismans are believed to bring good luck, whereas *amulets* are believed to offer protection from evil. An amulet among Catholics is the Saint Benedict Medal which includes the *Vade Retro Satana* formula to ward off Satan.

v. A *fetish* is an inanimate object that is worshiped for its supposed inherent magical powers.

Typically, a *fetish* is a man-made object that supposedly possesses supernatural or magical powers over other persons. A *fetish* can also be sexual in nature—*i.e.* an object that is believed by someone to possess powers of sexual stimulation. In psychology, the word *fetish* is used to represent a form of sexual desire in which gratification is linked to the possession or worship of a particular object. In religions, there are non-sexual *fetishes*, as well. In the Byfleet Murder, sexual stimulation does not appear to have played any role.

vi. A *totem* is a sacred object that symbolizes a group of people—such as a family or a clan. A *totem* is typically depicted as a carved pole, with faces of men or animals. As a sacred object, a *totem* may be believed to have supernatural powers granted by dead ancestors.

So, yes—a deceased wife's gold wedding ring, or the gold cufflinks that a victim may have worn to his wedding years earlier, could possibly have been stolen from George's lockbox as a trophy to mark a successful murder. Trophies can easily be mistaken for loot to be pawned or fenced for whatever monetary value these items might bring on the black market. To a ritualistic killer who has just successfully murdered his chosen victim and escaped without leaving a trace, the victim's intimate personal gold items can represent a victorious achievement and a source of supernatural power.

The twenty shillings contained in the lockbox were not personal items intimately connected to George's life. They were merely cold cash—impersonal items with no ostensible connection to George's innate being. Consequently, the killers had no interest in these coins as trophies, and they left these coins behind. Despite their monetary value, the shillings were not stolen because they did not possess any magical value to the killers. Also, James' money and valuable items had no direct spiritual connection to George—and so James' money and valuables were left untouched, even though they were lying in plain view on top of his dresser.

Was Anything Else Missing from the Crime Scene in Byfleet?

What else may have been taken by the killers upon their departure from George's house? The only missing item noted by the police was the gold and cash allegedly taken from the George's lockbox. However, was anything else removed from the cottage that the police never noticed? Possibly, yes!

In my opinion, the evidence documented thus far suggests that George Chuter was murdered for his blood. We know from Dr. Dealy that George bled profusely when his throat was slashed, and his skull was bashed. What happened to all that blood? Did all of it end up on the kitchen floor? Or might some of George's blood have been drained from his body by the killers and then removed from the scene in a flask or other container, for some as yet unknown use. The killers might even have stored some of George's blood in an old ginger beer bottle.

Following the commission of the murder and mutilation, the killers had no need to depart the residence immediately. They must have felt secure inside George's cottage with their advanced knowledge that James would not return home from band practice until 9:45 or so, at the earliest. The scheduled time that the rehearsal concluded was apparently 9:30 p.m. Add to that another quarter-hour to half-hour to walk home leisurely. As events actually transpired, James did not enter the kitchen until about 10:05-10:20 p.m. The killers would have felt even safer in the residence for several hours if the team had included a third member—who could serve as a lookout, stationed somewhere outside the cottage. Such a precaution would have been eminently reasonable—especially if an earlier attempt to murder and mutilate George in 1887 had to be aborted because of the unforeseen arrival of a potential witness.

With a torrent of blood flowing from George's slashed throat onto the kitchen floor; and with complete privacy inside the kitchen, the killers would have had ample time, opportunity and means to extract a considerable volume of George's blood and place it into a container. Did the killers bring with them a bottle or jar in which they could gather a substantial volume of George's blood? Did they take some of George's blood with them when they departed the scene? Where can we look for such evidence?

No More Clues?

Coroner Roumieu noted in his summation that "the police had no clue to guide them." That is not exactly true. There remained at least one Big Clue placed by the killers right in front of everyone's eyes. But the significance of this clue apparently never dawned on either Superintendent Bungard or Deputy-Chief Barker. Moreover, as I will eventually make evident, this clue was—undoubtedly—deliberately left in plain view by the killers as a gesture of their utter contempt for the intelligence and forensic abilities of the Surrey Constabulary.

This Big Clue was the deliberate placement of the two blood-covered murder weapons—the poker and carving knife owned by the victim—side-by-side, on top of the kitchen table, next to George's body. There, the weapons lay in plain sight, where they must have been seen by the police. That staged image was undoubtedly a message from the killers to the police. It had been the killers' obvious, deliberate intention to leave at the crime scene some clearly visible evidence that George's murder and mutilation were committed by two killers working in concert. Even the positioning of the bloody murder weapons had symbolic significance. The weapons were left together. What sort of burglar deliberately leaves symbolic evidence for the police? By placing the two weapons on the kitchen table, side by side, the killers told police: "Solve this, if you can." Had the Surrey Constabulary gotten this message, they might have dropped their illusory Lone Burglar Theory. The police investigation might have taken a far different turn.

What is not yet evident to me: for whom else was this symbolic message intended to be seen? In other words, for whose eyes--*besides those of the Surrey Constabulary*—might that staged evidence have been displayed?

There is no doubt in my mind: the killers planted this evidence to be seen, first of all, by the police. The killers were supremely confident that policemen—whom they viewed as hopelessly dumb--would never figure out the true significance of their staged evidence. But perhaps the killers had also planted the two murder weapons on top of the kitchen table so that they might also be seen by someone else. And who might that someone else have been? Perhaps, it was someone from whom they wanted some form of credit for their daring accomplishment: *i.e.*, the perfect murder. Perhaps it was someone who—they believed—had observed everything that they did. Perhaps, it was someone whom they worshipped?

The Motives for Murder and Mutilation.

The Byfleet Murder had, and still has, no apparent motive. That is: a credible motive for murder and *mutilation*, documented by authentic physical evidence, emanating from the crime scene. But, as in all murders—except those in which the killers are totally divorced from reality—this murder, undoubtedly, did have a motive. The crime was intricately planned in advance; and it was brilliantly executed. The over-riding question about the Byfleet Murder for us remains: *why did these killers murder and mutilate George?*

I have spent much of the previous chapters debunking the 'run-of-the-mill' motive proposed by the Surrey Constabulary: that the murder of George Chuter was the result of a robbery-gone-sour. I consider that motive unsupported by most of the known evidence—and powerfully contradicted by virtually all of the documented evidence. The police's proposed motive was merely conjecture based on their past experiences—which may or may not have been the same as what happened to George Chuter. The Robbery-Gone-Sour Theory was merely a hunch—groundless speculation derived from an inconsequential bit of incidental evidence. In my opinion, the Surrey Constabulary's fixation on their unsupported theory the main factor why the Byfleet Murder was never solved. This theory, shot full of holes by the police's own evidence, misled the police investigation from the onset.

What Are Credible Motives for Mutilation?

One must always keep in mind that George was mutilated, in addition to being murdered. The motives for deliberate mutilation are not necessarily the same as motives for murder. Murders in which the victim was deliberately mutilated form a category all their own. And mutilations have motives all their own.

Beginning in the 20th Century, criminologists, psychiatrists and psychologists have grouped motives for mutilation into various types, based on forensic examinations and interviews with captured serial killers. For example, *Dorland's Medical Dictionary, "The first and last word in medicine,"* lists four types of homicidal mutilations:

i. **Defensive mutilation** *(i.e.,* dismemberment to get rid of the body)
ii. **Aggressive mutilation** *(i.e.,* mutilation of the face or genitals in a state of outrage)
iii. **Offensive mutilation** *(i.e.,* fulfillment of a killer's sadistic need to inflict pain while indulging in sexual acts.)
iv. **Necromantic mutilation** *(i.e.,* mutilation with the purpose of obtaining a body part as a trophy or a fetish.)

Decapitation is the Symbolic Release of All Blood.

What can we say about the mutilation of George Chuter that was distinctive? Evidently, the killer who wielded the carving knife had attempted to decapitate George. The knife-wielding killer had attempted to cut off George's head—possibly in one symbolic stroke. Whether one slash or two, the knife-wielding killer did not fully succeed in severing George's head from his body—but not for lack of trying. The knife-wielder severed George's neck down to the spinal vertebrae. By itself, that was no mean accomplishment. He came very close to his symbolic goal, but ultimately, he failed—apparently as a result of unforeseen interference by the cravat that surrounded George's neck. However, this killer's intent determines his motive. His intent was clearly decapitation. And evidently, the knife-wielder intended to decapitate George symbolically in one stroke. His failure to cut off George's head in one stroke may have represented for him his only goal that he did not attain.

None of George's body parts were found missing by Dr. Sealy. However, a person's blood supply is also a body part. When George's neck was slashed by the carving knife, severing all the major blood vessels to and from his brain, a huge quantity of blood was released. Typically, an adult male contains around 5½ quarts of blood. Some of that blood was found in a huge pool of blood under and around George's body lying on the kitchen floor. Neither the doctor nor the police could assert that the blood on the kitchen floor accounted for all of George's blood. The doctor could not ascertain whether any of George's blood had been gathered by the killers and taken with them in a receptacle upon their departure from the scene.

Consequently, it is possible that the mutilation of George Chuter matches *Dorland Dictionary's* Type 4—necromantic mutilation with the purpose of obtaining a body part as a trophy or a fetish. Necromancy is defined here as relating to magic or communicating with a spirit or the dead. Blood has long been known in many religions as the key fetish that enables communication with a spirit or the dead. In religious rites, blood is often believed to be sacred. As established by numerous criminological studies of serial murders—blood is the ultimate goal of sacrificial murder.

Psychotic mutilation.

Dr. Scott A. Bonn, a professor of criminology at Drew University in Madison, New Jersey, wrote an article on ritualistic killers, published in *Psychology Today.* He describes another type of homicidal mutilation, which he calls 'psychotic mutilation.' He states these mutilations are sometimes associated with religious motives. The offender may drink body parts—by which Dr. Bonn is evidently referring to human blood: He wrote:

> **The offender may also eat, drink, or collect the body parts. Psychotic mutilation is often associated with bizarre, irrational, or religious motives on the part of the offender, who may have no connection or history with the victim.**

A New Kind of Killer Begins to Emerge in England around 1888.

Evidence is beginning to emerge in my investigation that George was the victim of a new type of killer that emerged to public view in England around 1888: a homicidal sociopath who kills for his own psychopathic pleasure. He feels no empathy for his victims, and no remorse for the mayhem and the misery he wreaks. Moreover, as we know now, in the 21st Century, under the rubric of homicidal sociopaths, there is a subculture of ritualistic killers who sacrifice their victims to their own fantasy religion of occult ideologies.

In the 21st Century, law enforcement officials and criminologists now know a great deal about this lethal phenomenon, based on physical evidence extracted from crime scenes and psychological interviews with serial killers who were captured alive and subsequently interviewed. In January of 1888, however, if the idea of such seemingly pointless murders ever arose at all in the minds of officials of the Surrey Constabulary, it was surely dismissed as nonsense.

No one in 2024 can expect the Surrey Constabulary to have known what was then not generally known. Nevertheless, the investigation by Superintendent Bungard and Deputy-Chief Constable Barker was fixated on a flawed theory, woefully cursory, utterly inadequate, and even incompetent. Aside from Dr. Sealy's testimony, there was no thorough, comprehensive forensic examination of the crime scene—even within the limited scientific forensics available in 1888. And there was no crime scene photography.

Crime Scene Photography.

Photography was by then readily available in England. In 1888, photography was already highly developed, in widespread use, and only moderately expensive. Inexcusably, no photographs of the crime scene in Byfleet were taken by the police, or by the press. Indeed, Surrey Constabulary historian Robert Bartlett wrote me that photography of crime scenes was not introduced in Surrey until the 1930s.

In 1888, crime scene photography and post-mortem photography were already sporadically employed practices in the police departments of London, Paris and New York. We know from the famous crime scene and mortuary photographs taken by the Metropolitan Police, and the City of London Police, of victims in the Whitechapel Murders, that photographs of crime scenes were already part of sporadic police procedures in some major cities in 1888. The Surrey Constabulary was way behind the times, and it remained so for many decades.

Clueless.

To be fair to the Surrey Constabulary, the police never had a clue that they could decipher. Surrey detectives had no idea what to make of many facts that they had gathered.

So, they ignored whatever facts did not fit neatly into their preconceived notions about run-of-the-mill murders. They fixated only on minor and possibly irrelevant evidence that vaguely supported their theory of a robbery-gone-sour. They focused solely on the fact that some unknown items of undetermined monetary value had allegedly been stolen from George's strongbox. The detectives failed to connect the dots of far more significant evidence that lay right before their eyes.

The police's failure to recognize the true significance of physical evidence at the scene of the crime, and its linkage to evidence in other contemporaneous crimes, are key issues that one must confront not only in this murder, but in many of the murders yet to be investigated in this series of volumes. We have already seen hints in the inquest summation by the Coroner that the Byfleet Murder resembled in some respects several other murders committed elsewhere in England not long before. A possible link was, apparently, never investigated by anyone in 1888—not by the Surrey Constabulary, and not later by the Met in London. Each police department was then an island unto itself. It seems like police officials in the 19th Century never imagined that a killer could board a train and perpetrate another murder elsewhere.

The Coroner's Summation.

The Coroner added that he "did not think there would be anything gained by an adjournment of the inquiry."

And so, the inquest was concluded—oblivious to what had actually happened that evening on January 12, 1888. Following the conclusion of the Coroner's Inquest on Jan. 16, 1888, more articles about the Byfleet Murder appeared in the county press. The journalists who wrote them were clearly unsatisfied by the inquest's inconclusive results.

On January 21, the *Surrey Advertiser* published this editorial report:

> **THE BYFLEET MURDER**
>
> **The horrible murder of a respectable and retired tradesman at Byfleet on Thursday night [last] week, reported in our last issue, has startled not only the village, but the whole country-side, while the escape so far of the murderer is another surprising element in the tragedy. The circumstances, so far as they can be gathered, are fully detailed in another column of the report of the inquest, but practically they add little to what we published last week. The poor man seems to have been first stunned by repeated blows from a poker, and then, while insensible, as Dr. Sealey states in his evidence, his throat was cut from ear to ear, in order either to make sure of the fell work, or to suggest suicide. Robbery seems to have been the motive of the crime. The case is one of exceptional horror, and although the police are making every exertion to track the murderer or murderers, we think the Home Office should**

> **offer a reward for information that will lead to his or their apprehension.**

Thus began the campaign for a reward for information about the perpetrator (or perpetrators.)

> **"There are more things in Heaven and Earth, Horatio, than are dreamt of in your philosophy."**
>
> William Shakespeare; *Hamlet* (Act I, Sc. v)

Chapter 8; The Classified Advertisement; No Reward; and the Letter from ANXIOUS.

A Strange Classified Advertisement Appears in the *London Standard.*

On January 20, 1888, a Friday, an advertisement mentioning the Byfleet Murder appeared on the classified advertisements page of the *London Standard.* I reproduce it, below, in **Figure 8-1.**

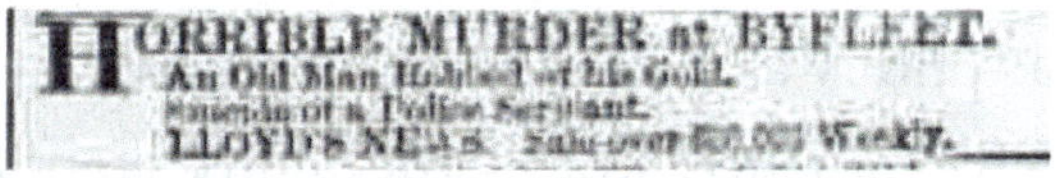

Figure 8-1. A classified advertisement placed in the London *Standard*, published on January 20, 1888 (one week after the Byfleet Murder.)

A surviving original copy of this ad—stored in the National Archives—is partly blurred. Some words are difficult to read. Here is my transcription, as best I could make out every word:

HORRIBLE MURDER at BYFLEET
An Old Man Robbed of his Gold.
Suicide of a Police Serjiant. *(sic)*
LLOYD'S NEWS. Sale over 120,001 Weekly

Several words (and numbers) in the original copy are almost illegible. "Sergeant" appears to be misspelled here as "Serjiant" (or possibly "Sergiant.") I had considerable difficulty in deciphering the word "suicide." Initially I thought it might be "suspicion." But after much enlargement and careful study, I decided the printed word was actually "suicide."

A Palpable Fraud.

It was immediately apparent to me, there was something very wrong with this ad—in addition to the embarrassing misspelling of the word "sergeant." *Lloyd's* management undoubtedly knew how to spell "sergeant." Indeed, the ad is clearly as phony as a $3 bill, as the old saying goes. Immediately, I smelled a rat. I am highly skeptical that this advertisement in the London *Standard* was ever placed by *Lloyd's Weekly Newspaper.* And here is why.

According to *Wikipedia,* the circulation of *Lloyd's Weekly Newspaper* was far above 120,001 around the year 1888. In fact, the newspaper's masthead in 1888 proclaimed in very large type: "Largest Circulation in the World."

Wikipedia's article on *Lloyd's* states:

> ***Lloyd's Weekly*'s circulation had risen to 170,000 by 1861, but it was soon to rise much more steeply. On 1 October 1861, the last duty on newspapers was abolished – the paper duty of a**

> **penny halfpenny per pound in weight. Lloyd lowered the price to a penny two weeks before the duty was lifted. Even with the much improved production, the first issue sold out at 350,000. Regular circulation had risen to 412,080 by 1865 and continued its upward path, passing the million mark in 1896 and reaching 1,500,000 during the 1914-18 war.**

Thus, *Lloyd's Weekly's* circulation in 1888 was somewhere in the range of 412,080 to 1,000,000. So, why would *Lloyd's Weekly Newspaper* greatly under-report its own paid circulation as 120,001 in a classified advertisement published in a rival London newspaper? Indeed, why would *Lloyd's Weekly Newspaper*—one of London's pre-eminent news journals—run a dinky classified advertisement in another newspaper, ostensibly to promote *Lloyd's* coverage of the Byfleet Murder in Surrey? A murder that had occurred eight days earlier in an obscure locale outside of London would hardly be of great interest to *Lloyd's* regular readers in London. This tiny amateurish ad purchased for a song in another London newspaper could hardly affect *Lloyd's* real circulation numbers. Moreover, what was that absurd number 1 doing at the end of 120,001, mentioned in the ad. Was that silly number '1' supposed to give this ad's paid circulation number some sort of verisimilitude?

Even stranger still is the attribution of this advertisement. LLOYD'S NEWS was not the official name of this publication. The name on the masthead was *Lloyd's Weekly Newspaper.* Why would a major news publication in London abbreviate its own name? Just to save a few pence in a classified ad by adding another line of type? Obviously, this ad was a crude forgery. It was never placed in the London *Standard* by *Lloyd's Weekly Newspaper.* So, questions arise: who created it? And who paid for its insertion into the London *Standard*? And why was it published? What possible purpose did it serve the person (or persons) who paid for its placement?

Horror!

The sensational first line, typeset in allcaps—"HORRIBLE MURDER at BYFLEET"—was apparently designed to attract readers' attention with the promise of gory, exciting details. Nothing attracts readers' attention more than the prospect of horror—except, of course, a **HORRIBLE MURDER!** If this ad had commenced **ROBBERY-GONE-SOUR**, then no one might have noticed it. *Lloyd's Weekly Newspaper* published its article on the Byfleet Murder on the previous Sunday, Jan. 15. So, the ad in the London *Standard,* published on Jan. 20, implored Londoners to find and read a five-day-old news report in a copy of last Sunday's *Lloyd's.* Evidently, someone on Jan. 20 was very keen on attracting the attention of residents of London to the Byfleet Murder in Surrey—and it was certainly not the management of *Lloyd's Weekly Newspaper.*

Although this tiny, classified ad in the London *Standard* could not have cost much money to insert, who—that is, who other than the management of *Lloyd's Weekly Newspaper*—might have had an incentive to spend his (or their) own money to purchase this deceptive ad? It had to be someone who felt that the murder and mutilation of George Chuter in Byfleet had not yet received the fervid attention of Londoners that it so deserved. The provincial press in Surrey had covered the murder thoroughly, and that was all well and good. But the London press, with the exception of *Lloyd's Weekly Newspaper*, had at this time generally buried news about the murder and mutilation of George Chuter in small articles deep inside the newspapers, or they had ignored the Byfleet Murder altogether.

With regard to news about murders, London was the big time. News about crime in rural Surrey—where murders were exceedingly rare—was like a school play in the suburbs compared to the Lyceum in London's West End. The publication of this classified ad made me think of an actor who had just received a brief mention in a small-town newspaper review for his walk-on role; and the following day he was contacting every important stage director, urging them to read his review.

If you were a sociopathic killer, intent on terrorizing the British public with an unsolved murder and mutilation of an old man in his locked kitchen, would you be satisfied with merely local press coverage in a rural county, located next to the nation's capital? If you had just committed the perfect murder and mutilation in Surrey, would you be satisfied if most of London had never heard about your triumph, even a week later?

More importantly, no one outside of Byfleet appeared panicked by news about the Byfleet Murder and Mutilation. If you and your cohorts had escaped from the crime scene without leaving an evidentiary clue that might be traced back to you, wouldn't you like to brag about that to a larger audience? If you were a narcissist who had left no trace to follow at the scene of the crime, wouldn't you enjoy some recognition in the London press? And wouldn't you crave an historical archive of some sort—such as the British Library or the National Archives—to preserve a permanent record of your victory?

And lastly, if you had just baffled and humiliated the Surrey Constabulary, wouldn't you desire to take on even bigger game—such as the Criminal Investigations Department at London's Scotland Yard? What better way to attract the scrutiny of the Met than by calling attention to the Byfleet Murder in the London *Standard*—a popular London newspaper. Surely, some policemen in London might see this ad—and that might indeed start the ball rolling. The Surrey Constabulary and Coroner Roumieu had consigned the Byfleet Murder to the category of unsolved run-of-the-mill crimes of plunder that had merely spun out of control. A psychopathic killer might reason: Scotland Yard—if somehow it could be enticed to intervene—would not similarly dismiss this crime. The Met's CID would give it the respect it merits. But Scotland Yard, too, would inevitably fail—the ad's authors undoubtedly believed.

What if the killers of George Chuter had secretly made other plans? What if they had conceived of perpetrating yet more crimes that, in January 1888, were still unimaginable to local law enforcement officers. What good were their fantasy plans be if Londoners were still largely unaware of their actual success in Byfleet, and all the gory details of their horrible accomplishment? What might these killers do to attract more attention? How about taking out a small, inexpensive, classified ad in the London *Standard?* That might stimulate Londoners to talk about the horrible murder and mutilation of an old man who was robbed of his gold in Surrey. That might prompt even more press coverage of the Byfleet Murder, especially in London.

Suicide of a Police Sergeant.

I should note that the classified ad in the London *Standard* also mentions the suicide of a police sergeant. Apparently, that line referred to the suicide of Sgt. Allin in Dartmouth, Devon on Jan. 15, 1888. This suicide was also in the news that week. According to the *Western Times* on Jan. 16, 1888, Sgt. Allin took his own life by poisoning after he was informed by officials that his rank would be demoted to that of constable, and he would be re-stationed at Ilfacombe, Devon. The following morning, Allin was found in his room by his landlady, writhing in pain. Dr. A. K. Crossfield was immediately sent for, but when he arrived there was nothing he could do to save Allin's life from the poison Allin had taken.

Thus, it is now clear to me: the line in the ad about the "Suicide of a Police Serjiant"*(sic)* published in the London *Standard* was merely a reference to an irrelevant news event. The mention of a current suicide was inserted into the ad merely to give the ad an appearance of authenticity. The creator(s) of this phony ad had hoped the line about the sergeant's suicide might convince readers the ad had indeed been placed by *Lloyd's Weekly Newspaper.* Here was a clumsy attempt to divert attention from the obvious fact: this ad was—undoubtedly—created and submitted to the London *Standard* for publication by the killers of George Chuter.

With the advantage of historical hindsight, I can say that there is no record that anyone in the Surrey Constabulary ever took note of this phony advertisement in the London *Standard.* Indeed, no one before now has ever realized the ad's true significance to the Byfleet Murder: it is the first known public communication by George's killers. It will not be the last.

No Government Reward.

On January 26, 1888, the London *Morning Post* published a letter related to the Byfleet Murder, from Godfrey Lushington, then Permanent Under-Secretary of State of the Home Office—who is shown below, in Figure 8-2.

Figure 8-2; Sir Godfrey Lushington, Permanent Under-Secretary of State in the Home Office.

Photographer unknown; Photo: Public Domain in U.S.

The letter was addressed to G. F. Roumieu, Coroner for West Surrey. Previously, Roumieu had written to the Home Office, requesting that a reward be offered for information about the Byfleet Murder. During Roumieu's summation at the inquest, he had stated: "At present, the police have no clue to guide them." With the investigation now at a standstill, and not one viable suspect to pursue, it must have seemed to the Coroner that the only hope for a breakthrough lay in offering a reward for additional information. Here, below, is the article that appeared in the London *Morning Post*:

GOVERNMENT REWARDS
FOR INFORMATION IN CRIMINAL CASES

The following letter has been received by the coroner for Surrey in regard to the proposed offer of a reward for further information respecting the Byfleet murder:

Whitehall, 23rd January 1888

"Sir, I am directed by the Secretary of State to return herewith the depositions forwarded with your letter of the 18th inst. in the matter of the murder of George Chuter; hand with reference to your recommendation, I am to say that the practice of offering rewards by Government for information in criminal cases has been discontinued for some time past; and that the Secretary of State, having carefully

> **considered the circumstances, does not feel justified in departing from the rule in the present case.**
>
> **I am your obedient servant.**
>
> **GODFREY LUSHINGTON**

Thus, the Coroner's hopes for a reward were dashed by the Home Office. Public opinion in Byfleet was at first disheartened, and then outraged.

On February 2, 1888, Rev. Granville Erskine Money, Rector of Byfleet, wrote about the murder in *Parish Magazine.* Beginning with a eulogy to George Chuter, he turned out an impassioned plea to the murderer. Quoting from scripture, he stated: "repent, confess, thou shalt be loosed from all. The blood of Jesus Christ cleanseth from ALL sin."

Here, below, are all the reverend's words about the crime:

> **The past month will long be remembered as a dark one in the annals of our peaceful village. George Chuter, born in the village on July 5th, 1820, was brutally murdered in it on January 12th, 1888. When we think of him, it is of one who was always known to be singularly inoffensive, gentle, kindly and playful.**
>
> **When we think of his murderer, we believe that he was betrayed first into one step, then into another, of this hellish deed, almost before he**

knew what he was doing. We pray mightily to God, from whom no secrets are hid, to save him from weeks or months of the heaviest and most agonizing load that any man can bear, by bringing him to confess his guilt to both God and man.

You, the murderer, if these words meet your eye, poor fellow sinner - I deliver this message to you from God.

"Repent, confess, thou shalt be loosed from all".

"The blood of Jesus Christ cleanseth from ALL sin."

A detective is after you, but another is after you, nearer to you than he - your Savior, who loved you when you lay innocent on your mother's breast, and loves you still. The Good Shepherd is out in front of the detective to seek and save this lost sheep. Give yourself up to Him, and then you need not, you *will not* fear to give yourself up to the law, and so rid yourself of this miserable load.

I beseech you, my fellow sinner, take this as a message from God, and "Lay hold on eternal life". We ourselves, when we think of ourselves, we are hard indeed if we do not take this as an awful warning not to make light of little sins, lest we go from bad to worse, and never leave home or return to our house unprepared to meet our God.

The reverend's imploring message apparently fell upon deaf ears, at least with regard to the murderers. No one ever gave himself up as a perpetrator; and no accomplice ever betrayed the killers.

Public Anger Grows.

As recorded in an undated *Coffee Shop Minute Book*, preserved by, and provided to me by Jim Allen, President of the Byfleet Heritage Society, leaders in Byfleet decided to pick up the issue of a reward where the Secretary of State had just dropped it.

> **BYFLEET MURDER**
>
> **A public meeting was held, in accordance to notice, in the National School room, to consider whether a reward should be offered for information leading to the discovery of the murderer. At this meeting, it was decided that a reward of not less than £100 should be offered, to be withdrawn after 12 months if the murderer should then be undiscovered.**
>
> **The following Committee were elected to receive subscriptions and to deal with the money as they thought best. Admiral the Hon. F. Egerton; J W Bashford, Esq.; G. Rice Holroyd, Esq.; G. B. Holroyd, Esq.; Rev. G. E. Money.**
>
> **It was resolved that notice was given that all subscriptions must be paid within one month**

from date. Mr. G. B. Holroyd appointed Treasurer, Mr. J. W. Bashford appointed Secretary.

Letter from Admiral Egerton, suggesting that as he is a Justice of the Peace, advisable not to sit on Committee.

Letter from Mr. Barnes read, as to form of reward. Sketch of reward Bill approved by Committee to be submitted by Mr. J. R. Holroyd to Supt. Bungard. Lists for reward to be printed and distributed.

The Home Secretary's decision not to offer a reward in the Byfleet Murder, as communicated to the Coroner by Godfrey Lushington, continued to rile the residents of Byfleet. The townsfolk gathered pledges for a reward totaling £100. On March 3, it was announced that the offer of a reward had been authorized in a public meeting.

On March 3, 1888, the *Pall Mall Gazette* in London reported:

Great dissatisfaction has been expressed in the neighbourhood of Byfleet at the refusal of the Government to offer a reward for the discovery of the Byfleet murderer. At a public meeting it was decided to offer a reward not exceeding £100, that amount having been promised in subscriptions.

Also on March 3, 1888, Rev. Money again commented in *Parish Magazine* on the current state of the murder investigation, stating:

> **The murderer is yet undiscovered. A reward for information leading to his discovery will shortly be placed in the hands of some responsible person. Meanwhile all who desire to contribute to this reward are requested to take or send their subscriptions *at once* to Mr. G. B. Holroyd.**
>
> **Let no one allow his suspicions to rest on anybody without sufficient grounds. It is most cruel. If the unhappy man who did this deed is in our midst, he is earnestly, yes lovingly, invited to come and unburden his crime and misery to either of his Clergy....**

Apparently, the reverend was worried that rumor and distrust might lead to mass violence against a resident of Byfleet. Anyone might come under suspicion. The threat of lynching was now being whispered about by residents of Byfleet. Although lynchings were, in the late 19th Century, a distinctly American racial phenomenon, they were not unknown in England. For example: here, below, is a drawing that appeared in the *Illustrated Police News* on July 11, 1896, entitled "An Englishman is Lynched to Save Expense"—as shown below, in **Figure 8-3.**

Figure 8-3; 'An Englishman is Lynched to Save Expense', detail from the *Illustrated Police News,* 11 July 1896

Artist unknown; Image: Public Domain in U.S.

The ire of Byfleet's residents continued to grow over the refusal of the national government to offer a reward. On March 17, 1888, the *London Evening Standard* published an article describing an acrimonious public meeting in which a letter from the Chief Constable of Surrey was read.

> **Great dissatisfaction has been expressed in the neighborhood of Byfleet at the refusal of the Government to offer a reward for the discovery of the Byfleet murderer. At a public meeting held in Byfleet on Thursday night to consider the advisability of the inhabitants offering a reward, a letter was read from the Chief Constable of Surrey, saying he considered a reward would be useless; and the employment of detectives of no**

> **avail. But the meeting unanimously resolved to offer a reward not exceeding 100*l*, that amount having been promised in subscriptions.**

Residents of Byfleet Organize Themselves to Raise a Reward.

On April 4, *Parish Magazine* reported on the same public meeting as the article in the *London Evening Standard* had described, above. *Parish Magazine* gave a more detailed description of the local subscription committee, evidently including many of Byfleet's most prominent citizens:

> **A PUBLIC MEETING attended by upwards of 150 men was held in the National School on Thursday 15th of March, at which it was resolved to offer a reward of £100 for information leading to the discovery of the perpetrator of the Byfleet murder. A Committee was elected, viz: Messrs. J. R. and G. B. Holroyd, J. W. Bashford, Admiral Egerton, and Rev. G. E. Money - with power to receive subscriptions and to deal with the money as they think best. Above £100 was announced in the room, as paid or promised, but much more is wanted to meet possible expenses. All subscriptions must be paid to one of the Committee before the 1st of April.**

On January 28, 1888, the *West Surrey Times* published a relatively short article, also entitled:

THE BYFLEET MURDER.

It is both surprising and disappointing to find that the Government are unwilling to take any special measures to promote the detection and capture of the miscreants guilty of the horrible murder at Byfleet. We publish elsewhere the letter received by Mr. Roumieu, the Coroner, from the Home Office, in reply to his suggestion that a reward should be offered for information which might lead to the offenders being brought to justice. And our readers will certainly share the surprise and regret expressed by Mr. Roumieu at the decision so announced. The offer of a substantial reward has in similar cases produced most satisfactory results. And it is difficult to imagine any case in which the newly-adopted doctrine of economy, which vetoes the expenditure of the public money for such a purpose could be less applicable than that under review. For without some special action such as this, there now seems but scant probability of the criminals being brought to book; and it will be at once a disgrace and a danger to the community should so flagrant a crime remain unpunished, and its perpetrators continue at large.

The editorial statement by the *West Surrey Times,* that "the offer of a substantial reward has in similar cases produced most satisfactory results" certainly raised my eyebrows. In all my research into the Byfleet Murder and into other possibly related 19th Century murders, I have yet to come across an instance where a reward was paid for information that led to the capture of the killers. It was with good reason the Home Office had decided not to issue rewards in murder cases. In the past, they had not proven themselves to be effective.

A few days later, on January 30, the *Surrey Advertiser* published a more detailed description of the local controversy over an offer of a reward. It began with a letter to the editor of the newspaper from the Coroner, Mr. G. F. Roumieu.

THE BYFLEET MURDER

TO THE EDITOR OF THE *SURREY ADVERTISER AND COUNTY TIMES:*

SIR—As the Byfleet murder has created a great deal of sensation in the neighborhood, the enclosed letter which I received from the Home Office, in reply to a communication of mine, will no doubt be of considerable interest to all parties concerned. I cannot help thinking in a case of such importance that a deviation from the rule might be made, and that a substantial reward should be offered in the

hope of gaining some clue to one of the most cold-blooded murders that has taken place in this county for some years. I understand that a subscription is being raised in Byfleet towards a reward; but I am of the opinion that, however good the intentions of the inhabitants there may be, they will not succeed in raising a sufficient sum to induce anyone implicated in the affair to give information.

I am, yours faithfully,
G. F. Roumieu

Whitehall, 23 January 1888
To G. F. Roumieu, Esq., Coroner for Surrey, Runwick House; Farnham, Surrey.

SIR—I am directed by the Secretary of State to return herewith the depositions, forwarded with your letter of the 18th instant, in the matter of the murder of George Chuter; and with reference to your recommendation, I am to say that the practice of offering rewards by Government for information in criminal cases has been discontinued for some time past; and that the Secretary of State, having carefully considered the circumstances, does not feel justified in departing from the rule in the present case.

I am, Sir, your obedient servant.

Nothing fresh has transpired in connection with this horrible event, and the police have obtained no clue upon which to work. Some surprise is expressed that the Home Office has declined to offer a reward, and some talk of getting up a sufficient sum in the village has taken place, but nothing has yet been done in the matter.

The Letter from ANXIOUS, Published in the *West Surrey Times* on March 2, 1888.

On March 2, 1888, something very fresh indeed transpired in Surrey. On that date, the *West Surrey Times* published a long, anonymous letter entitled "THE RECENT BYFLEET MURDER, dated Feb. 27, addressed to the editor of the newspaper, and signed ANXIOUS. After reading the first sentence, I stopped short. My blood suddenly ran cold. There was something oddly familiar about the letter's mysterious tone and its use of an enigmatic *nom-de-plume.* Here, below, is the full text of that letter, as published:

THE RECENT BYFLEET MURDER.

To the Editor of the 'West Surrey Times.'

Sir—On the 12th of January of the present year was perpetrated in this village about as cruel a murder as could be conceived. The victim, an inoffensive and respected old resident, named Chuter, was horribly

battered about the head with a poker, and his head was almost severed from his body. 'Coroner's quest' was held in due course, and the good men and true who sat thereon were unanimous in returning a verdict of 'Wilful murder against some person or persons unknown.' Unknown, I say. Unknown was the case then; and, although weeks have since elapsed, the murderer or murderers are unknown now, or, at any rate, are not under arrest.

You, sir, will remember from the evidence brought forward at the inquest that there was a strong presumption in favor of the theory that the fell murder of Chuter was committed by someone acquainted with his home, and who was known to the murdered man. I am bound to say that, after reading the reports which appeared in your paper, backed up by information which I have personally got, that I greatly incline to the same opinion.

We have been told that there was a clue, but I am not aware that anything has yet been done; and, as the weeks go on, the chances of securing the murderer become more and more remote. We have seen that the Government decline to offer a reward, and therefore I say—although I have no desire to force the hand of the police—that in the interest of the public some definite steps should be taken in order to endeavor to unravel this mystery. Only by taking some decisive action can public confidence be restored. If it is found that our own police are unable to cope with the case, then I would venture to suggest

that a detective from Scotland Yard should be allowed to take the matter up, and see if he can satisfactorily deal with it.

ANXIOUS

Byfleet, Feb. 27, 1888

The letter began by describing the events of Jan. 12 as "about as cruel a murder as could be conceived." ANXIOUS was not bothering, even for a moment, with the official nonsense about a robbery-gone-sour. With the authority of a Judge on the Supreme Court delivering a precedent-setting verdict, ANXIOUS declared not only that this event was a murder, but also that this murder had been "*cruelly conceived.*" Thus, the murder was not the accidental result of a panicked burglar attempting to hide his identity. It was a pre-planned murder. And the goal of this cruelly conceived murder was the sadistic infliction of pain.

Who was the only person (or persons) who could possibly know that the Byfleet Murder was perpetrated as part of a pre-conceived plan intent on cruelly inflicting pain? ANXIOUS could only be one of the two-or-more killers who had bludgeoned George's head with the poker or slashed his throat with the carving knife. From ANXIOUS' authoritative tone throughout the letter, he was evidently the leader of the team. He was the mastermind. ANXIOUS had conceived this plan to murder and mutilate George Chuter. And now, like a wolf in sheep's clothing, here in this elegantly phrased, published letter, he made his theatrical public entrance. He skillfully pretended to be a deeply concerned citizen, an upright local resident who was worried that "some person or persons unknown" were still at large and "not under arrest."

My dear readers: we are now face-to-face with the killer-in-chief of the Byfleet Murder. Let's examine each point in his devious letter to decipher what he really intended to accomplish by writing it, by appending a fictitious name to it, and by sending it to the editor of the *West Surrey Times.* Can we be absolutely certain that the anonymous author of this letter was, in fact, the leader of the team of killers who murdered and mutilated George Chuter? Of course, we can! And why is that? Because ANXIOUS has just told us so. In the second paragraph, ANXIOUS wrote:

> **You, sir, will remember from the evidence brought forward at the inquest that there was a strong presumption in favor of the theory that the fell murder of Chuter was committed by someone acquainted with his home, and who was known to the murdered man. I am bound to say that, after reading the reports which appeared in your paper, backed up by information which I have personally got, that I greatly incline to the same opinion.**

So, ANXIOUS had information *"which I have personally got,"* that the "fell murder of Chuter was committed by someone acquainted with his home." How could

ANXIOUS "personally" know that the killer was previously acquainted with George's home—unless ANXIOUS "personally" knew the "person or persons" who had murdered George Chuter. Evidently, ANXIOUS also knew the "person or persons" who had entered George's home on an earlier occasion. So, now it is confirmed: ANXIOUS possessed Special Knowledge about the killers who murdered and mutilated George. And in this case, his Special Knowledge is clear evidence of his complicity and guilt in the Byfleet Murder.

ANXIOUS' Arrogance and Contempt for the Police and the Press.

Why would ANXIOUS write anything so risky and daring as a letter to a newspaper—including information that contained clues to the murder and mutilation? These clues might reveal that he was one of the killers who murdered and mutilated George Chuter. He wrote and sent this letter because, as is all too apparent, virtually every word is dripping with his utter contempt for the intelligence of the editor of the *West Surrey Times*, for the readers of this newspaper, for the Surrey Constabulary, for the Coroner, and hopefully, one day for the detectives at Scotland Yard in London. ANXIOUS was convinced that these incriminating clues would slip past everyone who read them—unnoticed, their real import never comprehended. He was sure the true significance of these clues would be ignored. And—as we will see in the next section—his arrogant self-confidence would be proven to be absolutely justified.

"O villain, villain, smiling, damned villain!"
William Shakespeare; *Hamlet* (Act I, Sc. v)

ANXIOUS' Ulterior Motive.

Why would the leader of the killers who had so cruelly murdered George Chuter write this letter to the editor of the *West Surrey Times*—who, ANXIOUS already knew, was sure to publish it? What was ANXIOUS' hidden agenda in sending this anonymous letter? What was his ulterior motive? ANXIOUS contemptuously suggested that "our own police are unable to cope with the case." Then, he manipulatively added: "Only by taking some decisive action can public confidence be restored." And what, exactly, might that decisive action be?

ANXIOUS' initial purpose was to ridicule and humiliate the Surrey Constabulary as incompetent fools. He was "not aware that anything had yet been done; and, as the weeks go on, the chances of securing the murderer become more and more remote." His disdain for the local police is palpable. And so, ANXIOUS was yearning for a more worthy adversary to confront in mortal combat—someone renowned, whom he could also baffle and publicly humiliate. With oozing, false humility, ANXIOUS proposes: "I would venture to suggest that a detective from Scotland Yard should be allowed to take the matter up, and see if he can satisfactorily deal with it." ANXIOUS reminds me of those 19th Century bare-fisted boxers who, after knocking out cold one opponent, yells into the screaming crowd: "OK, Who's next?"

ANXIOUS' suggestion has a familiar ring. Didn't the fraudulent ad in the London *Standard*, published on January 20, 1888, also attempt to attract the attention of Londoners to the Byfleet Murder in Surrey? Someone in London was desperate to be noticed. Imagine a psychopath's thrill at defying and thwarting an investigation by the Metropolitan Police's famed CID at Scotland Yard. This killer clearly had his sights on bigger fish to fry. Safe in his anonymity, ANXIOUS knew that George's killers had not left any clues at the crime scene that detectives at Scotland Yard could utilize to trace back to him. Indeed, ANXIOUS wrote:

> **"We have been told that there was a clue, but I am not aware that anything has yet been done."**

"The Fell Murder of Chuter."

There is one more enigmatic clue embedded in the letter from ANXIOUS. It is a tiny clue, but one that will gradually prove highly significant in the Byfleet Murder—and elsewhere. It is but one four-letter word: *fell*. What's in a small word? Possibly a fatal wound.

To quote Shakespeare:

Marry, 'tis not so deep as a well, nor so wide as a church-door, but 'tis enough, 'twill serve: ask for me tomorrow, and you shall find me a grave man.

[Mercutio, in *Romeo and Juliet*]

ANXIOUS refers to the "the fell murder of Chuter." ANXIOUS' use of "fell" as an adjective is archaic, obsolete and literary. Today, and also in 1888, "fell" is almost invariably used as a verb, as the past tense of "fall' (except in Northern England where it is sometimes used as a noun to refer to an area of high, barren hillsides.)

However, in 13th Century Old English, "fell" was used as an adjective to mean "cruel" or "morally wrong." Shakespeare used "fell" in this manner in Act IV Scene 3 of *Macbeth* in the famous phrase "in one fell swoop." Thus, Shakespeare likened the murder and mutilation of Macduff's wife and children to a hawk swooping down on defenseless prey. Evidently, ANXIOUS knew his Shakespeare very well.

In 1819, the Shakespearean scholar and London playwright Horace Twiss also used "fell" as an adjective in a phrase that likewise became famous: "From what **fell demon** Learn'dst thou this damned subtlety of torture?" (from the five-act tragedy *Carib Chief.*) In this case, the adjective "fell" took on a double meaning. It derived not only from the Old English word meaning "cruel" or "morally wrong," it also alluded to the Biblical Fallen **Angels**—*i.e.,* the **fell demons** who were expelled from Heaven as rebels, together with Lucifer.

So, what is "a fell murder"? It is both a murder that was "cruelly conceived" and was committed by a "fell demon" (or by "fell demons.")

A Four-Letter Word.

Thanks to one small word embedded in this anonymous letter, we now know that George Chuter's chief killer believed he was a descendant of Lucifer's host of Fallen Angels. What do we know about the Fallen Angels?

The *Book of Revelation* describes a past war in Heaven between God's faithful host (two-thirds of all angels) led by the Archangel Michael, and Lucifer's host of rebellious angels (the remaining one-third of all angels) led by "the Dragon"—also known as the Devil. In the *New Testament,* Michael vanquished Lucifer, expelling him from Heaven, together with his rebellious army—as depicted below, in **Figure 8-4,** in the famous engraved image by Gustave Doré.

.

Figure 8-4. The Expulsion from Heaven of Lucifer and his host of rebellious angels. An engraving by Gustav Doré (1832-1883)

As recounted in *1 Enoch 7:2*, an apocalyptic text, when the **Rebel Angels** fell to Earth, they were transformed into demons. Then, they disappeared into Hell. In the painting shown in **Figure 8-5**, below, by Hieronymous Bosch, human sinners are consigned to Hell. There, they are devoured by the **Fallen Angels**, now transformed into **Fallen Demons.** These are the **Fell Demons,** in Old English. The name "Fallen Angels" was bestowed in traditional religious usage, not directly in the Bible. Here, below, in **Figure 8-5**, is a painting by Dutch artist Hieronymous Bosch depicting the **Fallen Demons** devouring human sinners in Hell.

Figure 8-5. **Demons devouring human sinners in Hell. A painting by Hieronymous Bosch (c. 1450-1516)**
Painting in Public Domain in U.S.

On Earth, male demons, called Nephilim, became enamored of human women and had sexual intercourse with them. The progeny of their unions was corrupt, and they inherited demonic knowledge. Their destiny was to wreak mayhem and murder on Mankind, and destruction upon the Earth. Here, below, in **Figure 8-6**, is another depiction by Dutch artist Hieronymous Bosch of three demons bludgeoning to death an innocent, defenseless traveler.

Figure 8-6. **Painting by Hieronymous Bosch (c. 1450-1516) of three demons bludgeoning to death an innocent, defenseless traveler.**

Painting in Public Domain in U.S.

3 *Enoch* mentions three Fallen Angels by name: Azazel, Azza and Uzza. The most prominent was Azazel, a master of the forbidden arts. He is specifically blamed for the

corruption of the Earth. Did ANXIOUS view himself as a descendant of Azazel?

Or did ANXIOUS see himself as Lucifer—just freed from the Lake of Fire after 1,000 years of captivity, now ready to take his rightful place as ruler of Heaven and Earth? In Figure 8-7, below, is displayed a once-banned sculpture in St. Paul's Cathedral in *Liège,* Belgium, known as *Le génie du mal;* or *The Spirit of Evil;* also as *Lucifer of Liege.* Here we see Lucifer with folded wings, presented seated, as a beautiful fallen angel. He is still a captive at the Lake of Fire, serving his imprisonment of 1000 years. His right ankle is bound to a rock by a heavy chain. He holds in his left hand half of his scepter of power; the other broken half lays on the ground at his feet. He also holds in his left hand his princely crown—which he intends to replace on top of his head when he is released, free again to retake power. With his right hand he feels the top of his head, which is bare. He longs for the day when his pointed crown will adorn his head.

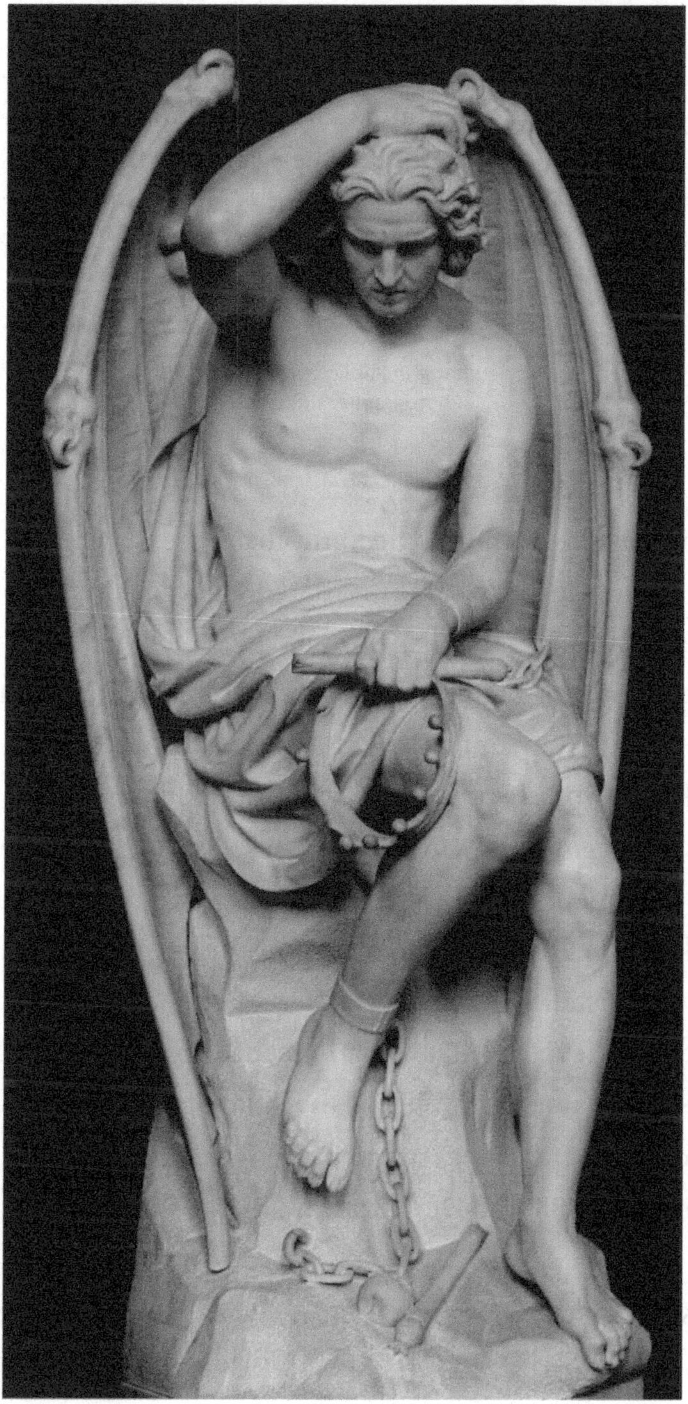

Figure 8-7. **Lucifer of Liège *(Le Genie du mal)***

in St. Paul's Cathedral, Liege; by Belgian sculptor Guillaume Geefs. (Note the chain of captivity around Lucifer's right ankle. He holds a crown and scepter—ready to take his rightful place as ruler of Heaven and Earth when his 1000 years of captivity comes to an end.)

Sculpture in Public Domain in U.S.
Photographer unknown.

A Cult of Killers.

It is now beginning to become clear: the two-or-more killers who murdered and mutilated George Chuter formed a homicidal religious cult. They believed they were descendants of Lucifer's rebel angels. They believed they were the progeny of the Fallen Angels, who had been expelled from Heaven together with Lucifer, as told in the *Book of Revelation.* Evidently, these killers believed it was their destiny on Earth to wreak murder and mayhem upon Mankind, in an attempt to gain power over Heaven and Earth, to install their deity, Lucifer, as ruler. Apparently, this cult believed the Devil had recently been freed from a thousand years of captivity at the Lake of Fire (as depicted above in the 18th Century sculpture *Le Genie du mal.*) And on Jan. 12, 1888, the Devil was in George's kitchen.

As Shakespeare observed in *Henry IV, Part 1*, **"Give the devil his due."**

A Psychopathic Guru.

It is now evident to me: ANXIOUS was not only the leader of the cult who murdered and mutilated George Chuter, he was also a sociopath, a manipulative narcissist, and a vicious sadist. As is apparent from his craftily constructed letter, he was certainly not insane. And he was no burglar. He was well-educated—although he wrote in a bizarre literary style that sounded somewhat stilted and theatrical, as though in a play from an earlier era.

For example, he wrote:

> "Unknown, I say."
> "Unknown was the case then; and, although weeks have since elapsed, the murderer or murderers are unknown now."
> "You, sir, will remember…"
> "The good men and true…"
> "The fell murder of Chuter…"
> "I am bound to say that…"
> "And therefore, I say…"

Above all, there is an element of Biblical grandiosity and elemental power to his statements.

> "Although I have no desire to force the hand of the police…" he wrote. Who was ANXIOUS that he believed he might have the power to force the hand of the police? Was he omnipotent?

> "We have been told that there was a clue, but I am not aware that anything has yet been done." And who was ANXIOUS to believe that he would know about any new clue uncovered by the police? Was he omniscient?

Did ANXIOUS believe he possessed supernatural powers? It looks that way, I'd say.

There is yet more evidence about the Byfleet Murder that we can deduce from this cryptic but highly revealing letter. Apparently, George's killers were familiar with every detail of the Coroner's Inquest. ANXIOUS knew that George's "head was almost severed from his body"—a fact revealed only in Dr. Sealey's direct testimony. Of course, ANXIOUS was well-aware that George's head had almost been severed from his body, since *decapitation* had been ANXIOUS' deliberate intention when he slashed, with all his might, George's throat from ear-to-ear, down to the vertebrae in the spinal column. Thus. ANXIOUS confirmed: decapitation was the unrealized goal of the mutilation with the carving knife. It remains to be seen what the killers took with them when they departed—instead of taking with them George's head, as originally planned.

Evidently, ANXIOUS was an avid reader of the press coverage of the Byfleet Murder. He cites the exact verbiage of the verdict in the Coroner's Inquest. He tells the editor of the *West Surrey Times*: "You, sir, will remember from the evidence brought forward at the inquest that there was a strong presumption in favor of the theory that the fell murder of Chuter was committed by someone acquainted with his home, and who was known to the murdered man." From Chapter 2 until this very spot in my book, I have repeatedly asserted that the killers of George Chuter must have visited George kitchen on an earlier occasion. That is how they knew where to find the two murder weapons: the poker and the carving knife. Evidently, ANXIOUS knew that, too.

From the classified ad in the London *Standard,* we know the author(s) of that ad yearned for more press attention in London. It sensationalized the "horrible" gruesome Byfleet Murder to attract viewers. From ANXIOUS' letter, we now know that he also wanted the investigation to be taken over by the Metropolitan Police in London, where it would inevitably be covered by the London press. The humiliation of Scotland Yard in the London press would be ANXIOUS' ultimate triumph. "Forcing the hand of the police" was exactly the aim of ANXIOUS' letter. His message is a transparent attempt to take control of the murder investigation and use it as a weapon against Scotland Yard. This letter was written by a man who was convinced that he was smarter than everyone else. In 1888, apparently he was.

Biblical Weapons of Sacrificial Murder.

Why was ANXIOUS focused on decapitation? Earlier, I speculated that the village of Byfleet may have been selected as the location for this symbolic murder and mutilation (and an attempted decapitation) because of historic decapitations associated with Henry VIII—who had owned and rebuilt Byfleet Manor. Now, more symbolic associations with the killers' selection of murder weapons come to mind. Why didn't they use a revolver to murder George? Or poison? Or a garrote for strangulation? These are not the weapons of ritualistic, sacrificial murder.

The two weapons employed by the killers to kill George were murder weapons of ritualistic sacrifices utilized many times in the Bible: *i.e.* a bludgeon and a long knife. The First Murder occurred in *Genesis* Chapter 4 when Cain killed Abel. The Bible does not specify the murder weapon employed by Cain. Nevertheless, traditional religious interpretation teaches that Cain bludgeoned Abel to death. He bashed in Abel's head—possibly with a stone, or possibly with a club. Here, below, in **Figure 8-8,** is an historic painting of Cain bludgeoning to death his brother Abel with a club, by 17th Century Italian artist Pietro Novelli, a.k.a. "Il Monrealese."

Figure 8-8. *Cain Kills Abel* (with a club)
by Pietro Novelli (1603-1647.)
Scottish National Gallery; Image in Public Domaine in US

In the New Testament, the most significant decapitation with a long knife (or sword) is the beheading of John the Baptist, by order of King Herod Antipas. Here, below, in Figure 8-9, is an engraving by German artist Albrecht Dürer, illustrating the story, as told in the books of *Matthew* and *Mark.*

Figure 8-9.The Beheading of John the Baptist
Albrecht Duhrer (1471-1528)

The most famous of all sacrificial decapitations with a long knife was the attempted beheading of Isaac by his father Abraham. As told in *Genesis* Chapter 21:1-19 in the Old Testament: Abraham took his knife to sacrifice his son. At the last moment, an angel of God told Abraham not to lay his hand on Isaac. Here, below, in **Figure 8-10**, is Rembrandt's celebrated painting of that Biblical event.

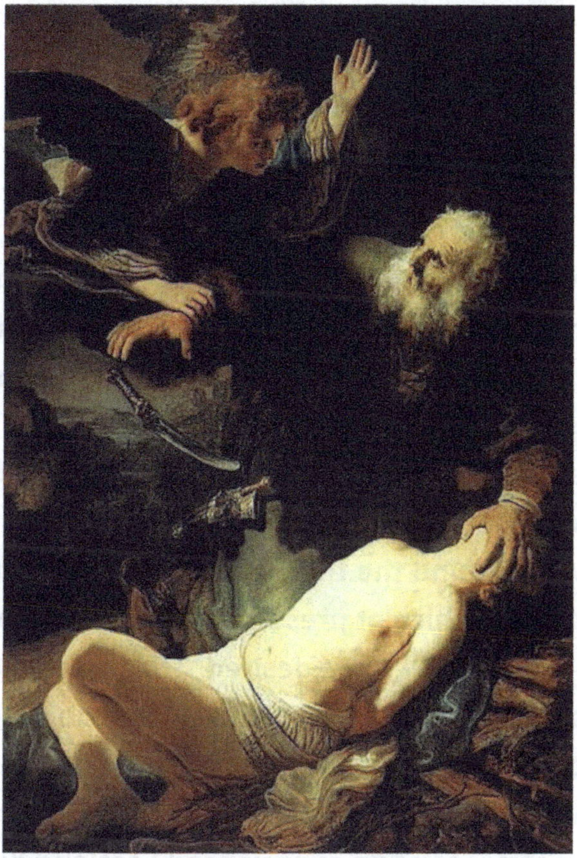

Figure 8-10. Abraham's [Attempted] Sacrifice of his Son, Isaac. Rembrandt van Rijn (1606-1669)

Hermitage Museum; St. Petersburg, Russia
Image and photo: public domain in US

Duped! —Hook, Line, and Sinker.

The letter from ANXIOUS was immediately followed by an editorial in the *West Surrey Times.* Utterly clueless about whom he was dealing with, the editor of the newspaper seconded ANXIOUS's helpful suggestion.

"Cannot the services of an experienced Scotland Yard detective be secured?" the editor asked plaintively:

> **THE BYFLEET MURDER.**
>
> **The correspondence we publish to-day indicates the natural feeling of disappointment prevailing in and near Byfleet respecting the failure to apprehend the person (or persons) guilty of the atrocious murder recently perpetrated in the district. No surprise will be expressed that this feeling is entertained, for on every ground the thorough clearing up of the mystery which at present surrounds the crime is most urgently to be desired. The county police, we have every reason to believe, have done their best, and have spared neither time nor pains in their efforts which might be forthcoming. Cannot the services of an experienced Scotland Yard detective be secured? The present position of affairs is wholly unsatisfactory.**

With the certitude of historical hindsight, we know today that the services of an experienced Scotland Yard detective were never secured to investigate the Byfleet Murder. There is not a scintilla of surviving documentary evidence of any contact between the Surrey Constabulary and London's Metropolitan Police concerning the Byfleet Murder. For Superintendent Bungard and Deputy-Chief Constable to have relinquished control of their investigation to the Met would have been viewed—by themselves, as well as by the public—as an admission of incompetence by the Surrey Constabulary. It would have meant ceding their turf to Scotland Yard—an unacceptable proposition for any independent British police force at the time.

Scotland Yard, Asleep at the Switch

Nor is there any surviving documentary evidence I have seen that, seven months after the publication of ANXIOUS' letter during the 'Autumn of Terror' in London, while the Whitechapel Murders raged across the East End, Scotland Yard ever contacted the Surrey Constabulary to inquire about the Byfleet Murder. Today, we have an unparalleled resource on the Internet about the Whitechapel Murders: casebook.org. Its archives contain thousands of press reports, police files, coroners' inquests, and official documents—as well as several decades worth of user forums—in which every known aspect of the Whitechapel Murders has been examined and documented.

In August 2023, I entered 'casebook.org Byfleet' into the search engine Bing.com. The response: "There are no results for **Byfleet site: casebook.org."** Then I entered **'casebook.org Chuter' into Bing.com. The response:** "There are no results for **chuter site: casebook.org."**

My conclusion: Scotland Yard never investigated the Byfleet Murder—not even during the Autumn of Terror. The rejection of ANXIOUS' suggestion must have been very frustrating for ANXIOUS and his cohorts. But after all, the Byfleet Murder was not in Scotland Yard's jurisdiction. One might assume that some official in the CID at Scotland Yard might have noticed reports in the London press of a "shocking" murder/mutilation in Surrey; and during the Whitechapel Murders later in 1888 thought it prudent to look into what had happened in Byfleet. If that ever happened, there appears to be no mention of it either in the press reports about the Surrey Constabulary, or at Scotland Yard. This seems to be a bald case of 'it's not my problem.'

Handbills for a Reward are Posted in Byfleet.

By the end of March 1888, the villagers of Byfleet took matters into their own hands with regard to a reward for the capture of the killer(s.) Through a public subscription organized by local bigwigs, at least £100 had been pledged. Interestingly, the handbill referred to "the murderer" in the singular.

On March 30, the *West Surrey Times* reported:

> **THE BYFLEET MURDER--Bills have been posted throughout the Chertsey Petty Sessional Division offering a reward of £100 to any person or persons who shall give such information as shall lead to the apprehension of the murderer of George Chuter at Byfleet. Information to be given**

to Supt. Bungard, at Chertsey, and the offer of the reward is to stand good for twelve months.

The End of the Beginning.

The reward was never given to anyone. No one ever came forward with information leading to the arrest of the murderers of George Chuter. Also, a killer never came forward to confess, repent, or face justice. Even though two-or-more killers working in concert perpetrated the Byfleet Murder and Mutilation, none of the team ever betrayed his cohort(s)—despite the issuance of the 100£ reward. Evidently, these killers had established a bond of trust among themselves that could never be broken—certainly not for 100£. Nor did any of them ever give away their cohort(s) by making an inadvertent slip of the tongue or undertaking some foolish action that might tip off the police. These daring but careful killers were always safe. They were never in jeopardy.

In a possibly apocryphal aphorism long attributed to William Shakespeare, the Bard (supposedly) but aptly said:

"In persons grafted in serious trust, negligence is a crime."

This standstill in the police's investigation appears to have been the end of the official Byfleet Murder case. There were no suspects to interrogate; no leads to pursue;

nothing but groundless speculation about the motive. Thus, the murder/mutilation of George Chuter was never solved—or ever re-investigated by anyone before the publication of this book.

Is it any wonder that the Surrey Constabulary always came up empty-handed in its investigation of this crime? From Day 1, they were looking for a lone, petty burglar, ostensibly a local resident of Byfleet. We saw in the earliest news reports about the Byfleet Murder, the police had already fixed upon a flawed theory of the crime—and they never wavered. They theorized that the crime could only have been committed by a burglar, and that burglar had to have been a local thief. In order to carry away his loot, he had to be a local resident—right? So, there was no point in searching for George's killer outside of Byfleet—or outside of Surrey, for that matter. The Surrey Constabulary always barked up the wrong tree. They wore blinders. For that reason, they remained—literally—clueless.

No one in Byfleet—except, for one brief moment, Coroner Roumieu—ever comprehended the true nature of this baffling crime. The Coroner momentarily reflected that, in recent years, other unsolved, exceptionally violent murders, assumed to be robberies-gone-sour, had occurred in various parts of England. When additional murder/mutilations occurred later in 1888 in London, and elsewhere in Britain—many of them with striking forensic similarities to the Byfleet Murder—it apparently never occurred to the Surrey Constabulary, or to Coroner

Roumieu, that these later crimes might somehow be linked to the murder/mutilation of George Chuter. The criminal investigation in Byfleet was never re-opened,

Superintendent Bungard and Inspector Barker wore blinders during their investigation. But we must also keep in mind the date: January 1888. At that precarious moment in British history, no police force had ever encountered a murder exactly like this one. What we have here in Byfleet is a new kind of crime. No one in the Surrey Constabulary had any previous experience with two-or-more peripatetic killers working in concert to murder and mutilate an ordinary victim with whom, apparently, they had no personal connection. The police saw no apparent motive, so they made one up out of thin air. They never considered the real significance of crime scene evidence that lay right before their eyes. Any alternative motive, other than a robbery-gone-sour, seemed too awful to contemplate seriously. The very thought of a human sacrifice would have appeared to them as ludicrous on its face.

It would not be until 1927 that Sir Arthur Conan Doyle would write in *The Case-Book of Sherlock Holmes:*

> **"Once you eliminate the impossible, whatever remains, no matter how improbable, must be the truth."**

Like the topsy-turvy world of Gilbert and Sullivan, the Surrey Constabulary eliminated the improbable but endorsed the impossible. They stuck with the run-of-the-mill robbery-gone-sour theory—despite the lack of credible evidence to support it in Byfleet. At the same time, there was strong, credible evidence that refuted the robbery-gone-sour theory. But the police ignored all that evidence, as did the Coroner in his summation. Thus, no one found the truth in January 1888—or even after that.

Coroner Roumieu's Discomfort.

Apparently, Coroner Roumieu was uncomfortable with his own directed verdict. He stated that: "The case was in an unsatisfactory position at the present moment." In summing up his thoughts on the Byfleet Murder, the Coroner declared: "A more wicked act one could not imagine." Then, he added:

> **They [the police] have heard of many [similar] cases about the country now, and I'm sorry to say they were getting more frequent. Now if men robbed the house, they seem to stand at nothing...**

So, the Coroner was aware of a recent increase in Britain of reported robberies-gone-sour in which the level of violence did not correspond to traditional robberies-gone-sour. The robbers "seem to stand at nothing," Roumieu said. Indeed, as my investigation progresses in future volumes of *A Trail of Blood,* we will encounter more unsolved murders with mutilations that already had begun to sprout up elsewhere in Britain—and outside of England, too. Despite the similarity of much crime scene evidence, they were usually dismissed by local police as unsolved robberies-gone-sour.

One might wonder: why would a killer (or more-than-one killer) travel from Surrey to other places around England, or around the globe, just to murder and mutilate random victims with whom he (or they) had no personal connection? The very idea was, at that moment in time, inconceivable. Even laughable.

And so, the murder and mutilation of George Chuter in Byfleet gradually disappeared from the public's view. The Byfleet Murder was—and, at this point, still is—a cold case, if ever there was one. For 136 years, nothing has been done to solve it. George Chuter still waits for his justice.

Tremble, thou wretch,
That hast within thee undivulged crimes
Unwhipped of justice.

William Shakespeare; King Lear—Act 3, Scene 2

***"All my pretty ones? Did you say all?
O hell-kite! All? What, all
my pretty chickens and their dam
at one fell swoop?"***

William Shakespeare, *Macbeth (Act 4, Scene 3)*
Macduff compares Macbeth to a cruel kite, a vicious type of hawk—who has swooped down and senselessly killed his entire brood of chicks, and their mother, in one fell stroke of his razor-sharp talons.

Chapter 9. Spreadeagled

At this point in my investigation, I thought I had written all that was known in the 19th Century about the Byfleet Murder. The crime was not solved, and it has remained unsolved to the present day. I was ready to move on, to investigate a similar murder/mutilation that occurred in Marylebone, committed soon after the murder and mutilation of George Chuter. Little did I know then that my investigation into the Byfleet Murder was just about to begin—*sul serio.*

I happened to notice a listing in the index of an archive of 19th Century British newspapers that struck me as rather odd. The index listed an article in the *Illustrated Police News* about the Byfleet Murder with a date of Jan. 28, 1888. I had already consulted the *Illustrated Police News* for the date of January 21, 1888. On that date, the *IPN* had published a long text article on the Byfleet Murder that evidently originated with a London news agency—as the identical article was also published in many other British newspapers. It described in considerable detail the testimony at the Coroner's Inquest in Byfleet on January 16, 1888. In the January 21 issue, there was no accompanying illustration; and so, I had assumed the *Illustrated Police News* had decided sometime before January 21 that the Byfleet Murder was not sufficiently newsworthy to deserve an illustration of its own.

Nevertheless, I remained curious about the January 28 date listed in the archive's index, so I decided to look up that issue, and track down the article about the Byfleet Murder. Sure enough, inside the *Illustrated Police News* on January 28, 1888, there was a lengthy article about the Byfleet Murder—but, upon examination, I saw it was the very same news agency article about the January 16 Coroner's Inquest that the *Illustrated Police News* had already published on January 21. Now I was confused. I wondered: why would a major London newsweekly re-run an old news agency story that it had already published a week earlier? On January 28, this text article was old news, and it took up a lot of space. The re-publication of an old news article—a Jan. 28 reprint of the report on the Jan. 16 inquest—made no sense to me.

One maxim I have often repeated to myself during this murder investigation: when something makes no sense, there must be a reason for it. I felt compelled to find that reason.

Front Page.

So, I decided to examine the front page of the Jan. 28 issue. The *Illustrated Police News* traditionally squeezed together a jumble of many sensational drawings illustrating the week's most violent crimes on its front page, mixed together with pugilistic news. I downloaded the entire front page. Here, below, in **Figure 9-1**, is that entire front page of the *Illustrated Police News*, as it appeared on Jan. 28, 1888.

Figure 9-1; Front page of the January 28, 1888 issue of the *Illustrated Police News*. The 'Byfleet Murder Drawing' is located in the bottom right-hand corner.

Image: Public Domain in US

The 'Byfleet Murder Drawing'

There, in the bottom right-hand corner of the front page, was a small but remarkably detailed drawing entitled "Murder at Byfleet." At first, I could hardly believe my eyes. Here was depicted, in minute detail, George Chuter's body, lying flat on his back in a pool of blood, on the floor of his kitchen, near his kitchen door. The two murder weapons—the carving knife and the poker—were pictured lying next to him, side-by-side, on the kitchen table. The drawing also depicted several minor, but important, details—such as blood dripping from the weapon handles onto the floor, as seen on the wooden floorboards, directly below the handles of the poker and the carving knife, lying on top of the kitchen table. Also shown—but partly obscured by the dark night sky—I could see, rushing out the kitchen door, a heavy-set man, as viewed from behind. Apparently, he was wearing a large, dark cape, or a long tailcoat, and he also wore a gigantic black hat.

Here, below, in **Figure 9-2**, is the *Illustrated Police News'* drawing "Murder at Byfleet," cropped from the front page and greatly enlarged. Incidentally, this drawing is unsigned. There is no indication anywhere on the drawing of the name or the identity of the sketch artist. Nor is there any information on the newspaper's masthead—or anywhere else in that issue that I could find—of the identity of the sketch artist who had illustrated the 'Byfleet Murder Drawing.'

However, two curious aspects of this drawing immediately struck me as quite odd. There were numerous small splotches of white on the dark shadows--almost everywhere in the kitchen—that gave the drawing a mysterious appearance of a mist-filled room. And on the floor of George's kitchen, his body was illuminated by a bright circle of light. What was the source of this bright circle of light? The murder and mutilation had occurred late in the evening of a particularly dark night in early January in Surrey, UK. Moreover, there was no lamp shown burning anywhere in the illustration.

Figure 9-2; "MURDER at BYFLEET," an illustration published by the *Illustrated Police News* on Jan. 28, 1888

Sketch artist: unknown. Image: Public domain in US

Did the Sketch Artist View George's Body *In Situ?*

The wealth of detail in this drawing was striking. Everything then known about the murder scene—as revealed in the news agency's article about the Coroner's Inquest—the sketch artist had included in the drawing; and he got everything right.

Also present in the drawing are many details that were not mentioned in the inquest testimony. Some of these details are not directly relevant to the murder—for example, the small door (perhaps a lavatory) to the right of the kitchen entrance door; the pottery on the kitchen table; the dishes, cups and jars on the shelves, the rug on the floor; the chair in the center of the image, the wood grain on the floor boards; the beams on the ceiling; and a strange, shiny object hung on the back of the chair. All these details, plus the complex perspective in the room, made me wonder: was the sketch artist actually present inside George's kitchen? Did he ever view the crime scene himself, or did he simply illustrate the facts, as reported in the news agency's story, and imagine the rest? Did the sketch artist ever see George's body lying on the kitchen floor? And if he did, when did he see it?

We know from inquest testimony that Dr. Sealy examined George's body only a few hours after James found it on the kitchen floor in the late evening hours of January 12. And we know from the news article in the *Surrey Advertiser* published on January 14 that the reporter for that newspaper had already viewed the mutilations on George's body and the blood on the floor—presumably sometime on January 13. So, evidently, the police were permitting reporters to view the crime scene by Jan. 13. Dr. Sealy had already finished examining the body by early morning hours, at the latest; and the police had completed inspecting the kitchen by then, as well. Reporters for the *Surrey Advertiser, Lloyd's Weekly Newspaper*, and a London news agency had all viewed George's body.

I wondered, did the sketch artist for the *Illustrated Police News,* based in London, also have an opportunity to view the corpse on the floor of the kitchen before George's mutilated body was taken away to a mortuary—presumably on late January 13 or early on the 14th? And if the sketch artist did view George's body *in situ* on Jan. 13 or 14, what took him so long to draw the sketch? Evidently, the sketch artist missed the newspaper's deadline for submission to make the Jan. 21 weekly edition of the *Illustrated Police News.* As we will soon see, this illustration is a very intricate and sophisticated drawing. The sketch artist must have gotten hung up on the remarkable wealth of details in this highly complex illustration. That seemed to me a reasonable explanation for the unprofessional delay in submitting it on time for publication on January 21. Or was this sketch artist otherwise occupied between January 13 and January 20, possibly with some other crime?

A Likeness of George Chuter's Face.

The most extraordinary detail in this newspaper sketch is undoubtedly the likeness of George's face. Here, below, in **Figure 9-3**, is a detail from the sketch showing George's face—rotated counter-clockwise, 90 degrees, for easier visibility.

Figure 9-3; A likeness of George Chuter's face, apparently drawn in death. (Rotated 90 degrees.)

Detail of drawing published by *Illustrated Police News* on Jan. 28, 1888.
Sketch artist: unknown. Image: Public Domain in US

While we cannot be certain that this likeness of George Chuter's face actually resembled the man, the verisimilitude of myriad other details in the drawing, and the indications that the sketch artist possibly viewed George's body *in situ,* suggest that this portrait may have been drawn directly from death. However, I was not able to locate any photograph of George, nor any other likeness of him, with which to make a comparison.

Note the expression of horror on George's face. His eyes are wide open. His eyeballs are bulging forward from their sockets in fright. His mouth is also wide open in a dark black circle, in a silent scream of terror. You can see George's tufted beard—which Coroner Roumieu specifically mentioned during the inquest. There is also visible a thin black slash across George's neck. Around the front of George neck, tissues from his esophagus and windpipe are protruding. The top of George's skull appears to be battered, with dark stuff oozing out of his wounds. A great quantity of blood is seen dripping onto the floor. George's 'greatcoat' is fully buttoned up to the top—as PC Thomas Mears testified at the inquest. PC Mears' evidence also established that George had been attacked immediately upon entering the kitchen door, even before he had an opportunity to unbutton his overcoat.

We can see in this sketch George's terrified facial expression soon after he was attacked in the dark, near his kitchen doorway—his horrible grimace in death now frozen in time. Was this the expression that remained on George's face—with his mouth open in a silent gasp for air, after his skull had been bludgeoned with the poker and his throat had been slashed with the carving knife, all in the dark? That is the impression we get by looking at this shocking portrait-in-death—akin to a death mask.

Flat on His Back, Face-Up.

Curiously, the sketch artist also got right that George must have been found by James lying flat on his back, *face-up*. Neither Dr. Sealy, nor the police, nor James, nor the Coroner, nor any other witness ever specifically mentioned that George had been found lying on his back, *face-up*. Recalling my own observations from Chapter 4, I had deduced from Dr. Sealy's testimony that George must have fallen forward after he was struck on the back of his head; then he fell to his knees and bruised his left knee. I reasoned: from that kneeling position, he could only have continued to fall forward onto his belly, or onto his side—but not flat onto his back. Then, in order to bash George's face with the poker, and slash George's neck down to his spinal vertebrae with the carving knife, it was my deduction: the killers would first have had to roll him over, flat onto his back, face up—as he is depicted in the 'Byfleet Murder Drawing.'.

Evidently, the sketch artist of this drawing had made the same deductions in 1888 that I did in 2023. How else, I thought, could this sketch artist have possibly known the body position in which George was found on the kitchen floor by James?—that is, unless the sketch artist had actually seen George's body lying in that position on the kitchen floor on January 13. Somehow, the sketch artist knew that George must have been rolled over onto his back by the killers. However, I was troubled by the fact that no witness testimony at the Coroner's Inquest had made that same deduction. It struck me as highly unusual that a newspaper illustrator would inject his own deductions—undocumented at the inquest—into his published drawing of the crime scene.

Spreadeagled.

It was then that I first noticed something in the sketch that shocked me to the core. Both of George's arms were fully outstretched at a 90-degree angle from his torso. And his legs were straight and somewhat spread apart. Evidently, George's body had been posed in this unnatural position by his killers before they departed the premises. It is inconceivable to me that, after he was remorselessly attacked with the poker and rendered unconscious, and then rolled over onto his back by the killers, George could have fallen into that highly symbolic position all by himself.

There is a special name for this particular body pose, *i.e.,* for a body lying flat on its back, face-up, with both arms fully extended at right angles to the body, and with legs straight and somewhat spread apart: *spreadeagled.* The pose gets its name from the pose an eagle assumes as it swoops down to the ground for the kill. A spreadeagled body is fraught with symbolism of violence and death.

It is a "fell swoop," as Shakespeare might have described it.

Princeton University's online *Wordnet* defines 'spread eagle,' when used as a verb, thus: "to defeat disastrously." Confinement of an enemy in the spreadeagle position has historically been associated with torture and serial murders. George was, undeniably, disastrously defeated. And he was tortured. After his head had been bludgeoned in the dark, his throat was slashed from ear-to-ear—as if it had been ripped by the razor-sharp talons of an eagle. Here below, in Figure 9-4, is a photograph of a golden eagle with its wings spread and its talons positioned, zooming in for the kill. I have outlined the pose in red.

Figure 9-4; A Golden Eagle in the spreadeagle pose. I have outlined here in red a golden eagle honing in on its prey for the kill—with its wings fully spread apart. As the eagle swoops down on its victim, it spreads its

legs down and slightly apart. This position is known as the spreadeagle pose. The sharp points at the ends of the eagle's talons sink into a wide area of flesh, tightening its grip on its prey. After the kill, the eagle hacks the prey to pieces with its sharp beak.

Photo credit: animalsbirds.com

Here, below, in **Figure 9-5**, is my outline in red of George Chuter's body, as depicted in the 'Byfleet Murder Drawing,' published by the *Illustrated Police News* on Jan. 28, 1888. I have rotated the image 90 degrees, counterclockwise, for direct comparison with the photo of the golden eagle, above. Note the dark and light-shaded bloodstains on the rug surrounding George's legs and feet. I have traced some of these outlined shapes of bloodstains in orange. Adding these shapes of bloodstains to the outlines of George's body, it appears to me that the sketch artist had simulated an eagle's tail feathers on George's overcoat, and talons on George's feet. Thus, the sketch artist evidently stressed the resemblance between George's body pose and that of an eagle with its wings fully spread and its legs slightly spread apart, coming in for the kill and mutilation. The Spreadeagle Pose is undeniable.

Figure 9-5; Illustration of George Chuter's body, rotated 90 degrees, in the spreadeagle pose (outlined in red, on the floor of his kitchen.) Outlines of bloodstains on the rug, traced

In orange, give his body the added appearance of tailfeathers and talons—thus making plain the resemblance of George's body pose to that of an eagle about to strike its prey in one fell swoop.

Original image published by *Illustrated Police News,* January 28, 1888; Sketch artist: unknown; Public domain in US. Tracing of outline of spreadeagle position;

Staging and Posing.

Professor of Criminology Scott A. Bonn, PhD—who has advised the FBI on serial killers—has written (in *Psychology Today* in 2015) about two types of positioning of murder victims' bodies by their killers: *staging and posing:*

> **The FBI profiler may also encounter deliberate alterations of the crime scene or the victim's body position at the scene of the murder. If these alterations are made for the purpose of confusing or otherwise misleading criminal investigators, then they are called staging, and they are considered to be part of the killer's MO. On the other hand, if the crime scene alterations only serve the fantasy needs of the offender, then they are considered part of the signature, and they are referred to as posing.**

Organized or Disorganized Killers?

Using Prof. Bonn's definitions, a mutilated body found in the unnatural spreadeagle pose is, by definition, a posed body. Thus, the posing of the body is linked directly to the killer's signature—*i.e.* his deepest motivation for killing based on his obsessive fantasies, not his MO. According to Prof. Bonn, the posing of a victim's body is a prime factor used to determine whether a murder was perpetrated by an organized or a disorganized killer.

> **The breakthrough idea of classifying serial homicide crime scenes according to an organized/disorganized dichotomy is credited to the former FBI agent and profiler Roy Hazelwood. This concept was based primarily on a study of 36 serial predators conducted by acclaimed FBI agents John Douglas and the late Robert Ressler.**
>
> **Profilers use a list of factors such as whether the victim's body was positioned or posed by the killer, whether sexual acts were performed before or after death, and whether cannibalism or mutilation was practiced on the body.**
>
> **These factors are used to predict whether an unknown offender is an organized or disorganized killer. The organized/disorganized classification of offenders is the centerpiece of the FBI profiling approach, and it is explained below.**
>
> **According to the offender and crime scene dichotomy, organized crimes are premeditated**

> **and carefully planned, so, little evidence is normally found at the scene. Organized criminals, according to the classification scheme, are antisocial (often psychopathic) but [they] know right from wrong, are not insane, and show no remorse.**
>
> **Based on historical patterns, organized killers are likely to be above-average intelligent, attractive, married or living with a domestic partner, employed, educated, skilled, orderly, cunning and controlled. They have some degree of social grace, may even be charming, and often talk and seduce their victims into being captured...Organized killers are very difficult to apprehend because they go to inordinate lengths to cover their tracks and often are forensically savvy, meaning they are familiar with police investigation methods.**

Modus Operandi or Signature?

Professor Bonn also defines two categories of crime scene evidence that describe a serial killer's actions: the MO *(Modus Operandi)* and the Signature.

> **In addition to the organized/disorganized dichotomy, a serial killer may leave traces of one or both of the following behavioral characteristics: MO (*i.e., modus operandi* or method of operation) and signature (the personal mark or imprint of the**

> offender.) While every crime has an MO, not all crimes have a signature.
>
> The MO is what the offender must do in order to commit the crime...For example, the killer must have a means to control his victims at the crime scene, such as tying them up. Significantly, the MO is a learned behavior that is subject to change. A serial killer will alter and refine his MO to accommodate new circumstances or to incorporate new skills and information. For example, instead of using rope to tie up a victim, the offender may learn that it is easier and more effective to bring handcuffs to the crime scene. The MO of Jack the Ripper, for example, was that he attacked prostitutes at night on the street with a knife.

[Not all of Jack the Ripper's victims, I hasten to interject, were attacked on the street. Mary Jane Kelly, for one, was a prostitute—but she was murdered and mutilated in her lodgings, on her bed—not on the street. MS]

> The signature, on the other hand, is not required in order to commit the crime. Rather; it serves the emotional or psychological needs of the offender. The signature comes from within the psyche of the offender and it reflects a deep fantasy need that the killer has about his victims. The essential core of the signature, when present,

> **is that it is always the same because it emerges out of an offender's fantasies that evolved long before killing his first victim. The signature may involve mutilation or dismemberment of the victim's body. [For example,] the signature of Jack the Ripper was the extensive hacking and mutilation of his victims' bodies that characterized all of his murders.**

[To the above extract, I would also add: to this day, we still do not know the motivation of Jack the Ripper. He was never caught. In his letters and postcards, he obviously played a phony literary role of a semi-literate Cockney. He was never interviewed by competent psychologists and criminologists. He never left us a confession of his motivation. We don't even know for sure which murders he committed, or how many.

Without knowing Jack the Ripper's true motivation, no one can determine his signature. To say that his signature was "extensive hacking and mutilation of his victims' bodies" is still speculation. The hacking and mutilations may have been merely a means to express a still unknown signature. The professor's statement does not explain, much less document, the fantasy beliefs that drove Jack the Ripper to commit these mutilations and hacking. The *why* is still missing in the Whitechapel Murders.]

Catherine Eddowes—an example of a famous murder victim, whose body was depicted in an ostensibly symbolic pose at her murder scene in Mitre Square, London, on Sept. 30, 1888.

Speaking of Jack the Ripper, an example of a body of a murder victim being posed by her killer in an ostensibly symbolic position is one of Jack the Ripper's canonical victims: Catherine Eddowes. In the early hours of September 30, 1888, Eddowes' mutilated corpse was sketched in Mitre Square, London, before her body was transported to a nearby mortuary. The sketch is attributed by some writers to Frederick Foster, a surveyor—but there is no report *in situ* or in any official document from that night that I could find, showing that Foster was actually present at the crime scene and drawing Eddowes' body, while her mutilated corpse was examined by the police and by Dr. Brown. There is no name of a sketch artist on this drawing. Here, below, in **Figure 9-6**, is the sketch of Eddowes' mutilated body in Mitre Square, drawn in two colors by an unknown artist. The detailed shadings suggest that this artist—whoever he may have been—was a skillful draftsman.

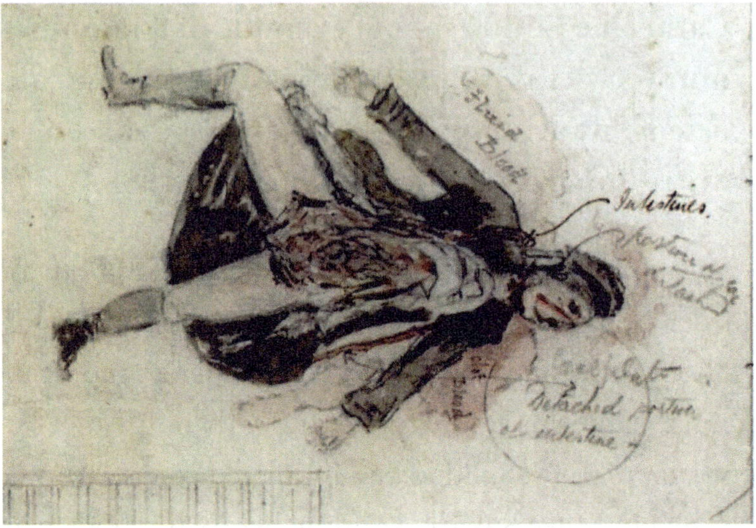

Figure 9-6; A famous example of a contemporary sketch of Catherine Eddowes' mutilated body, depicted as lying in Mitre Square on Sept. 30, 1888, in London, in an ostensibly symbolic pose.

Image created in 1888; sketch artist unknown, attributed to F. Foster; Public Domain in U. S.

Remarkably, this two-color sketch shows Eddowes body in an unnatural pose for a woman who has just been murdered and mutilated. Her right thigh extends away from her body at virtually 90 degrees, Her right leg extends away from her right thigh at virtually 90 degrees. Both arms—while not extended away from her torso at 90 degrees—have been posed in an exactly symmetrical placement at virtually 45 degrees. This pose is not the same as the Spreadeagle Pose that we viewed in the 'Byfleet Murder Drawing.' Nevertheless, Eddowes' body was clearly placed in this unnatural position by her killer as the expression of a symbolic statement. We don't know the killer's intended meaning of the symbolism in this case of a body posed by Jack the Ripper.

Comparing Prof. Bonn's Profile of an Organized Killer with the Crime Scene Evidence in Byfleet.

The posing of George Chuter's body in the spreadeagle posture has told us more about his killers' hidden motivation than all the groundless speculation by the Surrey Constabulary and Coroner Roumieu regarding a non-existent robbery-gone-sour. Evidently, George's killers were organized killers—indeed, they were highly organized, pre-meditated, and pre-planned killers. By posing George's body in the spreadeagled posture, they made a symbolic statement. But to whom was this statement addressed? Who was intended by the killers to see it?

Among several factors that possibly point to an organized murderer—according to Prof. Bonn—are: "whether the victim's body was positioned or posed by the killer; whether sexual acts were performed before or after death; and whether cannibalism or mutilation was practiced on the body." It appears to me that there was no sexual element whatsoever in George Chuter's murder; but certainly, there was mutilation practiced upon his body. So, in addition to the posing of George's body in the spreadeagle posture, we have a second factor indicating organized murderers: the mutilation of George's body.

The Spreadeagle Posture is a Symbolic Pose.

George's body was *symbolically* posed by the killers. According to Prof. Bonn, the posing of the victim's body, *alone,* is powerful evidence of an organized murderer. As Prof. Bonn made clear, in an organized murder, the chosen victim is posed according to the killer's signature. And a killer's signature is derived from his obsessive fantasies.

Thus, George was posed in the spreadeagle posture to fulfill the killers' fantasies. An eagle is a symbol of the highest form of avian raptor who mutilates its prey by slashing it with its razor-sharp talons and then picking it apart with its pointed beak. The spreadeagle position is also associated with symbolic ideas of imprisonment, defeat and torture.

While there was no evidence of any *cannibalism* in the Byfleet Murder, it is indeed possible that *vampirism* may have occurred. We know that a vast pool of George's blood was released onto the kitchen floor by the slash across his neck, from ear-to-ear, down to the vertebrae. Blood was also shed by the one and one-half inch wound and multiple fractures on the back of George's head. It remains to be seen whether any additional crime scene evidence will yet emerge to reveal that the killers intended to gather and use George's blood for occult purposes. If evidence of vampirism does eventually emerge, then we will have found three factors that indicate organized killers.

The symbolic spreadeagle pose is a fetish based on a belief in occult magic. Evidently, the killers believed that by posing George in this symbolic position his dead body then became a sacred object. It was then endowed with supernatural powers.

Comparing Prof. Bonn's Profile of an Organized Killer With the Letter from ANXIOUS.

In analyzing the Letter from ANXIOUS in Chapter 8, I noted that George Chuter's chief murderer was evidently of above-average intelligence, cunning, obviously well-educated and self-controlled—adjectives used by Prof. Bonn to describe organized killers.

In his letter, ANXIOUS told us that the plan to murder and mutilate George Chuter had been "cruelly conceived." Thus, the Byfleet Murder was pre-meditated. It was pre-planned—and every element of this plan was brilliantly successful in its execution. Such advanced planning and expert execution require above-average intelligence, cunning and control over every element in order for the plan to work smoothly. The plan to murder and mutilate George Chuter succeeded with nary a hitch.

ANXIOUS also told us that he and his cohort(s) had in fact been inside George Chuter's residence on a previous occasion. In his letter to the editor of the *Surrey Advertiser,* ANXIOUS stated:

> **"You, sir, will remember from the evidence brought forward at the inquest that there was a strong presumption in favor of the theory that the fell murder of Chuter was committed by someone acquainted with his home, and who was known to the murdered man. I am bound to say that, after reading the reports which appeared in your paper, backed up by information which I have personally got, that I greatly incline to the same opinion."**

So, now we've learned how the killers knew in advance that they could readily find a carving knife accessible in the kitchen table drawer and a poker accessible in an adjoining room (or in a corner of the kitchen near the fireplace.) According to the killer-in-chief—backed up by information which he had "personally got"—the killers were well-acquainted with the interior of George Chuter's home from an intrusion on an earlier occasion (possibly the break-in in 1887.) In that break-in, the killers had ample opportunity to check out the contents of the kitchen table drawer and a fireplace in an adjoining room (or in a corner of the kitchen)—and note the exact locations of the carving knife and the poker.

In addition to a previous break-in (possibly the one in 1887,) the killers also stalked George and James over a considerable span of time. Evidently, the members of this hermetic, homicidal team were frequent visitors to Byfleet. Perhaps their many visits explain why their presence in the village had not aroused the suspicions of residents wary of outsiders and strangers after the news broke about the murder and mutilation of George Chuter.

ANXIOUS was fully confident that the killers had left no clue at the crime scene on Jan. 12, 1888, that might now be traced back to them. In his letter, he informed us:

> **"We have been told that there was a clue, but I am not aware that anything has yet been done."**

Evidently, ever since the night of the murder and mutilation, ANXIOUS had closely followed in the press the progress—or rather, the lack of any progress—of the Surrey Constabulary. It is even conceivable that ANXIOUS was sitting in the public gallery at the Coroner's Inquest on Jan. 16, listening with intense psychopathic pleasure to the various witnesses give testimony about a crime that none of them could possibly comprehend. ANXIOUS knew for certain that he and his cohort(s) had left no incriminating evidence at the crime scene. Smugly, the arrogant ANXIOUS reveled in his invulnerability. He was not only smarter than everyone else, he also believed that he and his mate(s) were protected from capture by a supernatural power.

Insanity and Psychopathy.

Using an oft-used definition of 'insanity' as 'having lost contact with reality,' it is evident: George's killers were not insane. Apparently, however, they were psychopathic.

Psychopathy and insanity are not the same mental condition. According to one encyclopedia's definition of psychopathy:

> **Psychopathy is a neuropsychiatric disorder marked by deficient emotional responses, lack of empathy, and poor behavioral controls. It commonly results in persistent antisocial deviance and criminal behavior.**

Prof. Bonn indicated that organized killers are typically anti-social and psychopathic. They show no remorse. It is evident that the sadistic, manipulative and deceptive author of the Letter from ANXIOUS also showed no remorse for the commission of this "cruelly conceived" murder. It is also obvious to me: ANXIOUS knew the difference between right and wrong. He was fully aware that the killers' actions were illegal, as well as immoral.

The Attempted Decapitation.

ANXIOUS knew it was the killers' intention to sever George's head from his body. In his letter, ANXIOUS wrote:

> **The victim, an inoffensive and respected old resident, named Chuter, was horribly battered about the head with a poker, and his head was almost severed from his body.**

Of course, ANXIOUS knew that it had been the knife-wielding killer's intention to decapitate George. Indeed, it had been the intention of ANXIOUS—as the cult's guru—to symbolically decapitate George when he slashed George's throat down to the spinal vertebrae. If not for the unplanned interference of George's cravat, ANXIOUS might well have succeeded in severing George's head from his body in one stroke. Decapitation is not necessary to kill a victim. Simply slashing a victim from ear-to-ear with a large, long knife is sufficient to kill anyone. A decapitation in a murder—whether attempted or successful—is a symbolic act. In the mind of the killer, the decapitation held special meaning.

A Cultivated Killer.

Prof. Bonn indicated that organized killers are typically well-educated. The ornate prose evident in the Letter from ANXIOUS is a clear example of Prof. Bonn's criminological description. We are not looking for an illiterate thug. We are looking for an educated gentleman. We are also looking for an inveterate liar.

Fantasies and Delusions.

Prof. Bonn indicated that in cases of organized murders. the killers' motivations are expressions of their fantasies. These fantasies serve the emotional and psychological needs of the killers. Typically, organized killers live in fantasy worlds controlled by their delusions. The killers of

George Chuter lived in their diabolical fantasies of the **Fallen Angels**—or rather, **Fell Demons.**

The Media is the Message.

The professor also indicated that organized killers are typically media savvy. They not only closely follow every detail about their crimes, as reported in the press, they sometimes attempt to manipulate their own press coverage. They may leave cryptic notes at crime scenes, or send anonymous letters to newspapers.

It is evident from the published Letter from ANXIOUS—also from the self-published classified advertisement that appeared in the London *Standard*—that one of the emotional needs of the killers in Byfleet was the public humiliation of the police. Both documents sought greater public attention paid to the unsolved Byfleet Murder, particularly by readers in London. And the Letter from ANXIOUS overtly sought the entry of London's Scotland Yard detectives into the Byfleet investigation.

ANXIOUS was not satisfied with merely humiliating the rural, small Surrey Constabulary. He suggested that a detective from Scotland Yard take over the investigation into the Byfleet Murder. ANXIOUS had his sights set on defeating and humiliating the famed Metropolitan Police of London, and the world-class London press. Evidently, he craved recognition for his successful murder in Byfleet. He wanted a symbolic victory at the expense of all law enforcement.

Exactly what the Byfleet killers fantasized about has yet to be revealed by crime scene evidence. However, it is not sufficient, I believe, to say at this point that their signature was simply mutilation. *Why* mutilation? What was the nature of the fantasy that compelled the killers to mutilate George's body? Was it sex? Apparently not. So, what else might have driven the killers' fantasies and delusions in this case? From meagre evidence, we now have the beginnings of a theory: that the killers were driven by a religious fantasy about fell demons. We still need much more documented evidence to expand and corroborate this religious theory.

In 2024, we cannot interrogate these killers. So, we must look deeper into the documentation for original evidence that still survives in some form today. We must find evidence that reveals the true nature of the fantasy beliefs that drove George's killers to mutilate their chosen victim's body.

The Lone Robber vs. Two-or-More Killers.

Returning now to the 'Byfleet Murder Drawing,' I was particularly struck by the portion of the drawing that showed a heavy-set, large-framed, lone robber rushing out the kitchen door into the darkness outside. Here, below, in **Figure 9-7**, is a cropped detail—showing an enlargement of the solitary robber, as seen from behind.

Figure 9-7; Enlarged detail of a lone robber rushing out the kitchen door, after murdering and mutilating George Chuter.

Detail from Image published by *Illustrated Police News*, January 28,1888; Sketch artist: unknown; image: Public domain in US.

The lone robber is depicted in the drawing as grabbing the open door with his left hand, while exiting from the kitchen. We are looking at the lone robber's back. The image is shrouded in darkness—as is appropriate, since the attack on George occurred around 7:30 p.m. in January in the UK, with virtually no external illumination. The getaway could have occurred at any time following the murder and mutilation—up until the time of James' return from the band rehearsal, around 10 p.m. The man in the doorway appears to have been of very large build. He is wearing a long tailcoat—something like a conductor's set of tails. His hat is truly gigantic.

Because the image of this huge man is so dark, I decided to trace in red the man's outline with a computer paint program. Here, below, in **Figure 9-8,** is my result:

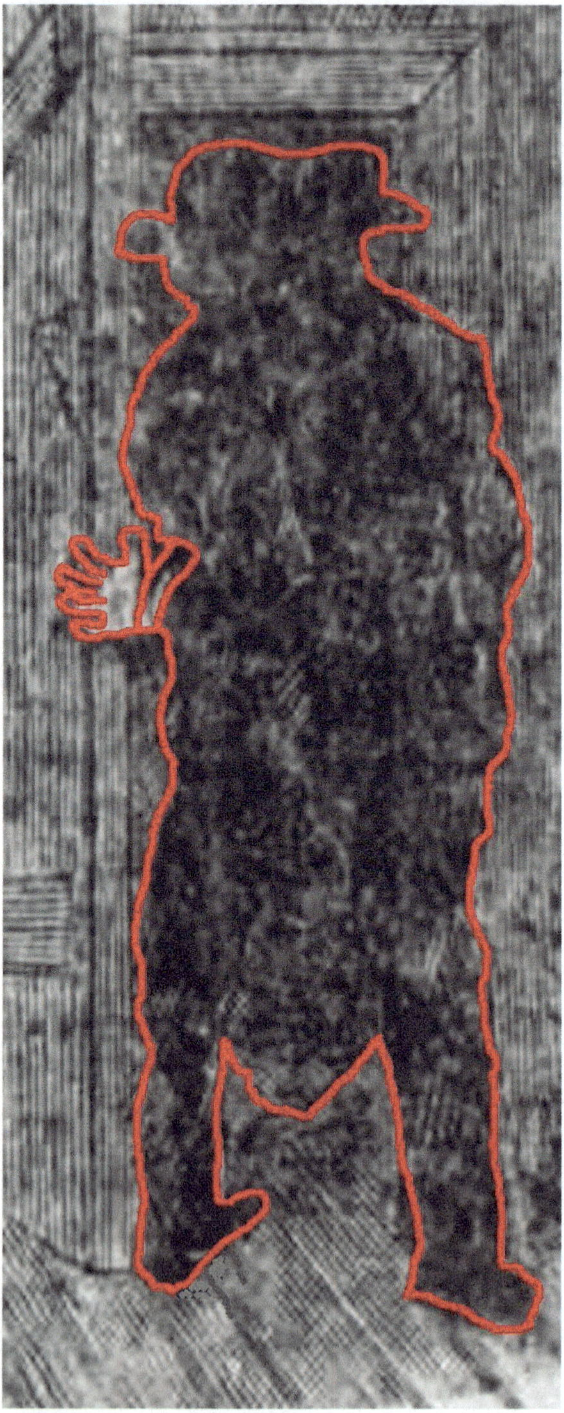

Figure 9-8; **Outline in red of illustration of lone killer rushing out the kitchen door. The image of this huge man is misshapen. It is impossible to accept as it appears. One foot points outside, the other foot points inside. The hat is far too wide. The head and neck are gigantic.**

Original image published by *Illustrated Police News*, January 28, 1888; Sketch artist: unknown; Image: Public domain in US.
Outline in red, traced by Mark Starr;

Upon viewing my red outline surrounding the heavy-set man rushing out the kitchen door, I saw immediately that something was wrong with this picture—very wrong. The man's proportions were impossible. The head was much too large for the body; and the neck was far too wide. The hat is as large as a giant sombrero. The man's back was also far too wide for his height. Moreover, the man's left foot faces the outside, while the man's right foot faces toward the interior of the kitchen—incongruously, like a ballet dancer at the *barre.* Many other details also look wrong. Oddly enough, I could discern details of other body parts embedded in grey smudges on the back of the robber's long tailcoat.

In sum, this drawing of a robber rushing out the door of George's kitchen made no sense to me as it appears in outlined form. It cannot be. The newspaper's sketch artist—who had drawn such a remarkably realistic depiction of George Chuter's face and body lying on the kitchen floor—was surely capable of drawing a properly proportioned man rushing out the door. So, I repeated to myself my mantra: when evidence in a murder investigation makes no sense, there must be a real reason for it.

Tracing the Outlines.

I decided to dive down deeper into this dark image using extreme magnification, outlining some of those whitish and grey smudged lines that you can see everywhere on the hat and on the back of the tailcoat, and on the legs of the trousers. First, I concentrated my efforts on the head area. It soon became evident to me that this man had two heads, and he was wearing two hats. Moreover, two men's faces were looking directly at me. They were not facing outside the kitchen door, as the outline of a lone robber rushing out the door had first appeared.

Here, below, in Figure 9-9, are my tracings of the outlines that I found embedded in the head and hat areas of the lone robber rushing out the kitchen door. To keep the outlines of the two heads separate, I traced those lines on our right in red; and those lines on our left in green.

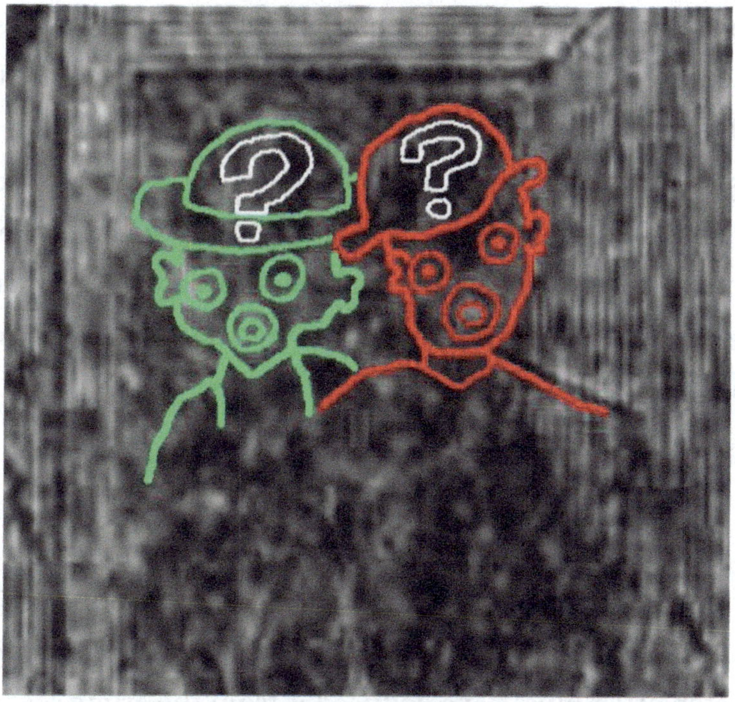

Figure 9-9; Tracing by Mark Starr of outlines of two men's heads, in the same place on the drawing as the lone robber's head and hat.

Drawing published by *Illustrated Police News*, January 28, 1888;
Sketch artist: unknown; Image: public domain in US.
Outlines in red and green traced by Mark Starr;

With the aid of my tracings, we can now see the outlines of two men, both wearing Bowler hats (in the US called a Derby hat.). Each man has eyes that consist of two concentric circles. Each man has a huge mouth, also made from two concentric circles. In the front and center of each man's hat is the outline of a very large question mark. I have traced these question marks in white, to distinguish them from the other outlines. The Man-in-Green on our left sports a pointed goatee beard. The Man-in-Red on our right is clean shaven. These two men—*i.e.*, the two killers—are obviously fantasy figures, not precise portraits of real human beings. Thus, their real identities are not revealed—as symbolized by the large question mark on the front of each man's hat.

Two (or-More) Killers Working in Concert.

How did the sketch artist for the *Illustrated Police News* know that at least two men acting in concert, not one, had murdered and mutilated George Chuter? Evidently, the sketch artist must have deduced it from the crime scene evidence—just as I did from the information uncovered in the newspaper articles and the inquest testimony. However, the sketch artist hid his deduction from viewers. He disguised the two killers who worked in concert as a lone robber rushing out the kitchen door after he had murdered and mutilated George.

If the sketch artist had actually seen two men in the kitchen doorway, that would mean he was present at the crime scene when the murder and mutilation were committed on the evening of Jan. 12. I put that stupefying thought out of my mind for the moment. At the time, it seemed to me ludicrous that the sketch artist for the *Illustrated Police News* could have been present at the murder scene when George was murdered and mutilated.

Nevertheless, I was encouraged that someone back in January 1888 had evidently agreed with my theory of the crime: *i.e.,* that it was committed by two-or-more killers working in concert.

My tracings of the two men in the doorway are not yet complete. All I had traced thus far were the faces of two men wearing hats. Now, I decided to trace the remaining outlines of the two men visible in the doorway—as depicted in the white and grayish smudges that I could see in the tailcoat, trousers and shoes of the huge dark man rushing out the kitchen door. I began with the Man-in-Red on our right. In **Figure 9-10**, shown below, I traced in red only those outlines that, apparently, belonged to him.

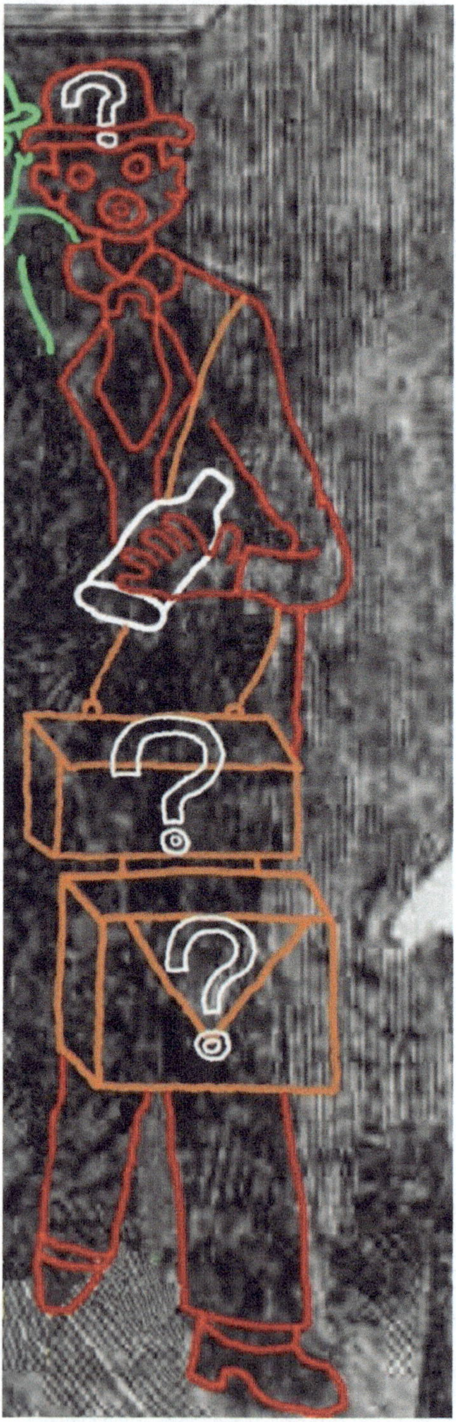

Figure 9-10; My tracings of the outlines of the body of the Man-in-Red.

Original image published by *Illustrated Police News* on Jan. 28, 1888; Sketch artist: unknown; Original image: public domain in US.

The Man-in-Red is Elegantly Dressed.

The Man-in-Red is dressed in an elegant coat, long pants and dress shoes. He wears a lucky horseshoe brooch to hold down his wide cravat. He carries two large cases strapped over his shoulder. I have traced these cases in orange. On each carrying case appears a large question mark—which I have traced in white (like the question marks on the two men's Bowler hats.) We can only guess what are the contents inside these two carrying cases, each marked with a large question mark on the front. In his left hand, the Man-in-Red holds a bottle about the size of a beer bottle. Is the Man-in-Red stealing a bottle of beer from George's kitchen, now that George is dead and mutilated? Or is this bottle one that the Man-in-Red brought with him to the scene of the crime, and then retrieved before he departed? I wondered: what conceivable relevance could this bottle and these two large carrying cases have to George's murder and mutilation?

The Man-in-Green Stands Behind the Man-in-Red.

Next, I attempted to trace the outlines of the body of the Man-in-Green. But I found I could not credibly attach the rest of the image in the doorway to the Man-in-Green. In Figure 9-7, the left leg of the lone killer rushing out the door is pointed to the outside. But the Man-in-Green is facing inside the kitchen. Thus, this large leg, next to the open kitchen door, could not possibly belong to the Man-in-Green. Nor could this pants' leg belong to the Man-in-Red—for the same reason.

Also in Figure 9-8, we can see a white hand grasping the edge of the open kitchen door. Attached to this hand, we can also see on the back of the huge man's cape the embedded outlines of a long arm. The hand and this long arm cannot possibly belong to the Man-in-Green. The Man-in-Green is facing toward us. The hand is facing away from us. Moreover, the long arm is much too low and too lengthy to be credibly attached to the right shoulder of the Man-in-Red. Again, the hand is facing the wrong way to belong to the Man-in-Red.

So, I wondered, to whom did the large leg next to the kitchen door--and the hand grasping the edge of the open door--belong?

Some Large Dark Object Blocks Our View of the Man-in-Green's Body.

Most of the body of the Man-in-Green is not visible to us. While attempting to trace the Man-in-Green, it became clear to me that the leg and the arm must belong to a third person in the doorway. This third killer blocked our view of the body of the Man-in-Green. Therefore,. I began to outline the leg and arm of the third killer in a different color: yellow.

A Third Man-in-Yellow Now Appears.

Suddenly, I saw there must be a complete outline of a third man in this picture—another killer who blocked our view of the body of the Man-in-Green. Examining under extreme magnification this outline embedded in the image of the lone robber rushing out the kitchen door, I found the image of a third man, complete, standing in the kitchen doorway. He was shown bending over, examining something on the wall behind he kitchen door.

Here, below, in **Figure 9-11**, are my tracings of the outlines of a third man, whom I outlined in yellow. He is not depicted in the drawing as wearing a hat. Nevertheless, he displays a question mark—on the left side of his head, instead of an ear. He wears a long tailcoat. He is somewhat shorter than the Man-in-Red and the Man-in-Green. Both his feet are pointed away from the viewer.

Figure 9-11; My tracing in yellow of the outline of a third man in the doorway.

Original image published by *Illustrated Police News* on Jan. 28, 1888;

We Were Duped! Yet Again!!

In Figure 9-8, we first saw the outline of a huge, lone robber rushing out the kitchen door—as viewed from behind. Then, in Figure 9-9, what we originally viewed as one very large dark man wearing a huge hat rushing out the kitchen door was revealed by my tracings actually to be the embedded images of two men standing in the kitchen doorway. Both of these men are depicted as facing us. Both men are depicted as wearing Bowler hats. Thus, we were duped by a devious sketch artist into believing the Surrey Constabulary's baseless theory of a robbery-gone-sour, committed by a lone burglar—shown here rushing out the kitchen door. This huge robber rushing out the kitchen door was actually an optical illusion.

In Figure 9-11, my tracings of outlines embedded on the body of this lone robber rushing out the kitchen door revealed outlines of a third man—whom I traced in yellow. According to the sketch artist, these three men are three killers. They are shown departing the scene after having murdered and mutilated George Chuter—who now lies spreadeagled on the kitchen floor. Two of these men, the Man-in-Red and the Man-in-Green, are facing us; and the third man, the Man-in-Yellow, is viewed from the side, bending down.

Thus, we have been fooled twice by the sketch artist—who was evidently adept at optical illusions. He skillfully cloaked the solution to the Byfleet Murder inside a mythical image of a lone burglar rushing out the kitchen door. The drawing appears to represent the police's Robbery-Gone-Sour Theory. However, the 'Byfleet Murder Drawing' actually reveals a much different description of George's murder and mutilation. This crime was no robbery-gone-sour perpetrated by a panicked lone burglar. The crime was a symbolic murder/mutilation perpetrated by three killers who all worked in concert.

Multi-Spectral Imaging Analysis.

By a remarkable coincidence, about a year after I first noticed the embedded images outlined in the 'Byfleet Murder Drawing,' curators at the British Library discovered a hidden drawing embedded in the *Codex Arundel 263* by Leonardo da Vinci. Using a technique that they called *multi spectral imaging analysis,* the curators found a drawing of a naked man that heretofore was not visible to casual viewers of the codex. Dr. Christina Duffy, an imaging scientist at the British Library, wrote that "the images raise fascinating questions about why the figure was drawn here, and why great efforts were made to erase it."

A scientific explanation of the technique was posted, and it boiled down to isolating different shades of colors in the light spectrum embedded in the background, reconstituted to create an ultra-high-resolution image. A recent article in the magazine of the Smithsonian Institution explains: multi-spectral imaging analysis is but one of several new imaging techniques developed in the past few years to explore hidden images embedded in works of art.

I have only my home computer and a UHD monitor (Ultra High Definition with a resolution of 3,840 x 2,160 pixels) available to me; and I work with widely available commercial imaging software. Nevertheless, I found that I had accomplished much the same thing with my desktop computer as Multi-Spectral Imaging Analysis—although admittedly on a more rudimentary level—as the curators at the British Library had done with their highly specialized multi-spectral equipment and programs. The crucial part of this technique of teasing out an embedded image is not so much dependent on the advanced optical capabilities of the equipment, but rather the human analysis to isolate varying shades of colors (including blacks, shades of gray, and whites) under intense magnification; and the detection of lines distinct from background visual noise.

Leonardo da Vinci

Here, below in **Figure 9-12,** is the British Library's restoration of Leonardo da Vinci's hidden drawing of a naked man, embedded on a page in the notebook called the *Codex Arundel 263.*

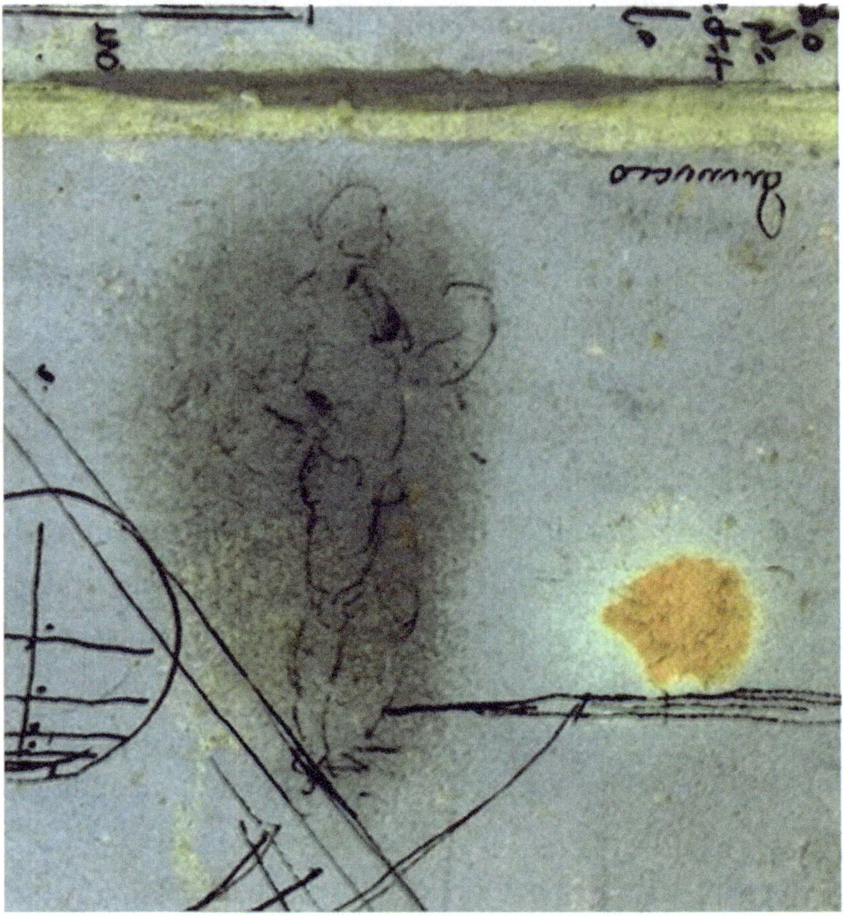

Figure 9-12; A restoration, by the British Library, of a hidden drawing of a naked man, embedded in Leonardo da Vinci's notebook called the *Codex Arundel 263.*

Nor is this naked man the sole example of an embedded image recently discovered in Leonardo's notebooks. In 2012, an Italian journalist, Piero Angela, discovered a drawing—a self-portrait by Leonardo—embedded in the *Codex on the Flight of Birds* (dating from 1490 to 1505.) Angela's initial inspection of the manuscript with a magnifying glass—*i.e.,* without the aid of computer technology—revealed the very faint embedded sketch of a face believed to be that of Leonardo as a young man. No one had ever observed this embedded drawing in the codex before—and written about it. Except for a slight reddish tinge on the paper, the image was virtually invisible. Mr. Angela explained: "After extrapolating the red-chalk portrait with the help of a graphic artist, a portrait of a Renaissance man emerged. Given the similarity, I thought this could well be Leonardo himself." Here, below, in **Figure 9-13**, is the restoration created by Mr. Angela's graphic artist, of the hidden self-portrait by Leonardo, embedded in his *Codex on the Flight of Birds.*

Figure 9-13; A graphic artist's restoration of a hidden self-portrait of Leonardo, embedded in a page of the Codex on the Flight of Birds.

Restored self-portrait of Leonardo; Museo de Milano
Image created by Leonardo in public domain in US.

Giuseppe Arcimboldo

Nor was Leonardo the only major artist to embed self-portraits in his artworks. Among famous artists known for their *trompe l'oeil* paintings was Giuseppe Arcimboldo (1526-1593,) the 16th Century Italian court painter to the Holy Roman Emperor Maximilian II and later Rudolf II in Prague. Arcimboldo was, and still is, renowned for creating imaginative and oft-times humorous portraits made entirely of common objects—such as fruits, animals, flowers and books.

Let's examine a typical example of his *trompe l'oeil* paintings, *The Jurist,* painted in 1566, and now housed in the Swedish National Museum—as displayed below, in **Figure 9-14.**

Figure 9-14; *The Jurist*, an oil-on-canvas painting by Giuseppe Arcimboldo (1526-1591); Court Painter to Emperors Maximilian II and Rudolf II

Swedish National Museum.

There are many outlines of animals and birds embedded in the huge, intricate fur collar that surrounds the jurist's neck and chest. But the most interesting embedded image is surely the one that I found on the upper right-hand side of the fur collar, between the jurist's shoulder and the white ruffle. I have traced Arcimboldo's outlined self-portrait, which is embedded in the hairs of the fur with thin dark lines. These outlines are distinguishable from the fur only under intense magnification. Of particular interest, for our purposes, is the large outline of a capital letter 'A' that I found, located on the front of the artist's cap. Presumably, the 'A' identifies the outlined head as belonging to Arcimboldo.

Here, below, in **Figure 9-15,** are my tracings of Arcimboldo's outlined self-portrait, embedded into the hairs of the fur collar in the oil painting of lawyer Ulrich Zasius, entitled *The Jurist.* The lines of Archimboldo's self-portrait are all dark brown in color, almost black—so they blend into the brown background of the fur collar and can be seen only under intense magnification. I traced these lines with various colors to increase their visibility.

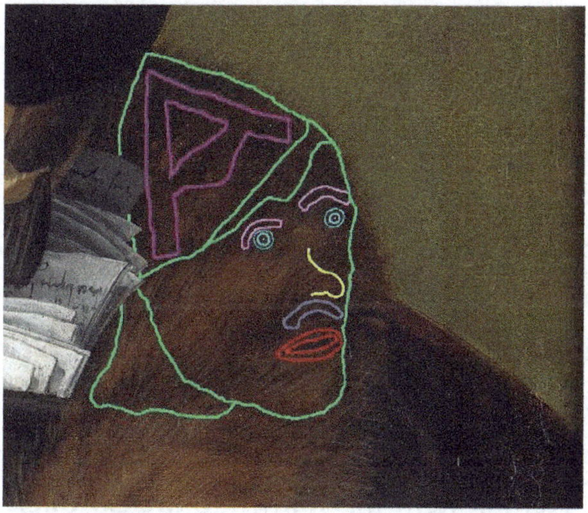

Figure 9-15; Image of a man's face embedded in the fur collar on the leather overcoat worn by jurist Ulrich Zasius. Presumably, the large capital letter 'A' on the man's cap identifies the outlined head as belonging to the artist, Giuseppe Arcimboldo.

The Jurist (an oil-on-canvas painting.) by Giuseppe Arcimboldo (1526-1591,) Court Painter to Emperors Maximilian II and Rudolf image of painting: Public domain in US. Swedish National Museum

"O serpent heart, hid within a flowering face."

William Shakespeare; *Romeo and Juliet* (Act III, Sc. ii)

Chapter 10; The Writing on the Wall

First, The Writing on George's Overcoat.

Thus far, we have learned from the 'Byfleet Murder Drawing' (published by the *Illustrated Police News* on January 28, 1888) two new items of highly valuable information about the murder and mutilation of George Chuter. Neither item was known to the Coroner, or to the Surrey Constabulary in 1888. First, that George's body was posed in the spreadeagle posture by the killers before they departed the scene. And second, that three killers, working in concert, murdered and mutilated George Chuter.

How can we know for sure that these new items of information were indeed true? Were they merely the ravings of an imaginative newspaper sketch artist? Or were they the faithful depictions of what actually transpired in George Chuter's kitchen on the evening of January 12, 1888? We need some credible, corroborative evidence to confirm these extraordinary revelations as fact.

Looking for new avenues of investigation to pursue, I returned to the 'Byfleet Murder Drawing,' this time examining every square inch methodically under extreme magnification. I began by cropping the image of George's spreadeagled, mutilated body, lying on his back, face-up, in a pool of blood, on the kitchen floor—as shown, below, in **Figure 10-1.** Like the deceptive image of the lone killer rushing out the kitchen door that later turned out to depict three killers standing in the kitchen doorway, the image of George's overcoat contains many smudged, faint white and black lines embedded into the dark fabric.

Figure 10-1; **A cropping of the body of George Chuter from the 'Byfleet Murder Drawing,' I could see many dark and light lines and white smudges embedded in the fabric of George's overcoat.**

Drawing published by *Illustrated Police News* on Jan. 28, 1888; sketch artist: unknown; Image: Public domain in US.

Now follows another discovery in the 'Byfleet Murder Drawing' perhaps even more remarkable than my revelation of the images of three men standing in the doorway. Indeed, this discovery is, I believe, so extraordinary, I feel obligated to describe, step-by-step, how I came upon it. While exploring the embedded lines and smudges that I saw on George's overcoat, I noticed embedded in these smudges two perfectly round concentric semi-circles. This struck me as odd, so I decided to trace these semi-circles in scarlet (for contrast.) Here, below, are my tracings, as shown in **Figure 10-2**. I found the ends of the two semi-circles were closed, thus forming a continuous outline of the letter 'C.'

Figure 10-2; My tracing in scarlet of the outline of the letter 'C,' embedded in the fabric of George's overcoat—as depicted by the sketch artist of the 'Byfleet Murder Drawing,'

Original image published by *Illustrated Police News* on Jan. 28,1888. Sketch artist: unknown. Original image: public domain in US.

I was perplexed by what I saw. What was an outline of the letter 'C' doing on George's overcoat in the 'Byfleet Murder Drawing'? Was this 'C' the sketch artist's initial, like the 'A' in Arcimboldo's cap? Was this 'C' the sketch artist's symbol identifying all his work, like a logo? The 'Byfleet Murder Drawing' bore no visible artist's signature. So, initially I conjectured: perhaps this was the sketch artist's hidden ID—like an identifying watermark.

However, once I had traced the outline of the letter 'C' on George's overcoat in **Figure 10-2**, I could see in the lighter smudges, the faint, embedded outlines of another, much larger instance of the letter 'C. This larger outline of the letter 'C' surrounded the smaller outline of the letter 'C' that I had already traced in Figure 2. In other words, the two outlines of the letter 'C' were nested. Here below, in **Figure 10-3**, is my tracing—also in scarlet—of the second, larger instance of the letter 'C,' embedded in the fabric of George's overcoat.

Figure 10-3; My tracing in scarlet of a second, larger outline of the letter 'C,' embedded in the fabric of George's overcoat. This larger outline of the letter 'C' surrounds the smaller

outline of the letter 'C' (shown in Figure 2.)

Original image published by *Illustrated Police News* on Jan. 28, 1888;
sketch artist: unknown; Original image: Public domain in US.

The two nested outlines of the letter 'C' no longer appeared to me to be the sketch artist's hidden ID symbol. The idea that his initials might be 'CC'—while not impossible—seemed to me unlikely. The two instances of the letter 'C' were closely nested—not consecutive, like initials. The lines of the larger 'C' enveloped and overlapped the smaller 'C', making the two letters, when viewed together, almost illegible, even under magnification. When viewed alone, however, each outline of a letter C was quite legible.

I resumed my search for any more letters embedded on the fabric of George's overcoat. To the left of the outlines of the letter 'C,' and partly superimposed upon them, I found embedded in the lighter smudges a dark triangle with straight sides. Thus, I saw a large equilateral triangle on the front of the overcoat, just above George's left hand. I marked the three apexes of this large triangle with small blue dots—as shown, below, in **Figure 10-4.**

Figure 10-4; My markings, with small blue dots, of three apexes of a large equilateral triangle. I found the lines of this triangle embedded in the fabric of George's overcoat, directly above George's left hand.

Original image published by *Illustrated Police News* on Jan. 28,1888;
Sketch artist: unknown. Original image: public domain in US.

Then, I connected the blue dots to draw two straight sides of this large equilateral triangle—but not yet the baseline. Under extreme magnification, I could see that the baseline was somewhat more complex than a simple straight line. Here, below, in **Figure 10-5**, below, are my tracings in blue of two sides of the equilateral triangle, as defined by the three blue dots shown above in **Figure 10-4.**

Figure 10-5; My tracing in blue of two straight sides of the large equilateral triangle that I found faintly embedded on top of George's overcoat. I left the baseline untraced, for now.

Original drawing published by *Illustrated Police News* on Jan. 28, 1888; Sketch artist: unknown; Original image: Public domain in US.

In the center of the large triangle, I saw a small whitish patch—which on closer inspection *(i.e.,* intense magnification) turned out to be surrounded by a small equilateral triangle with straight sides. I traced in blue the three sides of this small equilateral triangle—as shown in Figure 10-6, below.

Figure 10-6; My tracing in blue of a small equilateral triangle located inside the large equilateral triangle.

Like the multiple, nested instances of the letter 'C' displayed in Figures 10-2 & 10-3, I now found multiple instances of the triangles in progressively increasing sizes, superimposed on top of one another. Altogether, I found three matched pairs of equilateral triangles (although the largest triangle was incomplete where it overlapped onto the brightly illuminated floorboards.) To distinguish between the three matched pairs of triangles, I traced them in blue, yellow and green—as shown below, in Figure 10-7.

Figure 10-7; My tracings in blue, yellow and green of three matched pairs of equilateral triangles embedded in the image of George's overcoat.

Original image published by *Illustrated Police News* on Jan. 28,1888.
Sketch artist: unknown. Original image: public domain in US.

Focusing now exclusively on the matched pair of blue triangles, I could see under intense magnification that the baseline of the large blue triangle extended on either side a short distance at 90 degrees—as shown, below, **in Figure 10-8.**

Figure 10-8; My tracing in blue of the baseline of the large blue triangle. On either side, the baseline extends a short distance at 90 degrees.

Original image published by *Illustrated Police News* on Jan. 28,1888; Sketch artist: unknown. Original image: public domain in US. Additional tracing of outlines: © 2023 by Mark Starr – all rights reserved; license: CC 4.0 BY-ND.

Again, on either side, the blue baseline then turned upwards at 90 degrees—as shown below in Figure 10-9.

Figure 10-9; My tracing in blue of the baseline of the large blue triangle. On either side, the baseline now extended upwards a short distance at 90 degrees.

Original image published by *Illustrated Police News* on Jan. 28,1888;
Sketch artist: unknown. Original image: public domain in US.

The space in the center of the blue baseline is filled with a curved line that dips in the middle—as shown below, in Figure 10-10. Thus, we see a rather stylish outline of a capital letter 'A.'

Figure 10-10; My tracing in blue of the outline of a capital letter 'A.'

Original image published by *Illustrated Police News* on Jan. 28,1888;
Sketch artist: unknown. Original image: public domain in US.

This outline of a capital letter 'A" does not exist by itself. Like the nested instances of the letter "C" in **Figures 10-2** and **10-3**, three matched pairs of equilateral triangles are displayed in **Figure 10-7**. They form three nested instances of the capital letter 'A." I selected the instance of the capital letter 'C' that matched in size the blue capital letter 'A' shown in **Figure 10-10.** Thus, I traced these two selected capital letters (the 'A' and the 'C') together—as shown, below, in **Figure 10-11.**

Figure 10-11; My tracing in blue and scarlet of the outlines of the capital letters ‘A’ and ‘C’.

Original drawing published by *Illustrated Police News* on Jan. 28, 1888;
Sketch artist: unknown; Original image: Public domain in US.

To the right of the outline of the capital letter ‘C,’ I found multiple outlines of the capital letter ‘K.’ I selected the ‘K’ that closely matched in size the ‘C.’ I traced the ‘K’ in orange—as shown, below, in **Figure 10-12.**

Figure 10-12; My tracing in orange of the outline of a capital letter 'K.'

Original image published by *Illustrated Police News* on Jan. 28,1888; Sketch artist: unknown. Original image: public domain in US. Additional tracing of outlines: © 2023 by Mark Starr – all rights reserved; license: CC 4.0 BY-ND.

To the right of the outline of the capital letter 'K,' I found multiple outlines of the capital letter 'Y.' I selected the 'Y' that closely matched in size the 'K.' I traced the 'Y' in yellow—as shown, below, in **Figure 10-13.**

Figure 10-13; My tracing in yellow of the outline of the capital letter 'Y.'

To the left of the outline of the capital letter 'A,' I found multiple outlines of the capital letter 'J.' I selected the 'J' that closely matched in size the 'A.' I traced the 'J' in red—as shown, below, in **Figure 10-14.**

Figure 10-14; My tracing of the outline of a capital letter 'J' —thus forming the name JACKY. The five letters are all outlines of capital letters embedded by the sketch artist into the fabric of George's overcoat. I traced the five outlines in different colors to keep the overlapping letters visually distinct.

Original image published by *Illustrated Police News* on Jan. 28,1888;
Sketch artist: unknown. Original image: public domain in US.

Thus, an instance of the name **JACKY** appeared, embedded on George's overcoat. From here on, I will set **JACKY** in boldface—because it is evidence pertaining to the crime. The instance of **JACKY** embedded on George's overcoat is formed by the outlines of five capital letters spread over George Chuter's entire body. The five outlines are set on a baseline whose slope matches the slope of George's body in the sketch. These outlines were carefully drawn; they were not randomly nor haphazardly sketched.

It must be kept in mind that each of these five capital letters is embedded on George's overcoat multiple times, in increasing size, in nested groups. Moreover, the nested groups of capital letters are partially superimposed on top of one another. And, as we will see in a moment, these five letters are not the only characters embedded into the fabric of George's overcoat. Thus, the outlines are entangled and very difficult to discern without the aid of my colored tracings. It appears to me that the sketch artist's use of multiple instances of each letter, nested in groups of three, were a deliberate attempt at obfuscation—to make the various outlines of letters as difficult to observe as possible. Evidently, he did not want the readers of the *Illustrated Police News* to perceive these letters.

N.b., The multiple instances of the name **JACKY** were drawn by the sketch artist exclusively with upper-case letters. Moreover, these upper-case capital letters are exclusively *outlines.* There are no letters drawn as solids, cursives or stick figures.

There are three nested instances of the name **JACKY** embedded on George's overcoat. I have traced only one. The jumble of superimposed lines makes the names virtually illegible to the casual reader.

Who—or What--is JACKY?

Why are there three instances of **JACKY** embedded in the fabric of George's overcoat? Do these three instances correspond to the three killers standing in the kitchen door, as depicted in Figure 11 of Chapter 9? Was the image of George's overcoat intended to signify that each of the three killers depicted standing in the kitchen doorway was named **JACKY?** That seemed to me unlikely. Or was **JACKY** used here as a descriptive noun signifying a member of the cult of fell demons responsible for the murder and mutilation of George Chuter? Hmmmm, I wondered.

Who was **JACKY**? What was the significance of this name to the Byfleet Murder? No one at the Coroner's Inquest was named, or nicknamed, Jacky. Was **JACKY** the nickname of the sketch artist? Was his real name John (English); or Jean (French); or Johann (German); or Iain (Scottish/Gaelic)? Or was **JACKY** the nickname of someone in the sketch artist's family—such as his son, his father or his grandfather? No evidence was visible in the drawing to answer those questions. So, I will continue searching the 'Byfleet Murder Drawing' for additional evidence to clarify these questions.

JACKY & NINA.

The possibility that **JACKY** might be the name of a family member of the sketch artist reminded me of the drawings of American theatrical sketch artist and caricaturist Al Hirschfeld (1903-2003.) For 75 years, Hirschfeld drew sketches of theatrical celebrities in the *New York Times*—mainly on the front page of the drama section of the Sunday edition. Following the birth of his daughter, Nina, he embedded her name, in allcaps, in the lines of his drawings. For more than half a century, it became a regular weekly game for most readers of the *New York Times*—including me—to hunt for the hidden instances of NINA in Hirschfeld's drawing in the *Times'* Sunday edition.

The similarity of the embedded instance of **JACKY** in the 'Byfleet Murder Drawing' published in the *Illustrated Police News* on January 28, 1888, and Hirschfeld's countless embedded instances of NINA in his drawings published in the *New York Times* from 1945 to 2003, struck me as uncanny. Both embedded names—**JACKY** and NINA—were deliberately made difficult for readers to find by the respective sketch artists. NINA was Hirschfeld's daughter. Was **JACKY** also a member of the family of the *Illustrated Police News'* sketch artist? There's no evidence—yet—on that score.

Three Question Marks—The Unanswered Questions.

Another examination of the image of George's body lying on the floor of his kitchen revealed to me that I was not yet quite finished hunting for embedded characters on top of George's overcoat. I now found a large question mark embedded on top of the center of George's overcoat—which I traced in white, in Figure 10-15, below. Thus, the Sketch Artist had posed an unanswered question to his unknown viewer: who murdered and mutilated George Chuter? This outline of a question mark had an unusual dot at the bottom. Instead of a simple circle, it consisted of two concentric circles, like a donut.

Figure 10-15; My tracing in white of a large question mark, embedded in the fabric of George's overcoat, located in the center of George's body, which is spreadeagled on the floor of the kitchen.

Original image published by *Illustrated Police News* on Jan. 28,1888; Sketch artist: unknown. Original image: public domain in US.

While tracing the question mark shown above in Figure 15, I could plainly see that there were two more question marks embedded on George's overcoat—one on either side of the white question mark. I traced them in blue and in red. Here, below, in Figure 10-16, are my tracings of the three **question marks,** superimposed on top of George's entire body.

Figure 10-16; My tracings in white, blue and red, of three embedded question marks, superimposed by the sketch artist on top of the image of George Chuter's body. Note the idiosyncratic dots at the bottom of the question marks, each comprised of two concentric circles.

Did these three instances of **question marks** also refer to the three killers depicted as standing in the kitchen doorway? The killers' true identities were unknown. Was that, in fact, the obscure meaning signified by the three

question marks embedded in the fabric of George's overcoat? All three of these **question marks** were drawn in a peculiar way. The dot at the bottom of each **question mark** was formed by two concentric circles—as shown, above, in **Figure 10-16**. So, the dots under all three question marks were consistent. They were all shaped like donuts.

If these three **question marks** did indeed refer to the unknown identities of the three killers, then the progressively increasing size of these characters apparently indicated their relative status on the team of killers. The very large, white **question mark** in the middle apparently referred to the killer-in-chief—the man who undoubtedly had delivered the *coup de grâce* to George's throat with the carving knife, *i.e.*, the man whom we already know as ANXIOUS.

Multiple Outlines on the Wall of the Capital Letter 'P.'

On the wall, in between the large kitchen entrance and the small lavatory door, I came upon some lines embedded in the lighter smudges that looked to me like the outlines of a large capital letter 'P' (shown in **Figure 17A**, below.) In **Figure 17B,** I traced in red the small capital D-shaped space in the center of the outlined capital letter 'P.'

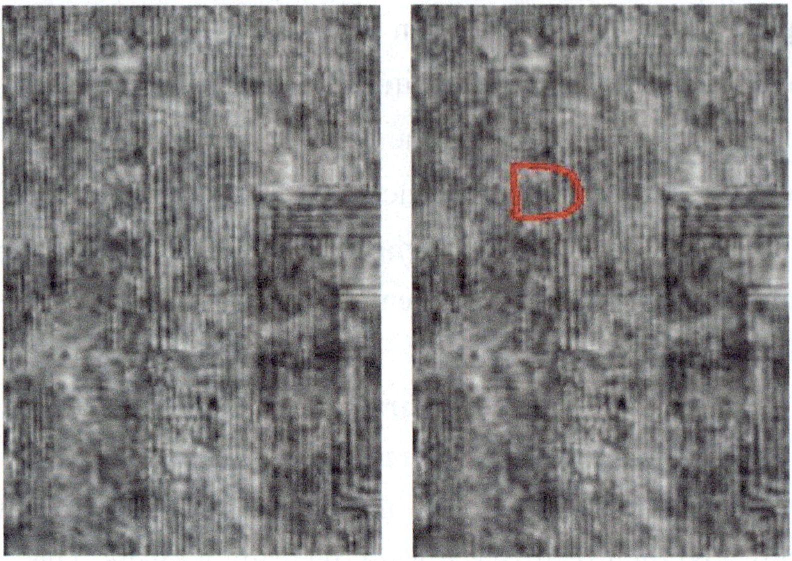

Figures 10-17A & 10-17B
The beginning of an embedded outline of a capital letter 'P.'

Then, in Figure 17C, below, I traced in red the remainder of the capital letter 'P.'

Figure 10-17C.
An embedded outline of a capital letter 'P.'

However, I noticed nearby there were additional multiple instances of the capital letter 'P.' And these multiple instances of the outline of a capital letter 'P' were all nested. Surrounding my red tracing of the capital letter 'P' in **Figure 17C**, I found a second, larger instance of the capital letter 'P'—which I traced in yellow (in **Figure 17D,** below.)

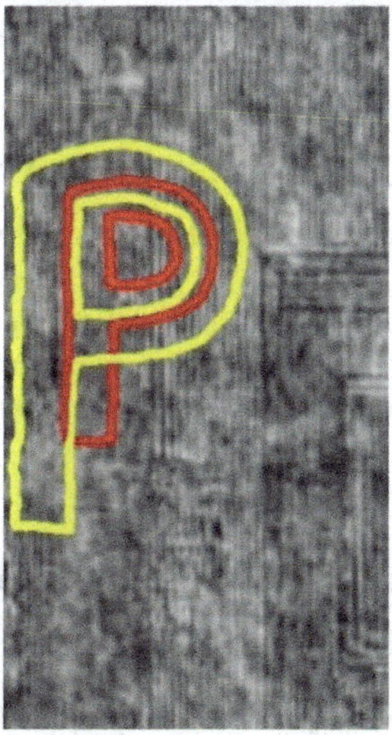

Figure 10-17D

Embedded outlines of two nested capital letters 'P.'

And surrounding the yellow instance of the capital letter 'P,' I found a third, huge instance of the capital letter 'P'—which I traced in blue (as shown, below, in **Figure 10-17E.**)

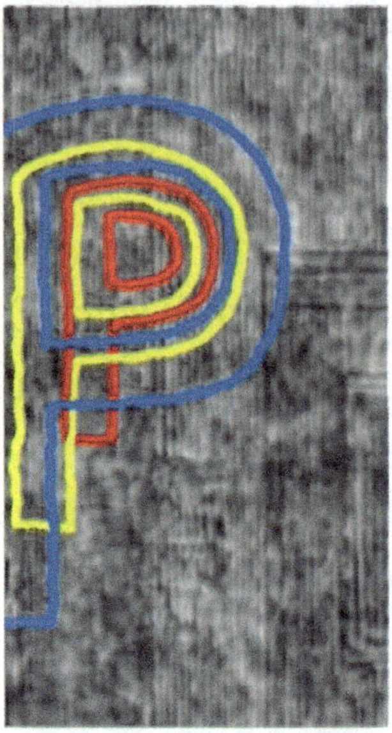

Figure 10-17E.
My tracings of three nested outlines of the capital letter 'P,' in red, yellow, and blue.

Original image published by *Illustrated Police News* on Jan. 28, 1888;
Sketch artist: unknown. Original image: public domain in US.

So, here once again, I had found three instances of the same outline of a capital letter, all nested together. From these three nested instances of the capital letter 'P,' as shown above in **Figure 17E,** I selected the small tracing in red—as shown below, in **Figure 10-18.**

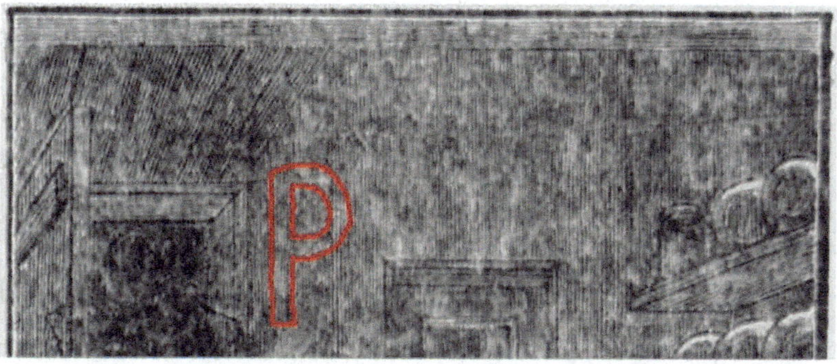

Figure 10-18; My tracing in red of the outline of a capital letter 'P'—located to the right of the open kitchen door.

More Writing on the Wall.

To the right of this capital letter 'P,' I found another instance of a capital letter 'P'—an exact duplicate of the first. I also traced this duplicate letter 'P' in red—as shown, below, in **Figure 10-19.**

Figure 10-19; My tracing in red of the outline of a duplicate capital letter 'P'—located

to the right of the first capital letter 'P.'

Next, I found an outlined capital letter to the right of the double 'P,'', an 'E', partly covered the framed mirror on the wall. Here, below, is my tracing of the outline of the capital letter 'E'—as shown, below, in **Figure 10-20.**

Figure 10-20; My tracing in red of the outline of the capital letter 'E'—located to the right of the double 'P.'

To the right of the outline of the capital letter 'E,' I found an outline of a capital letter 'R.' The 'R' was shaped and sized exactly like the 'P,' with the addition of the diagonal leg. Here, below, in **Figure 10-21,** is the outline of the capital letter 'R.'

Figure 10-21; My tracing in red of the outline of a capital letter 'R'—located to the right of the 'E.'

To the right of the capital letter 'R.' I found a surprise: a **question mark.** Because this character is a punctuation mark and not a letter, I colored it white—as shown, below, in **Figure 10-22.**

Figure 10-22; My tracing in white of the outline of a question mark—located to the right of the 'R' (displayed in Figure 21.)

To the left of the double capital letters 'P,' I found the outline of a capital letter 'I'—as shown, below, in **Figure 10-23.**

Figure 10-23; My tracing in red of the outline of a capital letter 'I'—located to the left of the double 'P.'

To the left of the capital letter 'I," I found the outline of a capital letter 'R', identical in shape to the capital letter 'R' that preceded the **question mark**—as shown, below, in **Figure 10-24.**

Figure 10-24; My tracing in red of the outline of a capital letter 'R'—located to the left of the capital letter 'I.'

Original image published by *Illustrated Police News* on Jan. 28,1888;
Sketch artist: unknown. Original image: public domain in US.

This Instance of the Word 'RIPPER' Potentially Affects Everything in My Murder Investigation, Thus Far.

In the 'Byfleet Murder Drawing,' an instance of the word **RIPPER** appeared on the kitchen wall**,** followed by a **question mark.** Note the uniformity in size and the perfect justification of the six letters. Evidently, these outlines were drawn by the sketch artist with great care. And they were concealed by embedding them in the complex texture of the kitchen wall. I found these lines only by examining the wall under intense magnification, using my computer and an ultra-high-resolution monitor. Undoubtedly, these embedded outlines of capital letters were not intended by the sketch artist to be seen by casual readers of the *Illustrated Police News.* On the front page of the newspaper, they were reduced to a tiny illustration that appeared in the bottom right-hand corner. Nor did the sketch artist intend for **JACKY** and **RIPPER** to be seen by the forensically-challenged Surrey Constabulary. The *Illustrated Police News* had a sensational and unsavory reputation. Yet, here they are, **JACKY** and **RIPPER**, printed together in that newspaper on September 28, 1888—for the first time in known history in 'The Byfleet Murder Drawing.'.

The Shock of Recognition: Instances of JACKY and 'RIPPER,' Appearing Together for the First Time In Recorded History. These Two Words are Embedded in the 'Byfleet Murder Drawing,' as Published in January 1888.

My discovery of instances of **JACKY** and **RIPPER?** embedded in the 'Byfleet Murder Drawing'—as published in the *Illustrated Police News* on January 28, 1888—was, for me, akin to being struck by a bolt of lightning. I wondered: what connection could there possibly be between the Byfleet Murder on January 12, 1888, and the Whitechapel Murder Series, which commenced seven months later, during the historic Autumn of Terror in London? These world-famous crimes were attributed by popular culture—but not by Assistant Chief Constable (CID) Melville Macnaghten of Scotland Yard, London—to a homicidal fiend self-named Jack the Ripper. Sir Melville always referred to the perpetrator as the Whitechapel Murderer. He never recognized a connection between the Whitechapel Murderer and the letter writer who signed his missives: Jack the Ripper. Macnaghten's *Memorandum*—*i.e.,* his notes on the Whitechapel Murders written in 1894—are still used today by many writers to define the parameters of the Whitechapel Murders. Macnaghten wrote:

> **"Now the Whitechapel murderer had 5 victims -- & 5 victims only..."**

Macnaghten five canonical victims did not include George Chuter. According to the Macnaghten *Memorandum,* the first murder/mutilation in this series was committed on:

> **"(1) 31st August, '88. Mary Ann Nichols—at Buck's Row— who was found with her throat cut-- & with (slight) stomach mutilation."**

Thus, the instances of **JACKY** and **RIPPER?**, embedded in the 'Byfleet Murder Drawing,' initially appear to be an anachronism, a paradox in time, a contradiction of virtually all that is presently known about the Whitechapel Murders and Jack the Ripper. Was it merely an improbable coincidence?

Jack the Ripper's Date of Birth.

On January 28, 1888 (the date the 'Byfleet Murder Drawing' was published in the *Illustrated Police News,)* the name "Jack the Ripper" had not yet been written down in any known letter or document published in any newspaper. The name "Jack the Ripper" was created eight months later in September 1888—possibly as the signature of the 'Dear Boss' Letter of Sept. 25. 1888; or possibly as the signature in the 'I am not a Yid' Letter of Sept. 17, 1888.

According to Casebook.org—the gargantuan website devoted to the Whitechapel Murders—Jack the Ripper made his spectacular public debut in the 'Dear Boss' Letter, dated Sept. 25, 1888, and signed "Jack the Ripper." This letter was received on Sept. 27 by the Central News Agency. Thus, it followed by seventeen days the murder and mutilation of Annie Chapman in London on Sept. 8, 1888. The 'Dear Boss' Letter was first published photographically in a handbill by Metropolitan Police on October 1. Later that same day, the identical facsimile was published by many London newspapers—including by the London *Daily News* in its late afternoon edition (possibly the earliest newspaper publication.)

Casebook.org website states:

> **Whether or not the [Dear Boss] letter is a hoax, it is the first written reference which uses the name "Jack the Ripper" in reference to the Whitechapel murderer.**

I should note now: I never found an instance of "Jack the Ripper" on the 'Byfleet Murder Drawing'—or anywhere else in Byfleet. I found only instances of **JACKY** and **RIPPER,** together with **question marks.** We don't know yet what connection there may be—if any—between "Jack the Ripper" and **JACKY, RIPPER,** & the symbolic **question marks.** I will also point out: the two names **JACKY** and **RIPPER** are not quite the same as "Jack the Ripper." So, possibly, the true significance of these monikers—**JACKY** and **RIPPER** on the one hand, and "Jack the Ripper" on the other—is not quite the same. There may be some explanation for the appearance of **JACKY** and **RIPPER** in the 'Byfleet Murder Drawing,' an explanation that I have not yet thought of. I do not see *yet* any evidence on the 'Byfleet Murder Drawing' that reveals the true significance of **JACKY** and **RIPPER**—and those strange **question marks.** Consequently, we must continue our search for yet more evidence in this regard.

Is the Claim on Casebook.org Accurate? Was the 'Dear Boss' Letter, Written on Sept. 25, 1888, in fact, the First Written Reference to "Jack the Ripper"?

There has long been general agreement among the majority of authors on the Whitechapel Murders that the claim stated on Casebook.org about the 'Dear Boss' Letter is indeed accurate. However, in relatively recent years, a new and earlier letter signed Jack the Ripper has surfaced.

This still controversial letter is the 'I am not a Yid' Letter of September 17, 1888—which was accidentally found in 1988, in an unopened, still sealed report envelope at the British Public Record Office by researcher Peter McCelland. This letter was subsequently published in a book by Paul Feldman. Immediately, this letter's authenticity was challenged by several noted authors.

The authenticity of the 'I am not a Yid' Letter is, even now, hotly debated. Nevertheless, I will take this opportunity to state my own opinion on the matter (which I have studied extensively.) In my opinion, I have absolutely no doubt the 'I am not a Yid' Letter was written by the same man who wrote and sent the 'Dear Boss' Letter. Also, in my opinion, there is no credible, documented evidence to establish that the 'I am not a Yid' Letter was a hoax of any kind—just as I also believe that the "Dear Boss" letter was not a hoax of any kind. In a later volume of the series *A Trail of Blood,* I will back up these assertions with new documented evidence. However, the first two volumes of *A Trail of Blood* are focused solely on the Byfleet murder and mutilation, not the Whitechapel Murders.

Both the 'Dear Boss' Letter and the 'I am Not a Yid' Letter' Were Written Seven Months After the 'Byfleet Murder Drawing' Was Published in the *Illustrated Police News.*

For the main purpose at hand—*i.e.*, evaluating the significance of my tracings of **JACKY** and **RIPPER?** in the 'Byfleet Murder Drawing—I will also state now that, in my opinion, the "I am not a Yid" Letter, signed Jack the Ripper, is irrelevant to the murder and mutilation of George Chuter. The 'Byfleet Murder Drawing' was published more than seven months before both the 'Dear Boss' Letter or the 'I am not a Yid' Letter were written, dated, sent and received. Thus, it is an impossibility that the 'Byfleet Murder Drawing,' published on Jan. 28, 1888, was a hoax, or a forgery, or a copycat illustration—based on knowledge of either of these two letters that were signed "Jack the Ripper" and dated in September 1888.

An original copy of the January 28, 1888 issue of the *Illustrated Police News*—in which the 'Byfleet Murder Drawing' was published—is stored inviolate in the newspaper collection at the National Archives at Kew. Thus, an original publication of the 'Byfleet Murder Drawing' survives today and is verifiable. For those who are skeptical of the embedded images that I have revealed thus far in the 'Byfleet Murder Drawing,' there are still more embedded images yet to come. Many more.

At this juncture in My Investigation, Is There Any Known Physical Evidence that Links the Byfleet Murder to the Whitechapel Murders?

Initially, it would appear there is not sufficient physical evidence to establish a connection between the Byfleet

Murder and the Whitechapel Murders. The similarity of JACKY and RIPPER to Jack the Ripper is still inexplicable.

i. Macnaghten's five Whitechapel canonical victims were all female. George Chuter was male. Two additional possible victims of the Whitechapel Murderer—Martha Tabram and Emma Smith—were also female.
ii. All of Macnaghten's victims resided in Whitechapel, London. George resided in Byfleet, Surrey—25 miles distance from Whitechapel, London.
iii. Macnaghten's five Whitechapel canonical victims were all prostitutes. George Chuter was not a male prostitute. He was a retired carpenter and an innkeeper—happily married for 43 years to Lucy, with whom he had four children. Tabram and Smith were also prostitutes.
iv. Four of Macnaghten's victims were murdered and mutilated by the Whitechapel fiend on the street; and one Whitechapel victim, Mary Kelly, was murdered and mutilated in her lodgings, on her bed. George Chuter was murdered and mutilated in his kitchen—ambushed (according to the sketch artist of the 'Byfleet Murder Drawing') by three killers lying-in-wait, hidden behind George's kitchen door. Thus, the MO in Byfleet was different.

However, according to Professor Bonn, the MO is not the deciding factor that links serial murders together. It is the signature of the killer or killers that establishes relevant links in serial crimes. In a series of crimes, the MO is not necessarily always the same. But—according to Dr. Bonn, Robert Ressler, John Douglas and many other criminologists, the signature is always the same in a series of murders, and it is present in some form in every murder committed by a serial killer. That raises the question: were outlined instances of **JACKY, RIPPER** and **question marks** the embedded signatures of these three killers?

Did Inspector Macnaghten of Scotland Yard Get It Wrong in His 1894 Memorandum about "Jack the Ripper"?

Perhaps Macnaghten got it wrong about "Jack the Ripper". Were there five victims and only five victims? Perhaps he based his list of canonical victims solely on the MO in each of these murders, and not on a signature that possibly unites them to other unsolved crimes. Perhaps, he missed the bigger picture. Did Scotland Yard's CID ignore evidence that links together more than five murders—or even more than seven—with a common signature?

Today, criminologists use the term 'Linkage Blindness' to describe the failure of law enforcement officials to perceive the symbolic signatures that link serial murders together. Did Magnaghten suffer from from 'linkage blindness.' That is a subject I will explore in Volume 3 of *A Trail of Blood.*

The variations in the MO in all these crimes might be accountable if "Jack the Ripper"—who was never directly observed by any eyewitness while perpetrating a murder—had actually been three killers working in concert under a common symbolic moniker. As Prof. Bonn has explained, the MO and the signature of a murder are two different manifestations of crime scene evidence. The MO may vary from murder to murder; but the signature is consistent in every case. The MO is comparatively easy to deduce from crime scene evidence. The symbolic signature, however, is much more difficult to discern. It may require a knowledge of semiotics—the study of symbols.

Perhaps, each of three hypothetical killers in Whitechapel had his own idiosyncrasies and preferences when it came to killing methods. But—if the Whitechapel Murderer was in fact more-than-one killer working in concert—is it possible all of the Whitechapel murders had a common signature. And if so, what was this signature, and how was it expressed with documented crime scene evidence?

For New Evidence about the Whitechapel Murders, Please Wait for the Publication of Volume 3 of *A Trail of Blood.*

The Whitechapel Murders are a subject so vast, any credible investigation about "Jack the Ripper" will require a book of its own—*i.e.*, a very large book. The evidence already known about the Whitechapel Murders is so extensive, many websites—and countless books—are completely devoted to their investigations. It will take a lengthy book to confront all the issues raised by many still unsolved murders—including the Byfleet Murder & Mutilation.

As the title of this initial volume in the series *A Trail of Blood* indicates, Volume 1 is focused solely on THE BYFLEET MURDER & MUTILATION. Volume 2 will also be focused on the murder and mutilation of George Chuter, but from the perspective of a 21st Century forensic investigation. In addition to revealing yet more 'new' evidence about the crime, Volume 2 will compare what is known about the Byfleet Murder and Mutilation with what is known today about ritualistic sacrificial murders.

In Volume 2, I will also display a large number of recent photographs that I commissioned in Byfleet, taken by a local professional photographer. These photographs will reveal new, authentic crime scene evidence about the murder and mutilation of George Chuter—evidence that still survives today. All the new evidence that I have discovered was unknown to the Surrey Constabulary and to Coroner Roumieu in 1888. All of it corroborates the 'new' evidence that I have already revealed in Volume 1: in the 'Byfleet Murder Drawing,' in the Classified Advertisement published in the London *Standard*, and in the Letter from ANXIOUS published in the *West Surrey Times.*

From the 'new' evidence that I will reveal in Volume 2, I will identify at least one of three killer who murdered and mutilated George Chuter. In the famous words of Paul Masson: "No wine before its time."

Before now, no book has ever been written about the Byfleet Murder. This mysterious, still-unsolved crime has never been re-investigated since 1888—not by the Surrey Constabulary, not by the Met in London, not by the press, and not by any previous author. It is my intention to give this murder and mutilation the undivided attention that it deserves in Volumes 1 & 2. I will not be distracted by any other contemporaneous unsolved murders. Let the chips of incriminatory evidence fall where they may without any recourse to any past speculative theories.

In Volume 3 of *A Trail of Blood,* I will explore any potential links between the Byfleet Murder and Mutilation and the Whitechapel Murders. I can assure my readers now that I already have new evidence about these notorious crimes. The last word about Jack the Ripper has not yet been written.

An Encrypted Confession to Document "A Perfect Crime."

The 'Byfleet Murder Drawing' is an encrypted confession left to us by the anonymous sketch artist of the *Illustrated Police News.* Possibly he was not a regular illustrator of the newspaper—but rather a per image contributor—similar to the independent *paparazzi* who sell photographs to magazines today. It is already clear to me: his creation, the 'Byfleet Murder Drawing,' contains Special Knowledge about the murder and mutilation of George Chuter. In this case, Special Knowledge indicates knowledge about the crime that could only have been known, in January 1888, by someone who had directly participated in the murder and mutilation of George Chuter. The sketch artist was—undoubtedly—one of the three killers depicted in the 'Byfleet Murder Drawing.' He was also ANXIOUS—who, on Feb. 27, 1888, sent the letter to the *West Surrey Times.* And he was the author of the phony classified advertisement placed in the London *Standard* on Jan. 20, 1888. Thus, the sketch artist is now my prime suspect. From now on, I will capitalize his moniker as the Sketch Artist. At this point in my investigation, all we definitely know about him is that he was a highly accomplished draftsman.

Yet More Instances of JACKY and RIPPER are embedded in the 'Byfleet Murder Drawing.'

I will now begin to search the 'Byfleet Murder Drawing' in earnest for yet more instances of **JACKY** and **RIPPER** and the symbolic **question marks.** Who knows whatever else I might find? On the kitchen wall, above the instance of **RIPPER?** I noticed a large, empty space on the wall. So, once again, with my high-resolution monitor and my imaging-painting software, I dived down amongst the pixels. Immediately, it became apparent to me, there were many more outlines of capital letters embedded in that same empty space on the kitchen wall. All together, these outlines of capital letters spelled **?JACKY.** In this instance, the symbolic **question mark** preceded the name **JACKY**—as displayed, below, in Figure 25.

Figure 10-25; **My tracing in multi-colors of the outlines of capital letters that spell ?JACKY—located at the top of the kitchen wall, above the two doors.**

In Figure 10-25, above, I have given the outline of each letter a different color. There is some overlapping of letters. I wanted to keep each letter distinct. This is a procedure that I will usually follow to keep letters as easily legible as possible. I have also colored the **question mark** in white—because it is a punctuation mark, not a letter. Moreover, a

question mark appears to me to have its own symbolic significance—as suggested by the three question marks on George's overcoat.

Each outline of a character displayed in Figure 25 is identical in shape to the characters displayed earlier in Figures 15 & 17. *N.b.*, in both Figures 10-17 and Figure 10-26, the idiosyncratic double dot consisting of two concentric circles at the bottom of the **question marks.** Note also the stylish dip on the bottom of the crossbar in the capital letter 'A.' Details like these make instances of **JACKY** and **RIPPER** the forensic equivalent of identifiable handwritten signatures in a letter.

A Logo of Authenticity.

The Sketch Artist's unique way of shaping the outlines of each character in **JACKY, RIPPER** and the **question mark** serves, in my opinion, like a unique watermark on a document. Even more accurately, these instances of **?JACKY** and **RIPPER?** serve as the Sketch Artist's logo. He has stamped his brand on the 'Murder at Byfleet' drawing. He has established his ownership and the drawing's authenticity. If we find yet more instances of **?JACKY** and **RIPPER?** outlined in allcaps of exactly the same shapes as those I have already displayed, we will know who made them.

Two Vertical Instances of RIPPER?.

Along the left edge of the 'Byfleet Murder Drawing' I found a small vertical instance of **RIPPER?**—as displayed, below, in **Figure 10-26.**

Figure 10-26; My tracing in multi-colors of a small vertical instance of RIPPER?.

Original image published by *Illustrated Police News* on Jan. 28,1888;
Sketch artist: unknown. Original image: public domain in US.

Superimposed on top of this small vertical instance of **RIPPER?** along the left edge of the 'Byfleet Murder Drawing,', I found a much larger vertical instance of **RIPPER?**—which I traced in red with a white question mark—as shown, below, in **Figure 10-27.**

Figure 10-27; My tracing in red of a much larger instance of RIPPER, with a white question mark.

It is superimposed on top of a small instance of RIPPER? displayed above, in Figure 26.

Original image published by *Illustrated Police News* on Jan. 28,1888;
Sketch artist: unknown. Original image: public domain in US.

**"In Nature's infinite book of secrecy,
a little I can read."**

William Shakespeare; *Antony and Cleopatra* (Act 1; Sc. II)

Chapter 11; O, My God!

The Man-in-Red Carries Two Cases Strapped to His Left Shoulder.

In my tracing of the three killers standing in the kitchen doorway, displayed earlier in Figure 10 of Chapter 9, we saw the Man-in-Red carrying two large box-like cases. They are strapped to his left shoulder. What was contained in these two cases? Of course, we cannot see inside these two cases to view their contents. The Sketch Artist placed a large **question mark** on the front of each case—as if he were teasing us about the contents contained inside the two cases. "Guess what's inside," these **question marks** appear to ask the viewer. Whatever might have been inside these two cases in reality, the contents must have been very important and highly relevant to the Byfleet Murder. Why else display the two cases and mark them with **question marks**? Let's see if I can form a reasonable speculation about the contents of the cases, based on the crime scene evidence thus far revealed in the 'Byfleet Murder Drawing.'

Here, below, in Figure 11-1, are my tracings of the three killers in the kitchen doorway, as they appeared in Figure 10 of Chapter 9. They include the Man-in-Red with two cases strapped to his left shoulder. He holds a bottle in his left hand—which I traced in white.

Figure 11-1 (the same image displayed as Figure 10 in Chapter 9); My tracing of the Man-in-Red carrying two cases, traced in orange. The two cases are strapped to his left shoulder.

Original image published by *Illustrated Police News* on Jan. 28,1888;
Sketch artist: unknown. Original image: public domain in US.

In Figures 2 through 27 of Chapter 10, I examined documentary evidence embedded in the 'Byfleet Murder Drawing' alleging that the three killers painted multiple instances of **JACKY, RIPPER** and symbolic **question marks** on George's overcoat, and on the kitchen walls, floor and rug. In order to have painted all these instances of **JACKY**, **RIPPER** and the **question marks** in George's kitchen on the evening of Jan. 12, two items would have been required: *paint* and *paintbrushes.* Indeed, they would have been indispensable.

Thus, according to the 'Byfleet Murder Drawing,' the killers must have brought with them a large supply of paint and paint brushes when they gained entrance into George's kitchen on the evening of January 12, 1888. We have already seen evidence that the killers knew in advance that the Chuters' poker and carving knife that the killers used to murder and mutilate George were readily available inside the residence. Apparently, the killers also knew in advance that George did not have any paint and paintbrushes on hand in his residence. Thus, the killers must have brought with them a supply of paint and paintbrushes to use on the walls and floor, and on George's overcoat.

We already know that the killers had available more than two hours' time alone in the kitchen after they had murdered and mutilated George. So, they had plenty of free time available to them to paint in the kitchen all the images I found embedded in the 'Byfleet Murder Drawing.'

Undoubtedly, the Sketch Artist of the 'Byfleet Murder Drawing' was depicted as the Man-in-Red with the carrying cases. Before going to George's cottage on the evening of Jan. 12, 1888, he must have prepared large quantities of paint of a suitable color and dilution. The Man-in-Red must have brought several containers of paint with him—which he carried into George's residence in the larger of the two cases depicted as strapped to his left shoulder. The Man-in-Red must have prepared earlier several cans of thinly diluted paint of a light greyish or brown color that would not show up much when applied to the walls and the wooden plank floor.

Evidently, it was the killers' planned intention to embed instances of **JACKY**, **RIPPER** and **question marks** on George's overcoat, and on the walls, rug and floor of George's kitchen. Why? This was their *raison d'être.* With these two fetish words and the symbolic question marks, the killers had marked the crime scene as a sacred space owned by their secret religious cult.

However, the killers did not want to make these painted fetishes readily visible to the Surrey Constabulary, or to readers of the *Illustrated Police News.* So, they disguised these fetishes as embedded, triple, nested images that were difficult to discern.

Nevertheless, these embedded characters must have been intended by the Man-in-Red to be viewed by someone. Or by something. And who might that someone or something have been? At this juncture in my investigation, I was still searching for evidence that would reveal for whom these embedded images were created on the walls of George's kitchen, and later embedded in the 'Byfleet Murder Drawing. I was still searching for whom the images painted inside George's kitchen were intended to be seen.

The killers must have brought with them several cans of paint and a sufficient quantity of paintbrushes when they entered George's kitchen as he was drinking a beer at the King's Head. Evidently, the Man-in-Red transported these art supplies in the two carrying cases strapped to his left shoulder. And the killers must have carried away these empty paint cans and the still-wet paintbrushes wrapped in rags in the two carrying cases when they departed the crime scene for a destination unknown. No empty cans of paint or wet paintbrushes were found on the premises by the Surrey Constabulary. So, the killers must have taken their used art supplies with them when they departed.

It is now apparent to me that the two carrying cases slung over the shoulder of the Man-in-Red, as depicted in the 'Byfleet Murder Drawing,' must have contained both a supply of paint brushes and also several cans of paint. Likely, the smaller, rectangular case on top contained the paint brushes. And the larger case, below, then contained empty cans of paint. The cans were then empty because the 'Byfleet Murder Drawing' shows the crime scene after George was murdered and mutilated, when the killers were departing.

Who Was the Killers' Intended Viewer of these Embedded Images?

Whether drawn in the 'Byfleet Murder Drawing' or painted on the interior of George's kitchen, these embedded instances of **JACKY, RIPPER** and the symbolic **question marks** were not intended to be seen by anyone. That is, anyone human—such as the readers of the *Illustrated Police News* or officers of the Surrey Constabulary. They were purposely made as difficult to discern as possible. So, whom did the killers intend to see their embedded images? These images could only have been viewed in George's kitchen by someone, or something, with supernatural powers. Thus, the killers' intended viewer was omniscient and omnipotent. The killers believed their intended viewer possessed supernatural powers that enabled him to see these embedded images that were artfully disguised and hidden in George's kitchen. The killers' intended viewer could only have been a supernatural being—perhaps even a deity.

The Eyes Have it.

Let's continue now our examination of the 'Byfleet Murder Drawing' to see if there are any more embedded clues regarding exactly whom the Sketch Artist was addressing with these fetish images. As noted earlier, when I first saw the 'Byfleet Murder Drawing,' the room looked to me rather mysterious—as if it was filled with wispy clouds of grey mist. The whitish-grey smudges on the dark areas create the impression of strange, translucent shapes floating about the kitchen. Also, I had an uncomfortable feeling that someone, or something, was staring directly at me.

Another exhaustive examination of the 'Byfleet Murder Drawing' under intense magnification revealed to me a pair of large eyes staring intently at the viewer. Each eye consisted of two concentric circles, with a solid dot in the center. I traced these eyes in dark blue—as shown, below, in Figure 11-2.

Figure 11-2; My tracing in dark blue of a pair of eyes embedded on the kitchen wall. Each eye consists of two concentric circles, with a solid dot at the center. The eyes stare directly at the viewer.

As I traced in blue the pair of eyes displayed in Figure 2, I could see there were many additional pairs of eyes embedded on the kitchen wall. Indeed, I found a total of five pairs of eyes embedded on the kitchen wall—but there may be even more than five that I did not find. These five pairs of eyes were neatly arranged by size. From bottom to top, the eyes increased in size, and the space between each pair grew larger—as shown, below, in **Figure 11-3.**

Figure 11-3; My tracings in multi-colors of five pairs of eyes. The pairs are neatly arranged in increasing

size, from bottom to top.

Original image published by *Illustrated Police News* on Jan. 28,1888;
Sketch artist: unknown. Original image: public domain in US.

Each pair of eyes is surrounded by an outline of a head. And each facial outline contains additional embedded facial features that match the outlined face in size. I selected the pair of dark blue eyes, displayed alone in Figure 11-2. Surrounding this pair of dark blue eyes, I traced the embedded outlines of a large face in which the ears were on the same level as the eyes. I traced the outline of the large face in green. Under intense magnification, I also traced in red the most prominent facial feature: the outlines of a gigantic mouth—which consists of two huge, concentric circles. Above the outlines of the mouth, I found a large outline of a **question mark** with a dot consisting of two concentric circles. A **question mark**—which I traced in white—took the place of a nose.

Here, below, in **Figure 11-4,** is my tracing of the great, semi-transparent face that fills the interior of George's kitchen in the 'Byfleet Murder Drawing.' Evidently, it, too, was drawn with great care—even reverence.

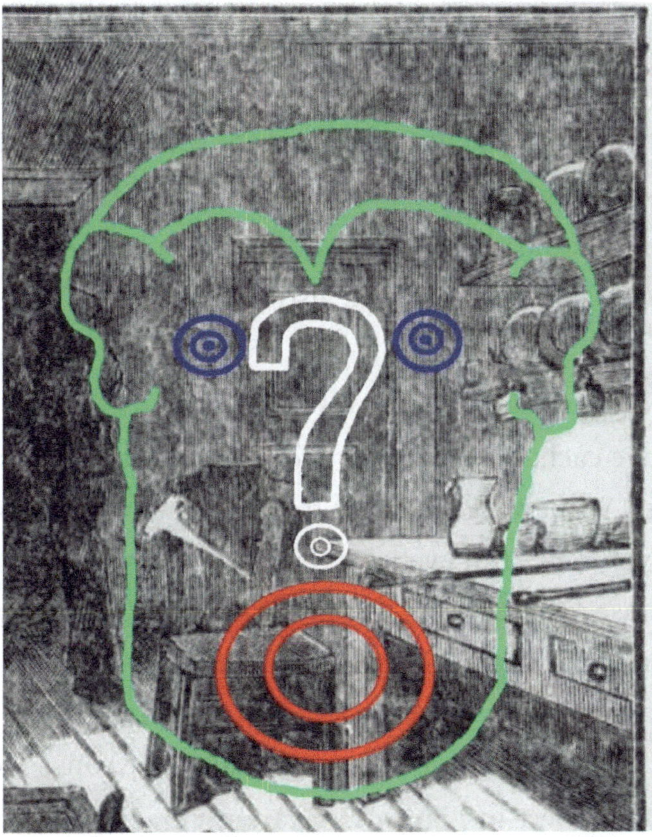

Figure 11-4; My tracing in green of the outline of a huge face, with two large ears protruding on either side. In addition to my tracings of the dark blue eyes, this enormous face contains a gigantic mouth made from two large concentric circles—which I traced in red. Above the mouth, I found the outline of a question mark, in place of a nose. I traced this question mark in white. This image of a supernatural being almost fills George's kitchen, but here it is still incomplete.

Original image published by *Illustrated Police News* on Jan. 28,1888; Sketch artist: unknown. Original image: public domain in US.

The image of the floating face—as shown above, in **Figure 11-4**—is still incomplete. While tracing these facial features, I could still see many more outlines embedded within the facial outline, and also some above it.

Chevrons, not Eyebrows

Above each dark blue eye, I found the outline of an inverted V-shaped object. At first, I thought these objects were eyebrows. But eyebrows are curved. Eyebrows made little sense as symbols in this face full of occult symbols. These angular shapes—bent at right angles—also made little sense to me as eyebrows. Then, I realized these inverted V-shaped objects were actually chevrons. Here, below, as shown in **Figure 11-5,** are my tracings in orange of the two chevrons.

Figure 11-5; My tracings in orange of two inverted V-shaped chevrons located above the dark blue eyes. These chevrons take the place of eyebrows.

A chevron is a symbolic insignia used in the military—and also in police forces—to designate an officer's rank. Of course, in the military and in police forces, rank means status and power. Here, below, in Figure 11-6, is a standard military chevron patch, usually sewn on the upper arm of an officer's uniform. It is virtually identical in shape to the chevrons above the eyes on the face of the supernatural being, displayed above in Figure 11-5,

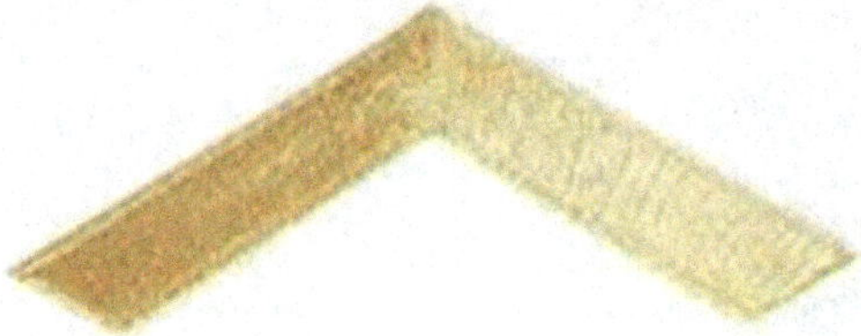

Figure 11-6; A gold-colored chevron patch, usually sewn on the upper arm of an officer's uniform. A chevron indicates rank in the military, and in police forces. This chevron is designed with straight lines in the shape of an inverted capital letter 'V.'

Photographer unknown

Chevrons are typically designed with a thin, sewn or colored border that forms an outline. The color of a chevron, as well as its shape and design, all indicate different ranks and status. Chevrons are often colored gold or silver. This one, above, shown in Figure 11-6, is made of straight lines—like the two chevrons I found above the eyes in the 'Murder at Byfleet' Drawing. (There are also many military chevrons designed with curved lines.)

What do the two chevrons that I found in the 'Murder at Byfleet' Drawing symbolize? Possibly, this occult face belongs to a high-ranking personage—who, in turn, belongs to some powerful military organization. Evidently, this face belongs to the commander-in-chief of an army of some sort. Could he have commanded the army of Fallen Angels that, according to the Bible, were expelled from Heaven by the Archangel Michael—with the aid of God's Host of Angels, in a cosmic battle described in the *Book of Revelation?* Apparently, the chevrons on this deity's face have religious as well as military significance. They are symbolic evidence pertaining to the killers' motive. And for that reason, I will now also set the word **'chevron'** in boldface.

A Disembodied Face Fills George's Kitchen.

In the 'Byfleet Murder Drawing,' this mysterious face hovers in the air, filling most of the space inside George's kitchen. This floating head can only be that of a supernatural deity. It is by now apparent, the outlined face embedded in the 'Byfleet Murder Drawing' has religious significance. This deity's face is filled with occult symbols, rather than human features—for example: the huge **Hellmouth** formed by two concentric circles (which I traced in red); the pairs of piercing **eyes** also formed by two concentric circles; the symbolic **question marks** (which I traced in white) with their unique dots formed of two concentric circles; the outlines of military **chevrons** (which I traced in white) indicating top rank in the host of Fallen Angels. There is even a touch of devilish humor to be found in the **widow's peak** hairline (traditionally linked to images of the Devil in popular culture.)

Does this face—composed of occult symbols—belong to a deity who is already well-known in religious literature, such as the Bible? If so, which deity's head is depicted as floating in George's kitchen? Can we identify him by his occult symbols? There have been thousands of deities named throughout history. The two chevrons have already established that this deity is a powerful and forceful supernatural being associated with the Fallen Angels. The huge question mark that appears in place of a nose informs us that his identity is still secret. Searching for a clue to his name, I examined—under extreme magnification—the area defined by the top of his head and the Widow's Peak Hairline. There, I found a large instance of **JACKY?**. I traced the six characters in multi-colors—as shown, below, in **Figure 11-7.**

Figure 11-7; My tracing in multi-colors of an instance of JACKY?, embedded above the widow's peak hairline. The outlines of the six characters in this instance of JACKY? are all drawn in the same shapes as the characters in the instance of JACKY and the three question marks that I found embedded in the fabric of George's overcoat (as displayed earlier in Figures 14 and 16 in Chapter 9.)

Original drawing published by *Illustrated Police News* on Jan. 28, 1888;
Sketch artist: unknown; Original image: Public domain in US.

??RIPPER JACKY?? (*not:* ??JACKY RIPPER??)

Above this instance of **JACKY?,** I found a large instance of **RIPPER**—surrounded by many **question marks**. All the characters were formed in the same shapes as the characters in the instance of **JACKY** and the three question marks that I found earlier embedded in the fabric of George's overcoat—as shown below in **Figure 11-8.**

The name **RIPPER JACKY** is surrounded by two **question marks** on either side. Thus, the complete name of this deity appears to be **??RIPPER JACKY??.** The four **question marks** are part of the deity's name. Indeed, it appears to me that the symbolic **question marks** are the source of the deity's supernatural powers. The four **question marks** protect this deity from attack by the Archangel Michael.

Moreover, the descriptive term **RIPPER** is located *above* the name **JACKY** in the drawing. Thus, the deity's name is **??RIPPER JACKY??**—not **??JACKY RIPPER??.** The deity's full name is an occult fetish, with supernatural power. Like the Devil in the Cornish folk tale *Terrytop* (also known as *Duffy and the Devil,*), the supernatural power of **??RIPPER JACKY??** rests inherent in his name.

Figure 11-8; My tracing in multi-colors of an instance of RIPPER, located directly above the instance of JACKY displayed in Figure 11-7. The name RIPPER JACKY atop the deity's head is both preceded and followed by a pair of question marks. Thus, the full name of the deity is ??RIPPER JACKY??.

Original drawing published by *Illustrated Police News* on Jan. 28, 1888;

??RIPPER JACKY?? is a Royal Deity.

Superimposed on top of the deity's name, I found an intricate image composed of many diagonal lines. When I traced these lines, they formed a multi-pointed crown. Thus, this deity is a king. Here, below, in **Figure 11-9**, is my tracing in yellow of the royal deity, **??RIPPER JACKY??**, wearing a crown.

Figure 11-9; My tracing in yellow of a crown atop the head of the royal deity ??RIPPER JACKY??.

Original image published by *Illustrated Police News* on Jan. 28,1888;
Sketch artist: unknown. Original image: public domain in US.

This multi-pointed crown is a royal crown. It has a total of 10 points in the front and in back. Thus, it is similar in shape to many of the multi-pointed crowns of kings of England in the past.

For example:

- the 11-point crown worn by **Edward I** (1239-1307), King of England in 1272-1307.

Edward I's crown is shown below, in Figure 11-10, in an official portrait:

Figure 11-10; Edward Longshanks, Edward I; King of England who reigned in 1272-1307. He wears an 11-pointed crown.

Artist unknown; Image: Public Domain in US.
National Portrait Gallery, UK; image in public domain in US

- the crown worn by **Henry II** (1133-1189,) King of England, who reigned from 1154 until his death in 1189. This 13-pointed crown is shown in Henry's portrait, displayed below, in **Figure 11-11.**

Figure 11-11; Portrait of Henry II, King of England, who reigned in 1154-1189. He wears a 13-point crown.

Artist unknown; Image: Public Domain in US.
National Portrait Gallery, UK; image in public domain in US

All Hail the King! ??RIPPER JACKY??.

Among the thousands of names of gods in hundreds of religions throughout history, the name **??RIPPER JACKY??** is absent from *Wikipedia's* compilation. *Wikipedia* also lists numerous "Kings of the gods in different cultures" and "Rulers of pantheons." The name **??RIPPER JACKY??** is absent from all these lists, as well. Thus, **??RIPPER JACKY??** must be a secret nickname—an alias for a royal god in some hermetic religion. In other words, **??RIPPER JACKY??** must be the supreme god in an occult religion known only to its adherents—who form a secretive cult. The three killers who murdered and mutilated George Chuter were members of such a cult—perhaps its only living members in 1888. Evidently, this cult's religious rituals included human sacrifices.

One supernatural being—one who has had more nicknames ascribed to him than any other—is the Devil. His royal nicknames—*i.e.,* those royal nicknames specifically mentioned the Bible—include Prince Satan, King of the Bottomless Pit, Prince of the Power of the Air, The Ruler of Demons, The Prince of Darkness, Ruler of this World, the Prince of Demons, and the King of Darkness. Besides those royal nicknames, the Bible also mentions many common nicknames for the Devil, for example: the Beast, the Deceiver, the Serpent, the Son of Perdition, the Son of Wickedness, the Antichrist, the Thief, Beelzebub, the Lawless One, the Fallen Angel, the Murderer, the Enemy, Lucifer, Satan, the Accuser, Belial, the Evil One, the Tempter. the Father of Lies, the Son of the Morning, the Roaring Lion and the Morning Star. Those are just nicknames for the Devil mentioned in English Bibles (for example, the King James Version.) In literature and in folklore—not to mention works in foreign languages—the nicknames for the Devil are legion. However, there is no written mention of the royal deity

??RIPPER JACKY?? anywhere—anywhere else, that is, other than in the 'Byfleet Murder Drawing.'

The Shiny White Object in the Center of the 'Byfleet Murder Drawing.'

At the exact center of the 'Byfleet Murder Drawing' shines a strange, white object that I have not examined thus far. It hangs from the top of the wooden chair located next to the kitchen table. It was on top of this tabletop that the two murder weapons were set by the killers. For the longest time, this unusually shaped, shiny white object defied all my attempts to identify it. Whatever this shiny white object was intended to represent in reality, its central location in the 'Byfleet Murder Drawing' seemed to me to indicate that this object must have been an important clue to the murder and mutilation of George Chuter. Here, below, in **Figure 11-12,** is that unidentified shiny white object hanging on the chair.

Figure 11-12; A shiny white object hangs from the back of the wooden chair, located next to the kitchen table.

Detail of image published by *Illustrated Police News* on Jan. 28,1888; Sketch artist: unknown. Original image: public domain in US.

Its symbolic location—at the exact center of the 'Byfleet Murder Drawing'—appears to me to be a statement by the Sketch Artist that this cylindrical object, whatever it was in reality, was a key to the solution of the Byfleet Murder. In **Figure 11-13,** below, I have drawn an 'X' over the entire 'Byfleet Murder Drawing.' The nexus is located at the bottom tip of this shiny, hollow, white object—at the very spot where any liquid inserted into the top of this round object would come out.

Figure 11-13; The shiny white object is located at the exact center of the 'Byfleet Murder Drawing.' The nexus of the 'X' that I drew on the drawing is located at the bottom end of the white object.

Original image published by *Illustrated Police News* on Jan. 28,1888; Sketch artist: unknown. Original image: public domain in US.

Shiny or Shining?

There are two curious circles of bright light visible in the kitchen. I say 'curious' because the 'Byfleet Murder Drawing' reveals no light source visible anywhere in the kitchen—such as a gas lamp on the wall, or an oil lamp sitting on the table, or light coming through a window from a streetlamp. This drawing takes place on a dark evening. And yet, George's body can be seen illuminated in a bright circle of light—as if he was an actor who had just died on stage and was now illuminated from above by a brilliant calcium oxide limelight.

In addition, there is a small, but bright, circle of light illuminating the top of the kitchen table that holds the two murder weapons. In **Figure 11-14,** shown below, I have traced in red the embedded circular border that marks the large circle of light that illuminates George's mutilated body. And I have traced in white the border of the small circle of light on the wall behind the kitchen table holding the two murder weapons. The top of the table with the murder weapons is also illuminated by a small spotlight striking the wall.

Figure 11-14; There are two curious circles of bright light visible in the kitchen. There is no light source visible anywhere in the kitchen in this drawing. What are the sources of these two circular beams of bright light?

Original image published by *Illustrated Police News* on Jan. 28,1888; Sketch artist: unknown. Original image: public domain in US.

What Are the Sources of these Two Circular Beams of Bright Light?

The large circle of light that illuminates George's mutilated body is located directly under the floating head of the deity **??RIPPER JACKY??,** displayed earlier in Figure 11-8. Evidently, light emitted by this deity's huge floating head illuminates George's body like a theatrical spotlight shining from above. Moreover, we can see under the wooden chair—and also under the kitchen table—dark shadows on the floorboards and on the wall under the table. The shape, location and direction of these shadows indicate that the large circle of light emanates like a beam of bright light from a lantern—the source of which is the floating head located directly above the body. So, evidently, one of this godhead's *magikal* powers was to emit a light around him wherever he went. (Please forgive the occult misspelling of *magikal.)*

The Small Circle of Light on the Wall Above the Kitchen Table.

What about that small circle of bright light that illuminates the two murder weapons lying on the top of the kitchen table? That small circle of light shining on the wall behind the table appears to emanate from the bright white shining object hanging on the back of the wooden chair. A circular beam of light, emitted from the circular part of the white object on the chair, would have an unobstructed path to illuminate the two murder weapons on top of the tabletop, and the wall behind them.

Did this mysterious white object in the exact center of the 'Byfleet Murder Drawing' also have *magikal* powers to emit light, just like the godhead? From the drawing, it would appear that it did. In that case, this white object was not *shiny—i.e.,* reflecting light that struck its surface, emanating from some other light source. It was *shining—i.e.,* glowing brightly, emitting light from its own source of energy. In other words, this shining white object played a mystical, sacred, critical role in the Byfleet Murder and Mutilation. It illuminated the two murder weapons. So, what, in reality, was this glowing, shining object, hanging on the back of the chair?

What Was the Shining White Object that Hangs on the Back of the Wooden Chair Intended to Represent in George's Kitchen?

At first glance—*i.e.,* before I realized that the white object on the wooden chair was *shining,* and not *shiny*—I had thought this object might be a trumpet. James played the clarinet in the village band. Perhaps, he also played the trumpet, I momentarily speculated—and he left his trumpet on the wooden chair during the band rehearsal. But, on closer inspection, I could see that this object was not a trumpet. It had no embouchure, no valves and no crooks. Natural trumpets had virtually disappeared from use in bands in England by 1888. And, by no stretch of the imagination would a trumpet be a significant clue in the 'Byfleet Murder Drawing.' Because of its exact, central position in the drawing, I had fully expected that this object would provide an answer to the mystery of the killers' signature.

Of What Material Was the Shining White Object Composed?

What was this bright white object made of? If it had been a shiny object—*i.e.*, one that *reflected light*—it probably would have been made of some shiny metal—such as polished silver or brass. However, it was a *shining* object—*i.e.*, one that *emitted its own light energy.* Thus, it would likely have been made of some transparent or translucent material, such as glass or crystal. Light emanated from within this object. The source of the light energy derived from what this mysterious object had once contained. It was now a sacred object that glowed white.

The Curved Lip.

Upon closer examination under intense magnification, I could see that the top of the white object was not perfectly circular. Protruding on one side, I could see a curved lip. It looked like a small extension that served as a handle for a finger to grasp and hold. Here below, as shown greatly magnified, in **Figure 11-15,** is the glass object that hangs on the back of the wooden chair, with the curved handle protruding from the top edge.

Figure 11-15; **Protruding from the circular top end of the glass object is a small, curled lip. This lip serves as a handle to hold the glass object upright with one finger.**

Original image published by *Illustrated Police News* on Jan. 28,1888; Sketch artist: unknown. Original image: public domain in US.

Eureka!

For many weeks, neither I nor some of my friends could pin down exactly what this object was designed to do. And then, one day, while browsing in a wine shop, I saw it. There it was, for sale: a wine funnel. In the 19th Century, the decanting of wine was a common practice—more than it is today with the current popularity of highly processed wines. One method of filtering sediment from wine is to strain it with a filter in a wine funnel. Another use for wine funnels is to facilitate the return of wine that remains in a glass, back into the original bottle.

Wine funnels were common kitchen utensils in Victorian England. They come in many different shapes and sizes, both straight and curved. They have long been made of glass, and also of various metals. These days, they are sometimes made of plastic. Some wine funnels have a small handle attached to the top—like the small, curled lip seen protruding from the top of the shining white object that hangs on the wooden chair, displayed in **Figure 11-15,** above. Here, below, as shown in **Figure 11-16,** are two examples of modern wine funnels made of glass.

Figure 11-16; Two examples of modern wine funnels in glass, one with a small handle, and one without.

Images: Photographers unknown.

The Connection.

What possible relevance does a wine funnel have with the murder and mutilation of George Chuter? When considered alone, a wine funnel has no relevance at all. However, when considered together with the drawing of the three killers standing in the kitchen doorway, displayed earlier in Figure 11-1, this shining, white wine funnel reveals the true motivation for the mutilation of George's body. It tells us what really happened in George's kitchen after he was bludgeoned and slain with the poker. It explains the location of the shining white object in the exact center of the 'Byfleet Murder Drawing.' The wine funnel represents the Sketch Artist's ultimate deception.

Return of the Man-in-Red.

One of three killers depicted in the 'Byfleet Murder Drawing' is the Man-in-Red. He is shown in my tracings in Figure 1 holding a bottle in his left hand. Comparing the bottle's size to the height of the Man-in-Red, I would estimate that this bottle might hold about a quart (or a liter) of liquid. Evidently, the Man-in-Red was holding forth this bottle as he prepared to depart the crime scene—after having participated in the murder and mutilation of George Chuter.

What Was Contained in the Bottle?

What liquid was contained inside that bottle? The Man-in-Red holds this bottle directly in front of him—

displaying it proudly and prominently to the godhead of the royal deity, floating inside the sacred space of George's kitchen. The Man-in-Red displays the bottle to King **??RIPPER JACKY??.** The Man-in-Red may even be symbolically offering the bottle to his royal deity with his outstretched left arm. The contents of this bottle must have been essential to the Byfleet Murder. It is a sacrificial offering of blood to propitiate this royal deity.

Here, below, in **Figure 11-17,** are my tracings of the Man-in-Red holding a bottle in his left hand, as he stands in the doorway of the kitchen. What is inside that bottle, displayed so prominently by the Man-in-Red? The bottle's contents were in fact the goal of the Byfleet Murder, the sole purpose for which George was slain. Everything we have read thus far was directed for one purpose only: to fill that bottle with George's blood.

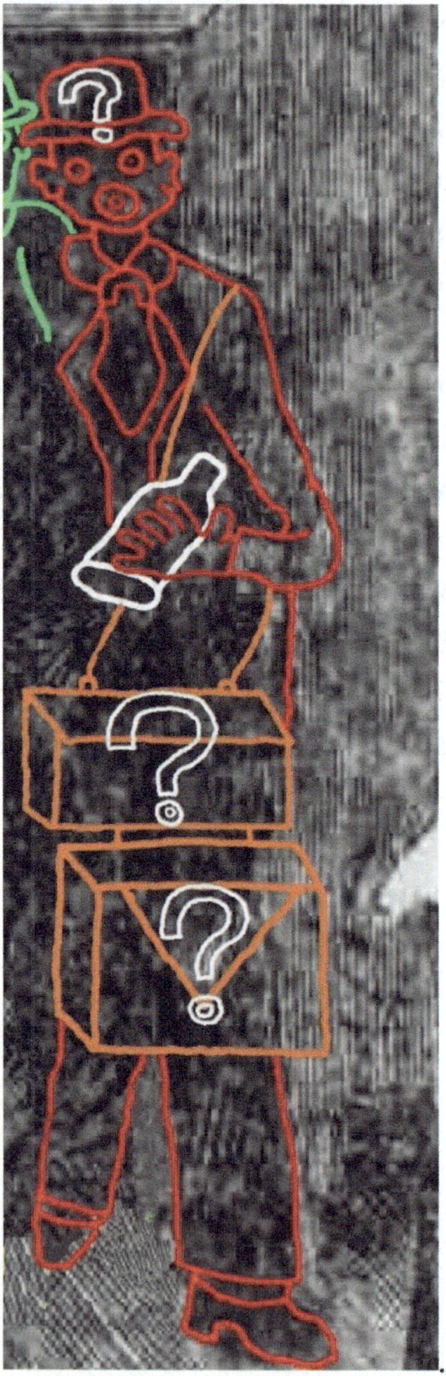

Figure 11-17. (same as Figure 10 in Chapter 9;)

The Man-in-Red stands in the doorway of George's kitchen—about to depart the scene after having participated in the murder and mutilation of George Chuter. He holds in his left hand a bottle that apparently contains about a quart of liquid. He prominently displays this bottle to the royal godhead that floats inside George's kitchen. He is offering his deity a bottle filled with George's blood.

Original image published by *Illustrated Police News* on Jan.28, 1888; Sketch artist: unknown. Original image: public domain in US.

Blood! Blood!! Blood!!!

At the Coroner's Inquest, Dr. Sealy testified that, following the repeated bludgeoning of George's head with the poker, George was insensible and dying—or, possibly, he was already dead. Thus, the subsequent slashing of George's throat with the carving knife served no lethal purpose other than to release a great flow of George's blood from his body onto the kitchen floor.

It is now obvious to me that George was murdered and mutilated so that three killers might obtain about a quart (or roughly a liter) of George's blood. As indicated in Figure 11-16, it was evidently the killers' intention to take this bottle of blood with them when they departed the scene, after they had made a symbolic offering of the bottle to the floating godhead. Equally obvious is the killers' intention to utilize George's blood for subsequent sacrificial worship of their royal deity, **??RIPPER JACKY??**. Or possibly, in future sacrificial murders, they would paint at the crime scenes many instances of the two fetish words and the symbolic question marks in George's blood—thus insuring their deity's protection.

One Minor Obstacle Remained.

However, one minor, practical obstacle still stood in the way of the killers realizing their ultimate goal. How did they get a quart of George's blood out of his body and into the bottle that was held in the hand of the Man-in-Red? There was a large pool of blood on the kitchen floor, under George's body. The killers could hardly scoop up this puddle of blood, spread on the wooden floorboards, with a spoon—to fill up a quart bottle. Much of George's blood had undoubtedly run through the cracks in the wooden floorboards, or had soaked into the wood and then disappeared. One small utensil was required to transfer the blood that gushed from George's slashed neck directly into the bottle held by the Man-in-Red. That indispensable utensil was the wine funnel.

And thus, the indispensable wine funnel now seen hanging from the back of the kitchen chair deserved a place of honor at the precise center of the 'Byfleet Murder Drawing.' The blood it had earlier transmitted from George's neck into the bottle was, in the minds of the three killers, sacred blood. The wine funnel radiated a sacred glow that illuminated the two murder weapons sitting on top of the kitchen table—and also the circle of light on the wall behind the table.

We Can Now Envision Exactly What Transpired in George's Kitchen After His Throat Was Slashed with the Carving Knife.

Now, it is possible to deduce from the crime scene evidence, as depicted in the 'Byfleet Murder Drawing,' just what happened when George opened his kitchen door upon returning home from the King's Head. He was immediately set upon by two killers who worked—quickly and efficiently—in concert. A third killer remained stationed outside, serving as a lookout for any pedestrians on Chertsey Road, or on the brick alley, who might hen be walking by. After George's throat was slashed with the carving knife, two of the three killers lifted up George's body and turned it upside down. With his neck now pointed downward, George's blood drained from his severed blood vessels. The third killer—likely the Man-in-Red—held the wine funnel under the blood gushing from George's slashed carotid artery. The wine funnel channeled George's blood into the glass bottle.

Thus, the wine funnel was a critical piece of equipment, without which the three killers would not have been able to attain their goal: *i.e.,* obtaining the blood of their chosen victim in a bottle, for later use in occult rituals, to pay ritualistic homage to their royal deity, **??RIPPER JACKY??**. For the three killers, George's blood was a sacred object in their occult rituals. The wine funnel—which had come in direct contact with George's blood—was also, for the three of them, a sacred object. It emitted a beam of light that pointed straight to the two murder weapons sitting on top of the kitchen table.

What Ritual Did the Three Killers Perform With George's Blood?

Earlier in this chapter, I quoted an article by Professor of Criminology Scott A. Bonn, PhD on the subject of identifying two types of killers with crime scene evidence. To identify an *ordered* killer. Dr. Bonn wrote:

> **Profilers use a list of factors such as whether the victim's body was positioned or posed by the killer, whether sexual acts were performed before or after death, and whether cannibalism or mutilation was practiced on the body.**

George Chuter's body was *posed* in the spreadeagle posture. His body was undoubtedly *mutilated* following his murder. There is no evidence that George was missing any body parts—so cannibalism is not apparent. But a person's blood is also a body part. A vital body part. *Vampirism* definitely is evident in the 'Byfleet Murder Drawing.' By 'vampirism,' I am not referring to bats flying through the window morphing into Dracula.

As a consequence of the deep slash(es) with the carving knife on George's throat, the victim's blood covered a small portion of the kitchen floor immediately surrounding his body. There was no logical reason for the killers to slash George's throat other than to gather some of George's blood into the bottle. The wine funnel permitted the three killers to raise up George's body and drain his blood—from his neck wound into the bottle. When the killers set down George's body on his back upon the kitchen floor, they carefully arranged his arms and legs in the Spreadeagle pose.

What Did the Three Killers Do with George's Blood After They Carried It Away In a Bottle?

What else? They drank it.

"The Devil can cite scripture for his purpose."

William Shakespeare; *The Merchant of Venice*; Act 1, Sc. 3)

Chapter 12; The RIPPER JACKY Outline Font.

"What's in a name?"

William Shakespeare, *Romeo and Juliet* (Act II, Sc. ii)

In Chapter 9 through Chapter 11, I traced multiple instances of **outlined capital letters** embedded in the 'Byfleet Murder Drawing,' as published by the *Illustrated Police News* on Jan. 28, 1888. I also traced multiple instances of symbolic **question marks** embedded in the drawing. The letters—all of which were upper-case letters—formed two words: **JACKY** and **RIPPER**. These words were invariably accompanied by **question marks**—sometimes placed in front of a word, sometimes placed following a word, sometimes located on both sides of a pair of words. The **question marks** appeared singly; or sometimes in groups of two; or even in a group of three—for example, the three question marks embedded into the fabric of George's overcoat.

.

Fetish Words

The context of these embedded characters made it plain to me that these two words and their associated question marks were all fetishes—that is, inanimate objects worshiped for their supposed magical (or, in occult jargon, *magikal)* powers. The words themselves were considered by the killers to be inhabited by a spirit, when these words were written on an object like the wall of a room. Thus, these fetishes, painted on the walls, converted George's kitchen into a sacred space. In the case of the 'Byfleet Murder Drawing,' it was undoubtedly the drawing's creator—*i.e.,* the Sketch Artist—who believed that these two words, and their associated question marks, were fetishes. These *magikal* fetishes gained their supernatural powers from the killers' royal deity, **??RIPPER JACKY??.**

The Royal Crown on the JACKYface is labeled ??RIPPER JACKY??.

The crime scene evidence embedded in the 'Byfleet Murder Drawing' establishes that three killers depicted in the kitchen doorway murdered and mutilated George Chuter; and that they did so as an act of sacrificial worship in fealty to their royal deity **??RIPPER JACKY??.** The name **??RIPPER JACKY??** appears inscribed on the deity's royal crown. The **JACKY**face is a godhead who floats in the air inside George's kitchen.

The Cognomen.

JACKY is a name; **RIPPER** is a description. Together, they form a cognomen, or alias. In **Figure 8 of Chapter 11,** these two words appeared superimposed on the royal crown, in the following order: **RIPPER JACKY,** and not **JACKY RIPPER.** The description **RIPPER** comes first; the name **JACKY** comes second.

Thus, the royal deity's cognomen is similar to *Bloody Mary*, for example, a.k.a. Mary I, Queen of England from 1553-1558 (shown, below, in **Figure 12-1.**)

Figure 12-1. 'Bloody Mary," Queen of England from 1553 to 1558, a.k.a. Mary I.
Portrait by Antonis Mor, 1554. Image: Public domain in U.S.
Mary was the only child of King Henry VIII and Catherine of Aragon to survive into adulthood. She restored Catholicism in England while her persecution of Protestants led to her nickname "Bloody Mary."

To reiterate: nowhere in the 'Byfleet Murder Drawing' does the cognomen Jack the Ripper ever appear. On Jan. 28, 1888, he was not yet born.

A RIPPER JACKY Font.

Moreover, while tracing these embedded characters in the 'Byfleet Murder Drawing,' it became apparent to me that each instance of a character was very carefully formed in an almost identical shape with well-defined proportions. The minor variations were due primarily to the constraints of fitting a character, or a word, into a limited space. Thus, each outline of a capital letter was formed in an almost identical shape to every other instance of that same outline of a capital letter. And, as we have already seen, the shapes of some of those embedded characters were quite idiosyncratic and distinctive. Thus, the unusual details of these hand-drawn, outlined characters, when considered in their entirety, are as unique as a handwritten signature.

The full name of the royal deity contains nine different letters plus a question mark—ten different characters, in all. It occurred to me that these ten characters formed a distinctive, partial, typographical outline font—almost as readily identifiable as any other typographical font. Thus, I undertook a detailed study of the precise form of each character that appeared in the 'Byfleet Murder Drawing' as an embedded outline.

The Characteristic Shape for the Outline of Each Capital Letter—an Analysis.

- The '**A**' (in Figure 12-2) in **JACKY** has a small equilateral triangle inside. This small triangle sits on top of a crossbar. The upper line of the cross bar is the straight line of the base of the small equilateral triangle. The lower line of the crossbar is formed by two curved lines, joined in the middle of the letter. Thus, the bottom of the crossbar dips in the center. This dip gives this outline of a capital letter '**A**' a stylish flair that is readily identifiable. The baselines of the two feet of the letter '**A**' are set at 90 degrees from the two legs. From repeated tracings, I could not help but notice the similarity of the dip in the center of the crossbar of the 'A" with the dip of the **widow's peak** hairline in the image of the royal deity.

Figure 12-2; Outline of capital letter 'A,' traced from an instance of JACKY, embedded in the 'Murder at Byfleet' Drawing.

After the 'Byfleet Murder Drawing, published by the *Illustrated Police News* on Jan. 28, 1888; Drawing in Public Domain in the US.

- The **'C'** (in Figure 12-3) in **JACKY** is made from two partial concentric circles. The two ends of the 'C' are set at right angles that are bent inward, toward the center of the circles.

Figure 12-3; Outline of capital letter 'C,' traced from an instance of JACKY, embedded in the 'Murder at Byfleet' Drawing.

After the 'Byfleet Murder Drawing, published by the *Illustrated Police News* on Jan. 28, 1888; Drawing in Public Domain in the US.

- The '**E**' (in Figure 12-4) in **RIPPER** is made entirely from straight lines set at right angles. The horizontal bar in the center is slightly shorter than the horizontal bars at the top and bottom.

Figure 12-4; Outline of capital letter 'E,' traced from an instance of RIPPER, embedded in the 'Murder at Byfleet' Drawing.

After the 'Byfleet Murder Drawing, published by the *Illustrated Police News* on Jan. 28, 1888; Drawing in Public Domain in the US.

- The 'I' (in Figure 12-5) in **RIPPER** is made in the shape of a dog bone or dog biscuit (set up vertically.) The top and bottom horizontal lines are not flat. The top line has a characteristic dip downward in the middle. And the bottom line has a characteristic hump upward in the middle. The outside corners are rounded.

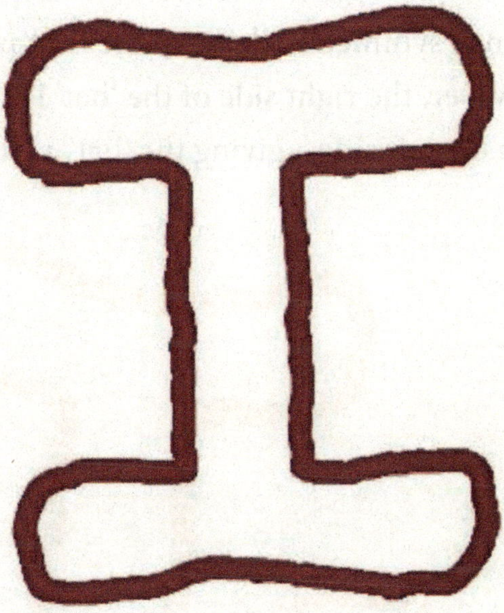

Figure 12-5; Outline of capital letter 'I,' traced from an instance of RIPPER, embedded in the 'Murder at Byfleet' Drawing.

After the 'Byfleet Murder Drawing, published by the *Illustrated Police News* on Jan. 28, 1888; Drawing in Public Domain in the US.

- The 'J' (in Figure 12-6) in **JACKY** is formed very much like the 'I' in **RIPPER**—except the lower half of the 'J' curves to the left. (The outline is shaped like a J-trap pipe that is typically located under a kitchen sink.) Significantly, the top horizontal line has the same characteristic dip in the middle as the top of the capital letter 'I.' The end of the curve on the left-hand side is a short horizontal line that forms right angles. The 'hat' at the top of the 'J' extends symmetrically from the mid-point. However, the right side of the 'hat' is slightly higher than the left side—giving the 'hat' a jaunty tilt.

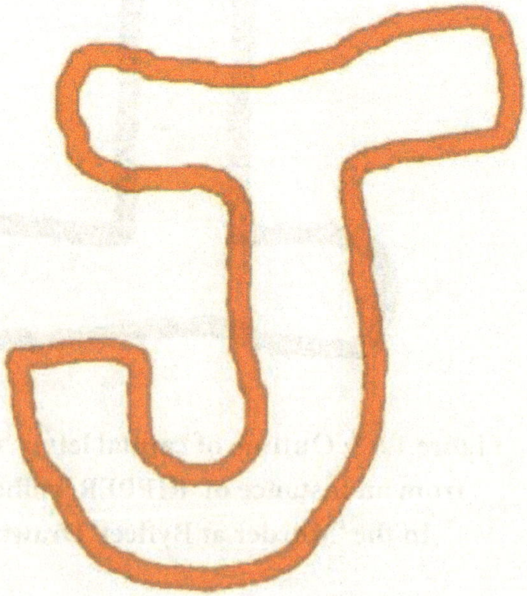

Figure 12-6; Outline of capital letter 'J,' traced from an instance of JACKY, embedded in the 'Murder at Byfleet' Drawing.

After the 'Byfleet Murder Drawing, published by the *Illustrated Police News* on Jan. 28, 1888; Drawing in Public Domain in the US.

- The **'K'** (in **Figure 12-7**) in **JACKY** is formed by a vertical post on the left side. The vertical post supports an arm that rises diagonally; and a leg that descends diagonally. The arm and the leg emanate at acute angles to the right of the side post, The top and bottom of the post are short horizontal lines. The arm, the leg and the post are all the same width. The end of the arm is set at right angles to the arm's sides. The end of the leg, however, lies flat on the baseline already determined by the bottom of the post on the left.

Figure 12-7; Outline of capital letter 'K,' traced from an instance of JACKY, embedded in the 'Murder at Byfleet' Drawing.

After the 'Byfleet Murder Drawing, published by the *Illustrated Police News* on Jan. 28, 1888; Drawing in Public Domain in the US.

- Each of the two instances of '**P**' (in Figure 12-8) in **RIPPER** encloses an empty space whose shape resembles that of a capital letter 'D.' Both the vertical post and the curved outline are of the same width.

Figure 12-8; Outline of capital letter 'P,' traced from an instance of RIPPER, embedded in the 'Murder at Byfleet' Drawing.

After the 'Byfleet Murder Drawing, published by the *Illustrated Police News* on Jan. 28, 1888; Drawing in Public Domain in the US.

Each of the two instances of '**R**' (in Figure 12-9) in **RIPPER** are virtually identical to the capital letter 'P,' displayed above, with the addition of a diagonal leg similar to the diagonal leg on the letter 'K.'

Figure 12-9; Outline of capital letter 'R,' traced from an instance of RIPPER, embedded in the 'Murder at Byfleet' Drawing.

After the 'Byfleet Murder Drawing, published by the *Illustrated Police News* on Jan. 28, 1888; Drawing in Public Domain in the US.

The '**Y**' (in **Figure 12-10**) in **JACKY** is formed by half of a vertical post, centered, supporting two diagonal arms. The two arms branch off at a right angle from one another. The baseline of the center post is horizontally flat. The ends of the two arms are diagonals; they are set at right angles to the sides.

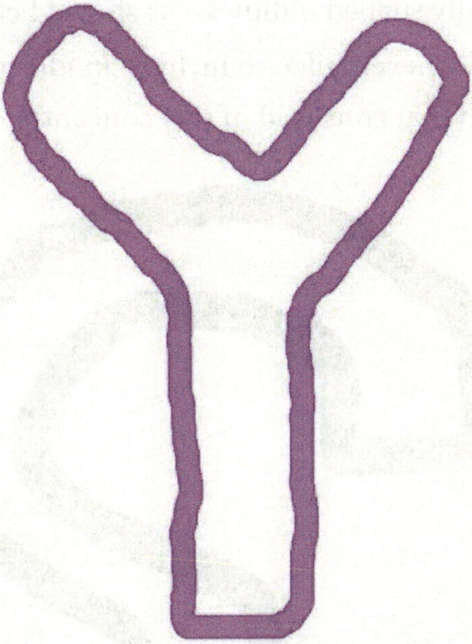

Figure 12-10; **Outline of capital letter 'Y,' traced from an instance of JACKY, embedded in the 'Murder at Byfleet' Drawing.**

After the 'Byfleet Murder Drawing, published by the *Illustrated Police News* on Jan. 28, 1888; Drawing in Public Domain in the US.

The Omnipresent Question Marks.

In addition to these nine outlines of capital letters, I also found multiple instances of a large **question mark**—drawn in conjunction with many instances of **JACKY, RIPPER,** and the **JACKYface.** All these **question marks** were drawn as identically shaped outlines—as shown below in Figure 12-11. They never failed to include an idiosyncratic dot at the bottom that consisted of two concentric circles.

Figure 12-11; Outline of question mark '?', traced from '?JACKY' and 'RIPPER?' on the 'Murder at Byfleet' Drawing. Note the dot at the bottom of the question mark. It is comprised of two concentric circles.

After the 'Byfleet Murder Drawing, published by the *Illustrated Police News* on Jan. 28, 1888; Drawing in Public Domain in the US.

The RIPPER JACKY Outline Font.

These nine outlines of capital letters and the outline of a question mark were drawn by the Sketch Artist of the *Illustrated Police News* in the same distinctive manner in every instance. Consequently, the various instances of **JACKY** and **RIPPER**—and their associated **question marks**—represent readily identifiable symbols of ownership. They serve as a brand, or a logo. Indeed, the fetish words **JACKY** and **RIPPER,** the symbolic **question marks,** and the **JACKYface,** are all part of the signature of the hermetic, diabolical, homicidal **Cult of ??RIPPER JACKY??.**

This typographical font—to which I have given the name the **RIPPER JACKY Outline Font**—consists solely of capital letters, of outlined characters, and of these nine letters and the question mark. My hand-traced font will serve as a highly useful evidentiary tool in later episodes of my investigation—especially in Volume 2 of *A Trail of Blood.* Because the font contains evidence, I will forthwith set the font name in boldface.

A Stamp of Authenticity.

The characters in the **RIPPER JACKY Outline Font** represent a secret stamp of authenticity. The idiosyncratic outlines of each character, as they were drawn by the Sketch Artist in the 'Byfleet Murder Drawing,' now stand as a reference. If and when future investigations into the Byfleet Murder and other unsolved murders reveal additional instances of these fetish words in crime scene evidence, we can utilize the **RIPPER JACKY Outline Font** to evaluate their authenticity. Here, below, is the complete **RIPPER JACKY Outline Font**, organized alphabetically—in **Figure 12-12**, below.).

Figure 12-12. The RIPPER JACKY Outline Font.

A Typographical RIPPER JACKY Outline Font.

I have also created a typographical **RIPPER JACKY Outline Font** for use in text. From here on—*when writing text*—whenever I write the words **JACKY** or **RIPPER,** or a symbolic **question mark** to indicate occult *fetishes*, I will employ my new typographical font. Thus, **RIPPER** now becomes RIPPER; **JACKY** now becomes JACKY; and a symbolic question mark'**?**' now becomes '?'**.**

The truth will out.

William Shakespeare

***The Merchant of Venice* (Act 2; scene 2)**

Intermezzo Leading into Volume 2, *A Trail of Blood;* The Byfleet Murder (Continued)

At this mid-point in my investigation of the Byfleet Murder and Mutilation, I think it is appropriate to take a step back and ask rhetorically: what does all this documented evidence actually prove?

In my view, the evidence documented thus far constitutes overwhelming proof that George Chuter was, in fact, murdered and mutilated by two-or-more killers who acted in concert. Moreover, it seems to me *certain* that the Byfleet Murder & Mutilation was a carefully planned assassination by ambush, intricately prepared, long in advance of the actual perpetration of the crime—and not a spontaneous robbery-gone-sour by a lone panicked burglar.

But what about all that other information embedded in the 'Byfleet Murder Drawing'—about a devil-worshipping cult of three perpetrators that killed and mutilated a random victim with whom they had no personal connection? From that information in the 'Byfleet Murder Drawing,' I deduced: that the killers' ultimate goal was solely to obtain a bottle full of George's blood to use in an occult sacrificial rite, to pay homage to their royal deity **??** RIPPER JACKY?? . Was that deduction proven true as documented fact by the embedded images in the 'Byfleet Murder Drawing"? Not yet.

And was it proven true that the killers had painted in George's kitchen (and perhaps elsewhere in George's residence) multiple instances of JACKY, RIPPER, symbolic **question marks.** and an iconic JACKY face? Not yet.

Or were these fetish words and the occult image of a royal deity named ??RIPPER JACKY?? merely the delusional ravings of the Sketch Artist for the *Illustrated Police News*? Did this Sketch Artist merely imagine a fanciful theory of the crime scene just to create confusion and make malicious mischief? There is no conclusive evidence yet on that score, either.

Does the 'Byfleet Murder Drawing' contain Special Knowledge? Does the drawing contain evidence of knowledge of the crime that could only have been known before January 28, 1888 (the date of publication) by someone who had directly participated in the perpetration of the murder and mutilation of George Chuter? Was the Sketch Artist a member—or even the leader—of this secret cult of killers who, as depicted in the 'Byfleet Murder Drawing,' murdered and mutilated George? We still need corroborative evidence to prove these deductions were, in fact, true.

What if the existence in 1888 of the Cult of ??RIPPER JACKY?? can be established with crime scene evidence that still survives today. If additional evidence can still be found today that links this homicidal cult to the perpetration of the Byfleet Murder & Mutilation, then the embedded images in the 'Byfleet Murder Drawing' will clearly qualify as Special Knowledge. That Special Knowledge would directly incriminate the Sketch Artist as one of the three killers who perpetrated the crime.

The only way to know today whether the fetish images embedded in the 'Byfleet Murder Drawing' constitute Special Knowledge of the crime would be to uncover additional physical evidence in Byfleet—evidence that dates from 1888, evidence that corroborated the occult images that I found in the 'Byfleet Murder Drawing.' Additional physical evidence, directly related to the perpetration of the murder and mutilation, would be convincing proof—at least for me—if it supported the killers' occult signature with more embedded drawings of fetishes.. Such evidence would be irrefutable, I believe, if these drawings were located in Byfleet at or near the murder scene, or related sites.

In other words, the question that still remains to be answered: did the killers mark the murder scene in Byfleet with their signature? And if they did mark the crime scene and its immediate environs, do traces of their markings still survive today in Byfleet? Where in Byfleet might such occult markings be found, even today?

One hundred and thirty-six years have now passed since George Chuter was murdered and mutilated in Byfleet. It might seem pointless even to hope that physical evidence pertaining to this horrendous crime still survives today in Byfleet. Nevertheless, one cannot dismiss that intriguing possibility until one actually searches for it—and photographs it. And reproduces it in detailed photographs in my Volume 2.

Clear and convincing evidence would also include trophy photographs, taken by the killers in the late 19th Century. Trophy photographs that confirmed the existence in 1888 of the homicidal Cult of ??RIPPER JACKY **?? would be conclusive evidence, at least for me.** Trophy photographs—if they could be found today—could establish beyond any doubt the participation of these killers in George Chuter's murder and mutilation.

Trophy photographs, if they could still be found today, might even lead to an identification of one or more of these cult killers. They might establish beyond a reasonable doubt the participation of named individuals in the murder and mutilation of George Chuter.

Above all, 'new' physical evidence—if it could be found today—might possibly establish the killers' motive for the crime—which now, only tentatively, appears in the 'Byfleet Murder Drawing' to be the procurement of the victim's sacred blood as a sacrificial offering to propitiate the royal deity ??RIPPER JACKY??.

In Chapters 9-11, I introduced three items of 'new' evidence about the murder. My 'new' evidence of three items were,, apparently, unknown in 1888—unknown to the Surrey Constabulary, to Coroner Roumieu, to the press, and to Scotland Yard in London during the Autumn of Terror later that year, All three items were published in newspapers, and thus they were available to anyone who might have searched for them and analyzed them, as I did in 2023. But there is no mention of them that I could find in any police records, or anywhere else.

Apparently, no one ever before has identified these three items as critical evidence directly linked to the members of the Cult of ??RIPPER JACKY??. who murdered and mutilated George Chuter. All three of these items were created in 1888 by the killers of George Chuter. All three items of 'new' physical evidence still survive today in their original form as newspapers stored in the National

Archives at Kew—and thus, they can be examined and verified by anyone so inclined.

The three items of 'new' evidence consist of

1. the occult images that I found embedded in the 'Byfleet Murder Drawing,' published on Jan. 28, 1888, located on the bottom right-hand corner of the front page of the *Illustrated Police News*;
2. the classified advertisement published in the London *Standard* on Jan. 20, 1888, evidently composed and placed by the killers of George Chuter; and
3. the Letter from ANXIOUS, who was the Killer-in-Chief. The letter was published in the *West Surrey Times* on March 2, 1888.

Even though all three items were published in the popular British press, no one before has ever brought them to public attention as critical evidence in the Byfleet Murder. No one before has established direct links from these publications to the perpetration of the crime. No one before has utilized these three evidentiary items to re-investigate the Byfleet Murder & Mutilation.

Following the publication of these three items in newspapers in 1888, the Coroner's Inquest in Byfleet was never re-convened. During the Autumn of Terror in London when the Whitechapel Murders, attributed by the press to Jack the Ripper, raged in the East End, there are no surviving documented communications between the London Metropolitan Police and the Surrey Constabulary regarding the Byfleet Murder. To this day, there is still no indication that I've seen in any official record stored in the National Archives that the Metropolitan Police ever investigated the Byfleet Murder on its own. Evidently, the Met remained oblivious of the suggestion of ANXIOUS in his letter to the West Surrey *Times* to take over the investigation..

If these 'new' documents had been known in 1888 to the police, to the Coroner or to the press, would any of them have helped 19th Century detectives to decipher the solution to this yet-unsolved murder. I doubt it. Why? Because, in January 1888, such a crime was *inconceivable*—that is impossible to conceive, based on past experience. Certainly, before September 1888, neither law enforcement nor the press had ever seen in Britain any comparable crimes involving a devil-worshipping, homicidal, secretive cult that murdered and mutilated a random victim to obtain his blood for ritual, sacrificial purposes.

In 2024, however, it is now general knowledge among the well-informed public that devil-worshipping homicidal cults do, in fact, exist. They exists in other countries, as well as the U.K.. To name only one example, in the late 20th

Century there was "The Order of Nine Angles a.k.a. ONA or O9A. This was was a militant Satanic left-hand path occultist network. According to *Wikipedia,* The Order of Nine Angles originated in the United Kingdom, but since then branched out into other parts of the world. "Claiming to have been established in the 1960s, it rose to public recognition in the early 1980s, attracting attention for its neo-Nazi ideology and activism. Describing its approach as "Traditional Satanism", it has also exhibits Hermetic and modern Pagan elements in its beliefs." The Order has been charged with multiple murders and other crimes. For example: "In the summer of 1997 two members of the Swedish O9A group called Misanthropic Luciferian Order perpetrated the so-called Keillers Park murder, an alleged ritual sacrifice of an Algerian man. The men were eventually convicted of a hate crime."

In the 20th and 21st Centuries, numerous criminal investigations and trial convictions of notorious perpetrators of ritualistic murders and mutilations have been documented. They are well publicized in the mass media. I suggest to those who are skeptical that such diabolical killers have in fact existed throughout past eras should read Randall Sullivan's new book *The Devil's Best Trick.* Killers who drink their victims' blood and eat their victims' body parts have been arrested, tried, and convicted. Moreover, some serial killers are now known to have worked in pairs or even in groups of three. In Volume 2 of *A Trail of Blood*, I will cite more specific examples.

We do not know yet whether the Byfleet Murder was an isolated example of a ritualistic murder in 1888, or whether it was part of a murder series. What could be the most persuasive evidence that possibly exists to convince us that the Byfleet Murder & Mutilation was, in fact, linked to other unsolved crimes? In my view, that would be the discovery of identical examples of the same, occult fetishes at the crime scenes of other 19th Century unsolved murder/mutilations. And perhaps, these same occult fetishes might be found in some unsolved murder/mutilations in the 20th Century, too.

The Byfleet Murder & Mutilation is not yet 'case closed.' With the wealth of new evidence that I have just revealed, the Byfleet Murder is now a gateway into the historical re-investigations of other unsolved murder/mutilations in Britain and elsewhere. Indeed, these re-investigations must include still-unsolved murder/mutilations that both preceded and followed the Byfleet Murder & Mutilation on January 12, 1888..

Lastly, we still do not know the identities of any of three killers who formed the cult of ??RIPPER JACKY??. The Byfleet Murder was a perfect crime. No clues were left at the crime scene to identify any of the killers. No mistakes were made by these killers during the flawless execution of their intricate plan. As indicated by all three items of 'new' evidence, the killers were very proud of their successful accomplishment. Perhaps, they left physical clues to their identities still hidden in Byfleet.

Why would they have done that? Perhaps, they wanted to get credit for the successful murder and mutilation, following their natural deaths, from their royal deity. Perhaps they wanted recognition from their royal deity for drinking their victim's blood as an offering. They craved recognition of the great sacrifices they had made in his name. The killers wanted to establish their claims for credit from their safe harbor in Hell, way beyond the time of their natural deaths. To do that, they would have needed a permanent record to show their deity what they had accomplished while on earth. As Fell Demons, they were loyal subjects to their royal deity, Lucifer. They had performed a sacrificial murder in tribute to ??RIPPER JACKY??. To claim their deity's protection, they would have needed documents and murder trophies as proof of their accomplishment. They needed evidence proving their service—evidence that would stand the test of time.

William Shakespeare*; Macbeth* (Act III, Sc. iv)

Acknowledgements & Thanks for Assistance

Isabelle Chapuis
Lulu de la Rue
Julia Wiland
Karen Hoy
Tessa Westlake
Pam Starling
Maurice Alder
National Archives, Kew
Donald Baraf
Jim Allen
Robert Bartlett
David Rose
Iain Wakeford
Jennifer Tuffs
Mike Chapman
Duncan Mirylees
Surrey History Centre
Byfleet Heritage Society
Byfleet Community Lib.
Surreycc.gov.uk
Casebook.org
British Library
British Newspaper-
Aarchive.org
Wikipedia.org
wokinghistory.org
Darren Kisner

Index
Of Chapters Names & Chapter Subheadings

Yet More Evidence Still Out There?

Dear Reader:
If you have any additional historical evidence about the Murder & Mutilation of George Chuter in Byfleet, and you would like to send it to me, Mark Starr, as an email attachment, for evaluation, and for possible inclusion in Volume 2 of this series, please contact the following email address:

noteworthyeditions@gmail.com

- Items of special interest would be photographs of George, Lucy or James Chuter. Also, photos of Coroner G. F. Roumieu, Dr. George Sealy, Superintendent Alfred Bungard, PC Dearlove. Deputy Chief Constable Barker.
- Also of great interest would be any photographs (published or unpublished) of notable locations in Byfleet (and its environs) taken around 1888.
- Any 19th Century drawings or paintings of historic locations in the Byfleet area;

- Any anonymous letters about the Byfleet Murder & Mutilation published in 19th Century newspapers;
- Any handwritten letters dated around 1888, about the Byfleet Murder & Mutilation.
- Press clippings about the Byfleet Murder from any newspapers or magazines published in Surrey or in London in the 19th Century that I may have missed.

Please include all pertinent information about this potential evidence, your name and location, and an email address where you can be contacted. Hopefully, Volume 2 will be published by KDP/Amazon before the end of 2024. Of course, any submissions included in Volume 2 will be fully credited. Any spam email or malware sent to the email address above will be deleted before I ever get to see it.

M.S.

Made in the USA
Las Vegas, NV
13 September 2024

95017802R00262